Plain
Life

ANTONIA PONT is Associate Professor in Writing, Literature and Culture at Deakin University, Australia. She publishes poetry, fiction and essays as well as theoretical work across writing, literature, philosophy and the creative arts. Her research is concerned with time, habit, ethical capacity, thought, movement and transformation. She is the author of *The Memory Library* (Spineless Wonders, 2024), *A Philosophy of Practising* (Edinburgh University Press, 2021) and a co-author of *Practising with Deleuze* (Edinburgh University Press, 2017). Her collection of poetry *You Will Not Know in Advance What You'll Feel* was published in 2019. She is the founder of Vijnana Yoga Australia (2009–), where she continues to practise, teach and lead retreats. Her essays have an international following, and have appeared in *Lit Hub*, *The Lifted Brow*, *Antithesis* and *Overland*.

'Read this precise, wild and tender offering,
and be sure to ask yourself how you feel after ...
Plain Life is challenging and generous.'

Debra Dank

'Fizzing with energy and ideas, *Plain Life* is a practical,
philosophical heart to heart with your most spirited friend.
Alain de Botton for hot anti-capitalists.'

Briohny Doyle

'Deeply alert to the challenges of our times, and
extraordinarily well read, Antonia Pont delivers us a
handbook for life that is politically radical, refreshingly
intellectual, and wholly attentive to embodiment and being.
Informed and informing, it is a seriously joyful tour de force.'

Julienne van Loon

Plain Life

On thinking, feeling and deciding

Antonia Pont

NEWSOUTH

UNSW Press acknowledges the Bedegal people, the Traditional Owners of the unceded territory on which the Randwick and Kensington campuses of UNSW are situated, and recognises the continuing connection to Country and culture. We pay our respects to Bedegal Elders past and present.

A NewSouth book

Published by
NewSouth Publishing
University of New South Wales Press Ltd
University of New South Wales
Sydney NSW 2052
AUSTRALIA
https://unsw.press/

Our authorised representative in the EU for product safety is Mare Nostrum Group B.V., Mauritskade 21D, 1091 GC Amsterdam, The Netherlands (gpsr@mare-nostrum.co.uk).

© Antonia Pont 2025
First published 2025

10 9 8 7 6 5 4 3 2 1

This book is copyright. Apart from any fair dealing for the purpose of private study, research, criticism or review, as permitted under the *Copyright Act*, no part of this book may be reproduced by any process without written permission. Inquiries should be addressed to the publisher.

A catalogue record for this book is available from the National Library of Australia

ISBN   9781761170164 (paperback)
          9781761179068 (ebook)
          9781761178320 (ePDF)

Cover design Regine Abos
Cover image Emma Cowan, www.wildstudio.co.nz
Internal design Josephine Pajor-Markus

All reasonable efforts were taken to obtain permission to use copyright material reproduced in this book, but in some cases copyright could not be traced. The author welcomes information in this regard.

Contents

In Praise of a Plain Life   1

Deciding Capacities   27

On Love and Making Ones   58

Being Bothered   93

Virtue: falling out of love with Awful   117

Envy: a case study   131

Four Nuances of 'Can'   138

Wanting, Affirmation and the Plain 'No' of Critique   156

Rigorous Kindness   183

The Middle: framing vastness   219

Risking Plainness   252

Coda   265

Works Mentioned   269

Acknowledgments   271

Notes   273

A 'plain life' is not another way of saying a 'natural life'.

In Praise of a Plain Life
*fear, wanting and the politics
of neoliberal anxiety*

Propositions &c.:

We can't live plain lives because we are afraid.
We mostly can't live plainer lives because of all the fear.
*We mostly can't relate to our lives plainly because fear hobbles
    this ability or repertoire.*
When I'm afraid, I replace curiosity with either/or thinking.
*When I'm afraid (and don't know I am afraid) my repertoire
    is puny.*
*I could be curious about being afraid, but this would involve
    noticing that fact, then a gear change.*
*It would mean abstaining (just long enough) from what or how
    I usually do.*
(Fear is very busy. One can end up paralysed with busyness.)
*Abstaining might involve making something – that is, swapping
    expectation for praxis.*
How is it that abstaining and making aren't opposites?
How could a plain life be not-the-opposite of a rich life?

These days, it's easy to get the impression that people are really very anxious. *Who?* you ask. Well, people you hear about. People who *tell* you they are. Friends. Lovers. Acquaintances. Colleagues. The Youth. The term is *around* and people are applying it to themselves, or having it applied to them, willy-nilly. People are talking about anxiety plenty, getting diagnosed by certified professionals as 'anxious'. It's concerning; it's distressing. Debilitating, often. It can dismantle a life, they say. It can erode your well-being and capacity for connection. You can become a real pain in the arse. Stuff like that.

Clearly, anxiety must be an umbrella term. There must be lots of species of anxiety. It means different things all the time. We could get far more precise about what we mean by the term, host a little tournament of semantics, but who's got time for that? Anxiety, in any case, goes to the heart of one's experience of time. And the term, we can affirm, gets thrown around as a new staple in the parlance of our times.

I didn't set out to write about anxiety. I wanted to contemplate something else, something I'm venturing to call a Plain Life. What I discovered, however, as I began writing, was how hard it was to avoid addressing this other thing. And it seems the two might be connected. Not in opposition – as one might assume – but more in a subtractive way: that's to say, they have that particular relation of no relation. A Plain Life might be that of which we can become capable (of recognising) when the conditions for anxiety are not operating so fiercely, or when we manage – even for a tiny interval – to abstain from colluding with these conditions.

And so, in order to explore this idea of plainness here, I find myself having to wrestle with the beastlier notion of anxiety – a thankless undertaking (I'm not qualified!), and a potentially hurtful one. In writing some of the things here below, I risk (ever so slightly, not so slightly) making you, the reader – an anxious person? Diagnosed, closeted, unsure? – feel blamed and judged. This might happen, and it would be neither my wish nor intention.

On the other hand, my intention is to ask slightly more probing questions about something that appears to be eating our collective faces off, or to be eating collectivity per se. I want to ask not so much about discrete instances of anxiety and whether the term is merited or not, but rather what the conditions might be in which a certain ilk of anxiety becomes more likely; in which it can gather momentum and flourish.

It seems to have been flourishing in recent times.

It could be, however, that I'm listening too earnestly to these declarations and self-diagnoses. Perhaps labelling oneself as 'suffering from anxiety' might be more a kind of style – like heroin chic – rather than something to worry about. It might just be one way a person likes to approach being a person. Going at life. Front on. With some edge. Nothing soggy. The anxious do not truck with soggy. That's the impression I've gleaned over time. Sans sog? Maybe there's a clue right there. Not so much middle ground.

I suspect it's both – an epidemic for many and a contemporary stance for some. And probably both at once.

In what follows, I may make some obnoxious arguments. Perhaps you'll find them obnoxious, or perhaps – ha! – I flatter myself prematurely. In this chapter, I'm going to talk two broad notions in two parts, and link them up. The first involves expectations about life (getting, having, feeling) that we tend to absorb unfiltered from our milieus. The latter seem also now almost inevitably global and neoliberal (with new formations threatening, crooning ...), and this will become important. Alongside that I'm going to explore a subtheme, namely: desire. Splendid, super-duper, never-the-problem, desire.

The second aspect I'll explore is fear (see propositions above), and in particular what unfelt fear does to one's thinking. In my own experience it tends to narrow my imaginative range, and then exaggerate the content of that range in unsettling ways. I think it's this – hyperbolic, polarised thinking – that constitutes a crucial element in the set of conditions in which anxiety can take root so operatically. Unfelt fear, then, really hinders the possibility of a Plain Life.

In this way, anxiety, and the conditions under which it flourishes, concerns us all and is therefore political. It is something we might consider collectively. Together. Although we may suffer the squalls of so-called mental health alone and in our own particular ways, as philosopher–activists Gilles Deleuze and Félix Guattari taught us, it is neither personal nor individual. We get sick in ways that are also specific to contexts and moments. It can be constructive to think about this as shared – to link it up with our moment and its mores, with our capacities and limitations.

Your suffering might be particular, but it also displays features, patterns, so-called idiosyncracies that are generalised. Given this, I reckon it's worth having a good shot at working out why that might be and if there is anything – anything at all – that we can do about it. Thinking about it together might be the first step to undermining one pillar that it relies on in order to operate.

Part I – What to Expect from a Life

'Am realizing whole myth of efficiency and no waste that is making this continent of countries we are in.' He exhales. 'You know myths?'

'Is that like a story?'

'Ach. A made-up story. For some children. An efficiency of Euclid only: flat. For flat children. Straight ahead! Plow ahead! Go! This is myth.'

'There aren't any flat children, really.'

'This myth of the competition and bestness ... they assume here always the efficient way is to plow in straight, go! The story that the shortest way between two places is the straight line, yes?'

David Foster Wallace, *Infinite Jest*, p. 80.

Firstly, let's debunk an easy assumption to make. Anxiety – despite appearances – mostly has very little to do with fear *directly*. Anxiety of a certain kind, I'd suggest, is far more a final confusing outcome: the cumulative result at the level of the body's cells and electricals of *contexts* in which unfelt (or unthinkable) fear operates to structure our imaginary along certain predictable lines.

Fear, when we don't feel it, when it mobilises us covertly, is one of the necessary ingredients for the conditions in which certain anxieties can flourish. The relation between fear and anxiety, then, may not necessarily be causal at all. In Part II of this chapter, I will talk more about unfelt fear. Firstly, however, I want to talk about something else. Something shared. Something ubiquitous, voracious, subterranean.

Expectations.

Let's consider for a moment to what degree our miseries might map to our shared and habitually harboured expectations, and how these are formed very much in relation to our sociohistorical moment. Another way to say it is that our expectations are not very personal or individual at all. We tend to expect what others expect – depending on our class, our cultural background, our choice of entertainment provider, our practices of information consumption, our own ethical/political attempts to think and decide. It's arguably, as E.G. suggested during edits (thank you!) an *immersive* learning that we've been in since forever. And let's face it: it takes quite a bit of contemplative spacetime to abstain from gobbling immediately and compulsively the prêt-à-porter expectations that our various worlds present to us as given, as natural, as being that to which we are entitled.

I expect many things that I don't know I'm expecting.

Years ago in India, I found it astonishing to walk past homes that had no doors, a dirt floor, and seemingly very few possessions, but which sported, on a single wall, an enormous flat screen. It's not that one shouldn't necessarily prioritise owning a gargantuan

TV, but what struck me was the thought of what that device would be pouring into that particular world: designer kitchens in sitcoms with brattish US teens; home improvement reality television from Australia; melodramas set in rural beach communities in far-off lands. UFC. Aerobic class re-runs. Infomercials. Ads for reformer beds. Crustacean foam and chocolate soil. Late capitalism is wild.

And, arguably, things could go in at least two broad directions with this kind of affluence dissonance. I guess viewers in the home could see that the world is tantalising and nauseatingly unfair (it is) and foment some serious social reform or crackling revolution (and many in India actually do this; grassroots politics there, as we know, can be breathtaking). Or, each individual viewer might absorb a strange cocktail of expectations and life vistas, disassociating a little, beginning to live in two or more registers – one embedded in, and constrained by, the socioeconomic conditions of their structural position and moment, and the other (which arrives reliably through the big, black portal) sizzling with the contents of an unmetabolisable disjunct.

India. Downtown or suburban Melbourne. Provincial France. Country South Australia. Java. Different? Maybe.

Expectations. They're great, right? They are the seeds of vision and ambition. We have to think bigger, no? We are promised rewards for thinking bigger. This is what the American Dream teaches at least half of the planet. From the moment we began vacuuming up Disney's narrative arcs, we've had to study it well and often. And the British Empire's expansion program before that. Expect more, and who knows what might happen! But the expectations we can see, the ones we take on with eyes-wide-open, operate within us very differently from those that we breathe in as part of the air that everybody's breathing.

What are those? we might ask. Could I even begin to track what they are, when I got them, and what they are doing to me?

They might leave a bad smell in the air, but one would struggle to practically identify their contours in any precise way.

Expectations, then, are more like Rohypnol than MDMA. The current moment (every current moment) sneaks them into our lime and sodas, and we slurp them down recklessly. We don't taste the drug among all the chilled citrus, but it's not a little dangerous. It can make for a bad night indeed. A blind and menacing night. Or, I want to argue – bringing my metaphor back 'round – for a potentially worse life.

Okay, so we aren't that passive. We have intense chats about stuff with people. We read. We write a little. We post the odd thing, gesturing at insight or critique. We can intervene in the slurping, surely? Some fortunate people have learned how to do this or evade the spiking – sometimes thanks to a sane upbringing, sometimes due to their own efforts of good questioning and contemplation, mixed in with some luck. Some people have a better and saner Expectation Immune System. Funnily, they tend to be the ones who end up with the appealing, enviable lives. They become the gold-standard for the life you're meant to expect. Curiously, they may have ended up with this life precisely by not swallowing down all the twaddle that came their way, and instead by inventing other programs; by setting off in other less mapped directions. Or, more likely again, they were also just privileged, and the dissonance between what was on offer and what their circumstances were likely to deliver was less exaggerated.

Without the practice of, and capacity for, resisting mass-produced expectation, there's a good-enough chance we'll have exactly the expectations of what a life is, how it should feel, and what it should 'offer' us, as those that our times offer to us.

Sound benign? Drink up.

When I conjure – right now – the idea that I should have or attain certain things in my own life, and then hold this idea up against some of the real material conditions and pragmatic limitations that exist in this same life, I can actually generate something very like anxiety; I can feel it starting to simmer and hiss. Try it for yourself, see what you'd call that feeling. I think it's a harrowing feeling, bloody awful mostly, sometimes transformable. Tolerating it, being able to stand it, while also processing it, and seeing through it, may be a crucial life skill for those of us living now – in among the bombardment of all the media, whether social, communication, information, entertainment or others. It's a matter of degree. A little sizzle is fine – a full-scale conflagration is another thing. Synapses melt. The body learns a heat that it may struggle to unremember. And as the yoga commentators tell us, pain (incidentally) is a heat pattern.

What expectation or cluster thereof, one might ask, is getting sown behind the scenes in any given exchange or consumption moment? Without my noticing. What expectation or bundle of expectations is twining itself around my circuitry and prompting processes down the track that, with a bit more critical mass behind them, might constellate something very close to the feeling of being wracked with 'anxiety'?

It's not fear. You see what I'm saying? It's not fear at all. Unless we say that we are 'frightened' our life isn't going to turn out to be what we are being sold that it should be. If that's what we mean by 'fear', then very well. But I think 'fear' deserves better; fear is far more serious and important. What I've just described above looks – I'm sorry to say it – far more like a tantrum, a kind of shared, generalised, systemically instilled tantrum that leaves us all bruised and with far less dignity.

We'd have to make some fairly serious decisions (something quite different from 'choosing between') if we wanted out of this little pickle. A detox program? Because the tantrum, as I'm ungenerously calling it, isn't even really conscious. It is at the level of something bigger than us, and we are its little, compliant nodes. If it's a meme, then we are its unwitting and colluding hosts.

We comply with being expectation mules, and then the damage plays out on our bodies, in our viscera and nerves. This anxiety can be a program that starts to run, that builds its momentum in an organism, able to start up easily and run again and further again. Psychology may or may not be able to help us here, and psychoanalysis could weigh in, to accompany certain personally rugged aspects, bringing all its deftest manoeuvres and most serious clinicians to bear.

However, we also might need politics, and then steady contexts to think through and say what that means.

∝

RECALLING OUR INTEREST IN WHAT INVITES OR WAYlays a Plain Life, we can ask questions about the kinds of expectations we tend to have right now, in the absence either of deliberate intervention or considered resistance. Are they (concealed) expectations about shelter and love? Are they (concealed) expectations around esteem and status? Expectations with regard to security and career? With regards to the categories of feelings we care to feel? Or kitchen tiles? Lifespan? Intimate or libidinal encounters? Offspring? Scope for expression, creative or otherwise?

Expectation, as one reads in Chapter 2 of Gilles Deleuze's *Difference and Repetition* (2004), is not a category of the future at all. Rather, expectation or anticipation is very much a mode that's proper to the stable (and sometimes interminable) present. We remain marooned in our (same-old) present when we dabble compulsively in expectation. It is part of what secures and petrifies our present. It is less the escape hatch to the future and more like the bolt on its door. We expect or anticipate from within the present and *as part of* its repertoire. And for neoliberalism this is more than ideal. No future. If we go via expectation, there's no way to get there.

But is expectation alone enough to account for our being shut out of a Plain Life – an inflection of life that I appear to be extolling? I think that something else accompanies this surreptitious absorption of expectations (which, after all, isn't so special, which isn't confined to our current moment; humans have always been susceptible to going along with stuff). No, there is an extra bit. It's the very fashionable, also-subterranean habit of insisting that if I desire it, it *should* happen. Smearing want into insistence. Not out loud. Never out loud. Just *de facto*.

Its antidote would involve turning desire back into desire, keeping fantasy in its wondrous, writhing place; and *then*, of watching accrued expectation reel before your eyes but without flipping silently into something like entitlement – an *ersatz* entitlement that the current world may not be able to deliver on.

Entitlement, then, acting as the hinge between want and need, is a kind of blurring that only a very select number of people can afford to indulge. You'd wanna be white, middle-class, male, straight, or have a lot of embodied or institutional capital that you are well versed in trafficking on your own terms, if you think you can get away unscathed with flipping your desires into needs.

But we do it. With wild enthusiasm.

One hears it all the time. People speak, are coached to speak (sometimes by well-meaning counsellors and the like) about their 'needs'. One of the best things anyone can teach you is to replace most instances of the word 'need' with the word 'want' and to watch what happens.

When we state 'I need', we coyly disguise an insistent 'I want' with something that implies terrible things will happen (they won't) if the 'need' isn't met. Insisting that sex is a 'need' is an old chestnut. Or saying our partner doesn't give us what we 'need' is another. Who hasn't tried having relationships where this sentence is a constant – going under the guise of transparency – which really means being oblivious and just a little bit hurtful?

So, we want stuff; we don't *need* it. Lots of stuff. We *want* feelings, experiences, scenarios, amplitudes, decelerations, expression, connections, interaction, scope, leeway, acknowledgment, entanglements, resistance, decompression and space.

Want, not need. And that's *gorgeous*. You know it is. The wanting is the best and most noble thing we do. It might be what Nietzsche wanted us to remember. Remember *that you want*, and learn to forget your pinched, resentful tendencies. But Nietzsche was not a Neoliberal *Wunderkind*. And, as much as wanting isn't need, this disambiguation is bad for business, right?

I stood on the platform at Flinders Street recently and marvelled at human ingenuity. A moment of awe. Across the rails, on the other platform, my short-sightedness could just make out the words 'Commute Refreshed'. I quite liked the turn of phrase: article-less noun with unanticipated adjectival denouement. The words adorned a dusty and very typical vending machine – full of fructose, sucrose, denatured fats, dairy from indentured creatures and curated carbohydrate inventions hostile to most post-adolescent intestinal tracts. Advertising genius … oh, let's not exaggerate … advertising *proficiency*, had managed to turn a big, sad metal box with indigestible crap in it into: *I've got answers for the tail-end of your 10-hour day and the terrible feelings in your body which are for the most part chemical, with some bacterial, circumstantial, skeletal, ontological and other arbitrary factors thrown in.*

Très competent. And the machine remains in this prime spot because people put money into it. They need/want a refreshed commute. Not only do we turn our wants into needs (because wanting would require us to step up, step out, be a little in the world's spotlight, to be a version of a vulnerable, messy human), but the world gives us wants we didn't have before and frames them as needs that it, conveniently, can satisfy for us.

Knowing *that* you want, and then *what* you want, is fairly bad for business. Not catastrophic, but it makes for slower, deeper economy, which isn't in *vogue* at the moment. For a quick buck, for rollicking neoliberal times, it's more conducive for people (I didn't say 'consumers') to feel pressured by some unseen force in relation to a whole gamut of things that they believe they need. The 'things', don't be fooled, are rarely objects. The 'things' we want, I reckon, are mostly *atmospheric*. It's only secondarily that we go looking for lots of props to get that ambiance happening just-so.

However, it's also hard to think thoroughly and well – to *feel* precisely in order to disambiguate wants from needs – when there are umpteen 'needs' that you *must* apparently and urgently guarantee now and into the future. There are immense numbers of things to be done, scenarios to instigate. No time to lose. Never any time to lose. No time. No losing.

A plain life, as I'd like to sketch it, would involve lots of wanting. Heaps of it. But with somewhat more of this wanting, this desire, being self-determined, and then acknowledged in its miraculous specificity and intangibleness. A Plain Life waits *a little* to see what it might really want, with deliberate hesitation – some moment of pause – to allow for the likelihood that the want is a manufactured one, cancerously shot through with mass-produced expectation. It might proceed anyway, with the seeking and getting and losing, but thanks to the pause, something is already other. There's been a minimal intervention, in the chink of which additional processes might also be able to roll.

Don't think you can suppress the want/need stuff. That's a fool's errand. No. You have to work surgically with it. Very closely. Stay close and repeat.

When I hear myself saying 'I want', then the life I'm living, with all its failures, tedium and moments of grace, is already a bit more *mine*. Try it. Try saying some needs as wants. (Your interlocutor will immediately feel more respected and probably find you much hotter all of a sudden.) Wanting comes with more responsibility; it is a bit weightier. Taking up responsibility (by saying 'want') can be like ballast for anxiety's zeppelin. It stops it floating away so horrifically. Doing the things you seem unable to stop and doing them *on purpose* – that's one way to read Nietzsche.

In order to explore the possibility of a Plain Life, it would seem to me that I have to get a bit curious about expectations that I might have absorbed over the course of my upbringing, the ones that I've absorbed through cultural artefacts (in my case probably *way* too much misogynistic French 20th-century literature, Euro, Japanese and American Indie cinema, British Pop of my parents' generation, and – thanks Dad – commercial country music from the late 80s – to name a selection of culprits), as well as the expectations that are getting farmed out and invented every moment in the neoliberal frenzy. Along with this, I could continue to practise vigilance around framing wants as needs. Needing is, well ... needy and coercive. And wanting is, well ... totally cool and vaguely adult. Wanting is sexy, and never invokes some transcendental order that hands down 'needs' to its minions, and which they, in turn, must pursue like dupes, until they perish from fatigue or get divorced.

But if it were that simple, about the expectations (interrupting them) and the needs (trying them out as wants), then we could say that *we* are the only obstacles to a Plain Life. We, in other words, each of us, would be the problem. But as you know, that would be a very boring conclusion; that would make the genre of this chapter, and this book, self help. God knows, no one wants that.

This is where the fear comes in.

We mostly can't live plainer lives because of all the fear.

So, why are we afraid?

We might be afraid, I want to emphasise (in upper case if necessary), because there has been a neoliberal program running and its nature is not to give a shit about us.

There's a reason for you. Right there. One answer to the question above.

Sometimes I say this word ('neoliberal') to intelligent friends, new acquaintances, or café table neighbours, of various generations, and I realise that they don't know this word. Fair enough. Following Wendy Brown, neoliberalisation involves the penetration of market logics into every sphere of life – trashing the membranes that make the world. She writes, in her 2006 article 'American Nightmare: Neoliberalism, Neo-conservatism and De-democritization', that neoliberalism:

> ... more than simply facilitating the economy, the state itself must construct and construe itself *in market terms*, as well as develop policies and promulgate a political culture that figures citizens exhaustively as rational *economic* actors in every sphere of life. (p. 694, emphasis mine)

Under neoliberalism's ghastly spell, our best vision seems to amount to making ourselves into small, competitive businesses who each long to become a large voracious corporation ('a successful start up'). As Brown says, 'governance talk increasingly becomes market speak' and 'business norms replace juridical principles' (p. 694). This has crept in slowly ('we' have also partially allowed it to, unable and under-equipped to fathom its sinister reach and its consequences). It has transformed how we view and speak of our health, our personality, our family, our vocations, justice, values, our futures. A crass but shocking example would be when you hear a finacée proudly explaining how certain sexual practices were 'sternly' held off until she got the diamond ring she wanted. We have been trained to call this kind of invasive transactionalism 'empowered', but it's more a sign of the depth of our capitulation to this regime that cares only to acknowledge one pinched and sorrowful aspect of the infinities that we are.

We are, furthermore, driven into valuing 'convenience' over everything else, even above our own survival, our own mutual care. Providing for the vulnerable (welfare), educating future human beings, health care, and the serious matter of incarceration are (have been) routinely privatised and outsourced so that a structural disconnect (that forecloses responsibility) is instated. Welfare, universities, medicine and prisons become sites to install an unscrupulous business model, rather than being institutions that ensure the continuity of civil society.

Neoliberalism leaves people behind (one of the explicit concerns of its founders in 1947 was the growing middle classes). It might talk inclusion, but it walks programs and policies that undermine all our belonging, leaving people of every ilk, creed, level of ability less and less space, and fewer options. We have, for some years now, been witnessing what such an extended experience of being overlooked and blocked from dignified ways to proceed can pave the way for ...

Altogether this might be a very valid reason to be afraid. Let's acknowledge this – no shirking and no recourse to magically thinking one's solo way out.

This question (about why we're afraid), however, may not be the only question to ask here, although it's pertinent, of course, and must not be elided. Not living more plainly, though, might also have to do with the fact that we don't know *how afraid* we are, with this ignorance, this state of being ignorant *of fearing*. Unfelt fear, I want to say, really *does* something to our brains, preventing us perhaps from imagining something else, from accessing a capacity for more generous, fresh, and autonomous thinking. For the purposes of neoliberalism and its cahooting with some heavy planetary shit (which *is* objectively frightening), this is very convenient indeed.

Part II: Emotional Precision

Lately, I've had a few moments of insight where I've managed to catch a glimpse of just how frightened I can be without knowing it. Without clocking it. I've had little glitches in perception – white rabbits of noticing darting through my peripheral vision. *Golly, I'm frightened*, I've been realising. *I'm really quite frightened right now.* And I've tried to catch the kinds of things I'd just been doing, just before the noticing – the style of thinking that I'd slid into. Hyperbolic thinking is one name for it. And the startling thing is always that the fearing *hadn't even felt like fear*.

Fear seems to be a blind spot in our current emotional repertoire. Or perhaps it's just me? *Because* it is so conspicuously absent, I suspect that something in our neoliberal moment relies on its being obscured.

When I'm frightened (i.e. in the *actual* throes – then and there – of fear), I don't tend to think that I'm frightened at all. I tend to think that I'm being realistic. Or decisive. Or doing tough-love. Or telling it like it is. Or saving everyone the trouble. Or looking after number one. Or getting on with things. Or facing life head on. You get the picture, right?

Fear doesn't tend to look like fear. It looks like being Hard-nosed. It looks Standoffish. It looks Self-interested. It looks Instrumentalist. It looks ambitious and a little cold. It looks overly cheerful, brassy. It looks a lot like *how we are told to be*, these days. It looks a lot like a Neoliberal Well-Adjusted Subject. Like a Winner.

Consider for a moment: a unit that is actually Frightened Deep Down corresponds rather too faithfully to the idea we are given of what a winner looks like, how winners behave and how they think. *Wild*, right?

In my family – and I realised this quite late – fear simply wasn't an admissible category. The impression I got, and to which in turn I conformed with my concept of self, was that no one felt any. We didn't *do* fear. We were impressively risk-inviting. Non-squeamish. Indifferent to consequence. That was how it *seemed*. In retrospect, knowing what I now know, what this has helped me to think is how 'intrepid' and 'pragmatic' the very frightened can appear.

Politicians? Business people? The pencil-skirted 27-year-old hired on contract to manage your restructure. Parents and authority figures of various flavours? We know all this.

It took years for me to understand that if you want to know what's really going on, one method is to spot what *doesn't* appear. If fear is what is 'never there', then *probably* it's the water everyone is swimming in. It isn't *there*, because it is the very fabric of the *there-ness*.

On a more encouraging note, fear changes its spots radically when it goes from being obscured and operating surreptitiously, to when it operates at the surface. Being openly frightened would be a great outcome. Our problem is how little we know about how frightened we are.

And it's less of a bad time – the noticing – it's engaging enough; I recommend it. It goes along with that competency in being alive that (depending on your generation, cultural context &c.) you may or may not have had adequate or any apprenticeship in. I'm led to believe that our smaller comrades, those currently in kinder and early primary, are getting something of this education in certain privileged enclaves. They are learning about feelings. How to name feelings. How to cultivate a bigger repertoire of feelings. A palate beyond salty and sweet.

There's something about fear's going under the radar, in good neoliberal form, that is pretty incompatible with a Plain Life. To this end, things to consider might include: how *much* fear we're feeling all the time, *that* this is no wonder, *how* fear (unmetabolised) hinders our chance to live plainer lives, *ways* to spot the fear, which tends to present in non-fearish ways, and just *to what extent* fear is wearing and battering (many people like to call some of its effects 'depression' – I used to).

We mostly can't relate to our lives plainly because fear hobbles this ability or repertoire.

Fear, as we know, often destroys a sense *of* – or a capacity *for* – perspective. When we are in the throes of fear (and how often *is* that? Weekly, daily, in tight cycles of seconds?), the options we can imagine tend to turn basic, to polarise.

When unknowingly frightened, there can seem to be only Zero or Hero. And of course, one will always choose Hero over its bad-sounding alternative, and thus it amounts to not really *choosing* at all. Fear creates a context that's ripe for ultimatums.

The brain can slip into a programmed state that flicks between two options – often one is terrifying and the other almost-impossible. And we remain there, flipping back and forth like a suffocating fish, our aperture for living a big, plain life radically narrowed.

The hype-thinking that tends to accompany unfelt fear (and which is enabled by the very fact of its being unfelt) often also, in these moments, comes to seem natural and reasonable, and the answers we envisage tend to be *quantitative* ones. The pathology, then, is not our being frightened. Fear is not optional in a life; it is intrinsic and perfectly wholesome. However, existing in contexts that feed off what fear becomes when consistently elided ... *that* is what is both personally harrowing and system-reinforcing in disturbing ways.

Fear tends to have the odd side effect of making us imagine that the only life that would count, the only tolerable, memorable and respectable life, is a hulking, behemothal one. A bloated, brash, brattish one. A life on 'roids.

Blimp. Blimp.

Fear triggers a kind of oedema in our imaginations, in our perspectives and visions. Our projections and fantasies swell up – fatter, towering, bursting. Everything needs to be upsold, uplifted. We upsell ourselves and end up with large buckets of seething carbohydrates that nobody wanted. Inhuman-sized receptacles that weren't about a nuanced solution at all. They just happened to match the proportions of our fear in the moment.

I know because I know this in myself.

And the atmosphere that I'm risking calling 'plainness' is one that miraculously rises up, just sometimes, when our slant on the world slips beyond the reach of these grim opposites. It might be miraculous, but it isn't 'special'; at least, not in the special/irrelevant binary that currently rules our airwaves and media feeds. Contemporary French philosopher, writer and activist, Alain Badiou, offers a parallel conceptual structure in the opening to the second volume of his *Being and Event*, with the interesting title, for our purposes, *Logics of Worlds* (2009). He writes:

'There are only bodies and languages, except that there are truths.' (p. 4)

There are only winners and losers, except that there is your life. There is only perfection or disgrace, except that there is experience, accident, grace and generosity. There is only fame or anonymity, except that there is decision and practice. There is only missing out, or raking it in, except that there is service and the pleasure of losing interest in the identified self.

'Plainness', then, starts to look more like something true (in that Badiouian sense of truth) since it slips between the extremes that make the stakes of life so unpleasantly high – the kind of thought that we don't know to think for the very reason that a lot of untrained thinking happens in binaries.

Our parents, for all their authority, were frightened too – and when frightened we tend to reach for vivid illustrations, examples with a lot of *punch*. If you are a parent, check how much fear you can peddle, under the guise of guidance. Getting better at being explicitly frightened, and therefore more responsible for what we leak when frightened – would that be what makes plainness more likely, at least for those for whom we care, whom we teach, raise and mentor?

Of course, I want to give you examples. I want to paint 'plainness' for you – so that you can sense, for a brief nourishing second, its characteristic atmosphere of relief; the decompression it introduces into the familiar atmospheres of quantitative competitiveness and scarcity.

It can be the feeling that attends the conclusion of a decent therapy session (if you have a competent, ethical therapist). It can be the feeling you get when you've had some space from being a Productive Unit (your workaday life) and you're not organising yourself around economic categories, but rather creaturely ones. After camping. After a benign rainstorm that intervenes on the usual unfolding of time, on your weekend 'jobs list'. It's the feeling that practising brings (more on this later). It's reading poetry, wandering without aim in a city, or in a national park. It's all this, but *not quite*. Because you can go camping and bring your inner-neoliberal schmuck along inside. You can bushwalk competitively. Hahaha. Examples help, but we need other ways to invite the vibe of its 'otherly' logics. (How do you think I ended up wading knee-deep into this book you're holding...?)

As Badiou shows, you have to be able to imagine a world that has more than just bodies and languages (or what's the point?); more than just success and esteem in a certain paradigm of what makes a life. If you don't (and excuse me for saying), you're basically fucked. And not in that nice slippery way, with the sheets around your shins and late morning light coming in through the blinds. Oh no, you're basically fucked in that *other* way. You're fucked in the way that you think you're avoiding when you subject yourself – earnest and compliant – to the paradigm of 'one-or-the-other', all or nothing. This is the bad habit of masturbating secretly that the binary is *fine* – it's fine because you magical-think how you're going to fall on the right side of its gnashing fangs – how you're going to be one of the winners.

Neoliberal life, as many are starting to cotton on, is all about promising the very things that its mechanisms explicitly undermine. Lauren Berlant explores this in her work *Cruel Optimism* (2011). Neoliberal life coaches us to think that we are loving shit that we aren't loving at all. Vicious competition – it says – well, who doesn't *love* that? Well, most of us, I'd like to say. And in neoliberalism, the odds are stacked. It's not really a fun game. No one mentions *how much fun it isn't*. Those who champion it don't mention that at all. And: ask them in 55 years, when their store of embodied capital, or whatever, has waned somewhat. Ask them after a natural disaster has trashed their security, arrogance, family ties. To love *only* competition is to believe one is immune to misfortune, to time, to the very tissue of being alive.

So, I was thinking about fear – my own, other people's, the planet's – and I was also sitting in a minibus, being chauffeured around the Werribee Water Treatment Plant, as part of a public art piece called *Flight Lines* (because of all the birds at Werribee who feel safe there). It was Saturday, and it was nice being driven around.

In the bus, I huddled next to my then-partner, listening as some other attendees (French) spoke about their impressions of the works (in French), and I gazed out the window. If you've ever been to the treatment plant – as either a registered birdwatcher with permits to enter, or as a past attendee at a *Treatment* public art event – you'll recall how many roads and gates and turns there are inside this expanse of land not very far from Melbourne's closely mapped metropolis. It's enormous and feels labyrinthine.

We would drive along some roads, and then meet a security gate, and then find ourselves outside the plant for some minutes before entering another section, via another gate. Like a tardis, the expanses inside didn't seem to reflect the perimeter. With no bird's-eye view via the iDevice, the bumpy, communal touring-about felt all the more intriguing – like being in a sequence from Tarkovsky's *Stalker*. The topography arrived to me as both strange and ordinary. Traversing it passively, I could let it stretch and morph for the purposes of the reconfigured version it would later become in memory.

There wasn't too much fear on the minibus, as far as I could sense. Just Saturday morning sleepiness, some vague impatience (because aren't we always grappling with it) and something very ordinary going on alongside something extraordinary. (Dancers far ahead in the landscape, rehearsing the gestures of birds. Deafening guitar in a disused water tower. Visceral sculptures of foam and foods, moving slowly, becoming different, more alive through decay.)

It's this I want to try to say something about here – in what you're reading here (where are you reading it? in what state are you reading it?) – about an atmosphere. Not quite nameable. It is this atmosphere that this book you're holding is seeking *both* to account for and to be an experience of. It wants to not-shut-out this atmosphere, which tends to loiter around the edges of usual language, typical description, or habituated ways of thinking and saying. It's perhaps like when a white noise to which you'd become too accustomed goes quiet. It must be a kind of 'negativity' – the allowance for what doesn't so brashly *appear*, the grace of including that which eludes attention.

It's like when you pick yourself up after a crisis, bin the handfuls of tissues, and head out into chilly dusk air, without your phone, for an untracked walk. (The double timbre of sobbing *and* of also being done with sobbing?)

Plainness. A kind of ceasing. Refusing to play a certain game anymore. A pause in those other atmospheres thrown up by fright, by compacted fear never given enough room or the right words.

It's just the way a life might feel, if we weren't so (blind to being) frightened some of the time, and then acting out of this invisible, wettish medium. It would involve inventing other kinds of action, ones not powered by logics of self-harm, exhaustion and gutting competitiveness.

Simon Springer, theorist and critic of neoliberalisation, describes direct action as no longer appealing to an indifferent (and corrupt) authority of elites, a politics that can also be called prefigurative. He writes that '[w]e begin organizing alternatives by following our bliss and opening ourselves to the possibilities that serendipity and experimentation have to offer' and by 'reject[ing] the politics of waiting outright, where we no longer make demands of a political system that has never listened to us and has never been democratic'. '[T]o live well', he explains, 'means to fully express one's power in attendance with, rather than over others.'[1] (In the coming chapters, I'll speak about this internal disambiguation within the English word 'power'.)

The habitually and secretly frightened can struggle to imagine how a different life might feel, because they (we) are exiled at the poles of either catastrophe or forever-deferred (but fantasised) indemnifying affirmation by those in power. The link between anxiety and capricious authority. Either/or. Only this or that.

(Another way I've learned to notice that I'm frightened is by feeling myself slide into Knowing Everything. Fear seems to spawn opinion. But it's unfunny opinion, with no sense of humour about its preoccupations.)

When I'm afraid (and don't know I am afraid) my repertoire is puny.

As I rumbled along on the minibus, along one of the roads that went outside the gates, we passed a new housing estate going up. Suddenly, as I looked at the area divisions made by those string markers in the mud, I imagined myself living there and a feeling that I would call 'plainness' rose up in me. The thought involved just living somewhere, and that this would be enough. It would be a life with all its variations and encounters. With its machinations and diversions. With its cycles of valid, yet not life-shattering, emotions. It would be neither hyperbolic nor disappointing. It would not be straining to be exceptional in any way, nor would it be a sad, meaningless catastrophe.

I have no intention of purchasing off the plan in Werribee,

but I realised that it was a valid idea and that, if I had the money and did follow through (even though there is nothing impressive, exceptional or redemptive about the idea particularly), I would have a life. Not the best life, or the biggest life, or the most astounding life. Just a life – one that I would care for, tend, improvise and come to cherish, find disappointing at times, reminisce over. Not because of its objective, exceptional quality or credentials, but because it was what I would have made, what I had decided to live, what I could be bothered noticing and acknowledging in its unique ordinariness.

And so, the idea of living on the new Werribee estate was accompanied by a disquieting *and* steadying feeling, one which I wanted to catch and ponder. In that moment, something fell away, dropped out, went quiet as I allowed myself to entertain that fairly ordinary thought of buying or renting a fairly ordinary place to dwell, in a fairly ordinary part of the world (next to a world-heritage bird sanctuary, no less, but that aside).

The question I'm asking, if you haven't already guessed, is about what it feels like to lose the habit of thinking that there is *only* amazing *or* there is nothing (failure, ignominy, irrelevance, obsolescence, squalor) and of second-guessing a world that might seek to make us believe this logic. My inkling is that this logic has plenty to answer for in terms of the epidemic of unhappiness that our friends and loved ones are deafeningly declaring in more and less articulate ways.

We might call the manifestations of the bind we are in 'anxiety', but more important than name-calling, I'd like to think of ways to intervene in it. To do it deftly, for the sake of the plain lives we're capable of inventing – with enough dignity, more generosity, and far less self-involved and blinkered suffering.

The delicate part is that some of it we *do*, in fact, do to ourselves (the issue of consent) *and* some of it is really, truly happening and is larger than our solo selves; we are complicit victims in complicated ways in this self-(in)forming system. The world is doing stuff to us, and we also need to take that on – but together. If the world is peddling fear, while also appearing truly frightening, how can we catch this program and abstain from running with it?

I've tried to offer some tips for political practice in this chapter: knowing your fear (not discounting or demeaning it), learning to fall out of love with the hyperbolic binaries, and the trap of imagining that one will be the exception, overlooked by a brutish system, even cashing in on its violence. We've learned, inevitably, some nasty little habits of thinking from our neoliberal classroom (in which we are not accidental students), and our characters are none the nicer for the learning. I'd prefer to excel in another kind of classroom. With a better curriculum.

Sometimes, although it may be undiplomatic to say it, we suffer a lot because we've become a little bit horrible, or because we've cultivated for too long the company and traits of horrible people. Neoliberalisation relies on us admiring horrible people. It relies on our finding them titillating, and seeking to emulate, them. So, stop it.

Horrible people are those who have taken fear into their very fibres and without alchemy. They are often proud of how they've trampled over the conditions of their fear (while still having it, acting out of it, operatically). Without vigilance and creativity, we are all at risk of joining their ranks. But you can attend to this fear for some time each day – to get it out of your system, to acknowledge that you don't create the world all alone, and that, to a very large extent, you are subject to the times in which you live, but, also that you are *more* than only a product of the times in which you live.

Those who profit from neoliberalisation may well want you to ignore *and* coast along with concealed fear, and it is here that we can abstain from complying. It takes a particular kind of effort, and its practice may be called a particular kind of life.

I've called it, for want of a better name, a Plain Life.

Neoliberalism is terrifying, and you've every reason to be frightened. Be frightened and feel it, so that you comply a little less. Neoliberalism and its gig-economy moguls *want* our love of convenience, our fantasies of separateness and mastery, our reluctance to withdraw from shitty scenarios with atrophied imaginaries.

Neoliberalism affirms and ramifies the impoverished and high-stakes imaginaries that fear produces, and which it has, of course, always produced. The imaginaries aren't new, but the way they can be mobilised and intensified – set into self-fulfilling motion – under neoliberalism might well be. Neoliberalism takes the binaries that smothered fear throws up and conjures them in the real. By affirming and promising to reward the worst of that of which we're capable, it lures us into affirming that we are only the worst versions of ourselves and that the way forward is to intensify and cultivate this worst-ness.

If this is true, then we can only suffer. Except that it isn't. It isn't true – we can also uncomply.

I've tried to intimate why a Plain Life would be something else. Minimally and radically *other*, not in opposition, not even deigning. Deciding that a plain life can also be a big, rich, intense life steps outside of neoliberalism's usual take.

Plain but not impoverished. Singular but not individualised. It is going on all the while, indefatigably, despite the noise of the neoliberal circus, its crisis thinking, and convenience logics. A plain life. It might sound like birds, like being accountable and saying sorry, like learning something well and slowly, or like the kettle boiling in another room.

Excuse me for a moment. I'll be back shortly ...

Deciding Capacities
moves we make

I don't know about you, but subcontracting out *too* many choices tends to leave me feeling weird. That said, I'm no purist. If you tell me there's a restaurant and a time to be ready, dressed suitably and with an appetite, I'm all there. That's a deliberate relinquishing of administrative burden, and an occasion. No, I mean the other kind of surreptitious subcontracting that has sneaked into our contemporary lives.

When I say to a thirteen-year-old at a New Year's family event: 'I'm not sure I love what the music platforms do to my "taste"', they answer that they love having all these playlists created for them. 'A playlist for when I'm sad, when I want to focus, when I'm motivated.' We're both right, of course. I may, however, be contemplating within a longer arc of temporality.

You see, I don't always know that I'm doing it (the subcontracting), and it can be regarding things including but far beyond music. I can't, therefore, spot the source of the uneasiness that it tends to unleash. I can end up liking myself less, with the day getting queasier by the minute. Or I might get snappier, at once more intolerant *and* listless. It's as if I want to *have* my irresponsibility *and* disavow it, too.

A contrived confusion about 'not feeling good', where I fail to apply my intelligence about why this *wouldn't entirely* feel good.

We've become arguably quite accustomed to modes of *not* choosing and *not quite* deciding. Tired, tetchy, living on borrowed vitality, we don't mind when something else – our music algorithm, our socials feed, sheer accident, or the whims of our partner and kids, social pressure/convention – forces our hand for us. Worn out from the drone of quasi-decision, this relieves us. We may falsely believe it absolves us. *I guess that's just what's happened*. One's active role evaporates, and agency becomes opaque, slipping beneath the blistering horizon of *that which concerns me*.

There are, however (and more seldomly), passages when we make intricate origami shapes of interleaved decisions. *Actual* decisions. All grown-up like.

One could be tempted to swap out 'decision' for the word 'choice', as if they worked as synonyms. But perhaps we need at least two words. *Choice* could suggest choosing-between, whereas we could let decision imply a mechanism of both content and follow-through, which we ourselves, to some extent, determine or invent.[1]

Thus, our current lives involve lots of micro, tinny faux-choices, benign or otherwise. If too relentless, too saturating, these can *dwindle* our reserves, sapping verve and meaning. Consider the feeling of looking at a lot of, say, hundreds of potential running shoes online. *Oosh*. Or shopping to spend a birthday voucher, also online. Or selecting a gelato flavour when you're poorly slept and platform addled. *So hard for me right now* – the vegan lychee lime, or the buttered gluten-free popcorn. It's a new kind of malaise. Truly, a new invention in human feeling.

People!

There *are* genuine choices where we choose between something and something else, and where these two things are not effectively just versions of each other. Alain Badiou includes such choosings in the process he calls a *truth procedure*. In order to remain faithful to a truth that we want to follow through on, there are daily, humble choices that involve yes or no responses. Repeatedly. In ongoing contexts. Will I go to the demo? Will I write a letter to my local member? Will I attend the strike? Will I call up a person I have been thinking about, simply but insistently, for months now to propose a meeting? Will I risk this phrasing in a poem that might not yet be legible in the canon? These are genuine choices, and to construct a truth, Badiou says, we will embark on this process of fidelity, which isn't glamorous, and is difficult and meaningful. It involves a labour of choosing, yes or no, in each instance, in each situation.

Finally, there are *actual* decisions. These might merit the term 'audacious' that Badiou offers. They are rarer, more resounding, and often difficult. The philosopher Jacques Derrida has a confronting and persuasive take on decisions in *The Gift of Death*. Drawing on Kierkegaard, Derrida explains that what makes a decision a decision (and not a program, not the most obvious thing to do) is its undecidability – wow! – its risk and a kind of faith. He explains that there are two moments to any decision. There is the one wherein we might research the pros and cons; we might indeed make a list or a spreadsheet of possible consequences, &c. However, if the spreadsheet told us simply what to do, then we aren't in the realms of decision. We are in the realms of cost–benefit analysis. That's something – *sure* – but it isn't a decision. Decision has this *other* moment. We do analyse, think, research and 'weigh things up', however, to be involved in a decision *per se*, after and alongside informing ourselves with these sane actions, we also leap. We enter into informed madness ...

If we *only* leapt, with no deliberation or thought, then we would be verily mad. Thus, we must leap (because something of us is required for proper decisions), *and* this cannot exactly be derived. We cannot indemnify our decisions by referring to a chart, report, table, &c. that *told us to*. We are included, and *we decide*. We, not any ghost in the spreadsheet, contribute to the future that will then unfold.

So, there are a lot of shades and degrees and levels in this Choosing–Deciding business.

Kind parents often present young children with benign quasi-choices, in those moments when it's not really a matter of a genuine choosing. Putting on underpants to go to school is not a truth procedure. Sometimes parents invent an appropriately fake choice in a skilful way: 'Would you like to wear the green ones or the purple ones?'

It's unkind to present a six-year-old with something too decision-like for the circumstances. The bus is leaving, and your mum needs to be in a Zoom at 9.10am. To ask (at 7.37am), 'Darling, what do you think about humans wearing coverings when attending an educational institution called a "school"; do you want to get educated in the current system and according to this recent curriculum?' is not a kindness. (It might be a parent who struggles with not being liked in every moment.)

As an adult, I *appreciate* a decent choice coming along, to supplement the imitation ones that most of our days are cluttered with, the condescending, time-gobbling faux-choices that we blunt our best teeth on. How much, I want to ask, do we conspire with being infantilised in the sandpit we call our current techno-economic predicament?

If we primarily exist in that charmless category known as the Prosumer (by which I mean Alwin Toffler's term describing how we create value for companies without receiving any wages for this labour – daily, addictive labour, often – and without being aware we do this), then many of the 'choices' with which we're presented won't even make the grade as meriting the name. In Australia, it might be Bunnings or Mitre 10 … *yep.* Airbnb or Booking.com. Amazon or whatever.

These are less choices than a same–same. *Purple or green, sweetheart.* Like a scattered Grade One-er, sometimes we're a bit cornered in our nude, sleepy vulnerability. However, if you paid attention in the first chapter, you'd see that it's still Not Nothing if you're able to notice *the fact of* how there wasn't really much of a genuine choice on offer in that instance. Notice playfully; just to clock it.

Decisions, on the other hand, could be seen as opening space *for us*, out in front of us. Where a *choice* plonks a suite of options down in front of us (or seems to ...), the decision clears an unknown space and whispers: *what do you want to put here?* Decisions signal that there is wriggle room, breathing space among the molecules of necessity, habit and assumption. Decisions can include us, *and* they ask more of us.

Terrifying, no?

The room-to-move in a decision is less the gap *between* the existing options (although in its stages we might have to choose-between as part of the broader decision). The feeling of real space in a decision might have to do with its being a moment of shimmering potential. Vertiginous. Once decided, we will collapse this aspect of its wave. The space *before* deciding is often tinged with risk's anxious wondering, since the future hovers on the threshold of existing, unseen *and* ripe to be filled in with colour, texture. We will cast our decision – an *act*, in fact – forward like a weighted line to hook a different future we don't yet know. Nothing guarantees it for us, not even platitudes uttered *post hoc*, such as: 'it was meant to be'.

Thus, we are choosing and deciding – in among all the constrained and energy-squandering pseudo-choices – *all the time*. I don't want to list stuff. It's better you make your own inventory of the possible micro-decisions that waste your time. You could say, we are often not very free, *and* we are *not* wholly and *not* always unfree.

A question might be whether there any principles to inform how we position ourselves in such decisions? And, also, to wonder whether there are ways I can *form* myself that would reduce the likelihood of my squandering these tiny openings when they blink freshly out of obscurity? Are there worse and better models by which one can apply some thinking to the situation? Better for me, worse for me? Better for the collective? Worse for the collective?

Is better/worse even a useful frame? (We will see, with the philosopher Baruch Spinoza, that all binaries are not equal ...)

The more intimidating question (I'll hold off on grappling with it thoroughly for now): *where am I giving ground without understanding that I am?* Where am I adding to life's being unliveable (for me, for others ...)? This sends a nasty shudder through ... and, like me, you might be feeling tired now.

How about I tell you a story about deciding?

∝

IN MY EARLY TWENTIES, I LIVED IN NORTHERN Germany. It was across the university winter semester – October through February. I celebrated my 21st birthday there. Three friends back in Australia arranged for a bunch of flowers to be delivered that morning. I thought it the most wonderful gift imaginable. There was no party; there was a bouquet.

It came at the end of a longer trip through Europe. I'd saved hard for it, working at the gym and the Italian restaurant. I must have been fleeing some age-appropriate confusion and bad feelings (about which I had little insight), as well as getting distance from Australia and its bleak settler vibes. I was probably curious about, hungry for, what, without having words for it, I hoped was a *big enough life*. For sure, I would have been under the sway of some heavy cultural cringe that made Everything Elsewhere more desirable, more likely to emancipate me, more stylish and alive.

After the usual bussing and training around the continent – hostels, loneliness, weight gain (it turns out Nutella *isn't* high protein), epiphanies, awkward encounters and artless poetry – I managed to get some kind of study place, via a chain of confusing snail mail in German, at the main university in my destination city. I wasn't enrolled for credit, but I wasn't *not* enrolled. I qualified, for example, for a student card, which granted free travel on inner-city transport and near-regional trains. I could enrol in scheduled subjects or join others in designing and proposing reading courses for credit (it was that kind of university!). The set-up offered just enough gentleness and just enough structure and purpose. I could collapse at some level, while still appearing to be Doing Something. In some part of myself, I was so deeply exhausted. In those days I had neither the language of psychoanalysis, nor of yoga (practising). I had little political critique, and no real insight into the vicissitudes of my upbringing.

The exhaustion, too, could have been from all the unfelt fear. It could have stemmed from a certain kind of rhythm of surviving/striving that I hadn't yet managed to spot and query. I see now that I was poised on a seriously delicate cusp in a younger person's trajectory. *Mine*. Viewed retrospectively, I was certainly teetering on a brink – existential, psychological, socioeconomic, physical ...

At this university, I made a friend.

I'd lived overseas alone once before and had been very lonely. That time, I'd read a lot of books, done singing practice, cried myself to sleep, gone for long walks, found a way to lose my virginity on my own terms, and other antics not inappropriate for a late teen. This second time, I decided to be more proactive. Rather than waiting for friends to find me, I thought I'd place myself in spaces where I might meet other people, where it was more expected that people might chat and encounter one another.

The German university had a strong history of communist politics, emancipatory thinking and practice. In the building cluster labelled *Geisteswissenschaft* (which means 'humanities', but literally translates to 'Spirit/Mind Science') there was a space called the *Frauenraum*. Women's Room. It was one of those gender-segregated experiments of that era. These days one sees fewer of them in this same shape, and it would be more complicated now. *Then*, however, the idea of such a room, as I grasped it, was that women (straight or unsure, queer or just tired) could go to this room and experiment with how they might interact if there wasn't a male gaze going on. If they'd been on the end of gendered violence, there was one space in which they didn't have to steel themselves. Or if one had instead been mostly on the velvet-glove end of patriarchy, one generally didn't need to manufacture oneself to meet the expectations of a shifting and capricious Heteronorm. You might think this last idea is bonkers, but it also isn't. Many women (straight and not) still alter their comportment massively when a man, or certain cipher for dominating man-vibe, enters the space. Call it Being Strategic. Call it 'My father was awesome' (or 'a total train wreck'). Call it Oppression. Call it the Unconscious. In any case, *certain* conversations or ways of being don't tend to take place in spaces mapped too-starkly by a Hegemonic Masculinity, or with someone around who is straining to maintain allegiance to it.

My experience of that particular *Frauenraum* (as someone white, cis, foreign) was that I could go there and be around other women, or lie silently on the ground with period pain, or have a cup of free tea-bag tea in a chipped mug. I could go there and unwrap a sweaty, homemade cheese sandwich and eat it while staring into space, on a lumpy couch, surrounded by posters advertising protests, demos, strikes, gigs and reading groups. I cannot say whether it was a safe space for everyone who considered themselves a woman in that moment. I was an outsider for a short time, and probably missed a lot of subtleties. It's likely the space had inevitable blind spots, flaws and inconsistencies, its sly ways of excluding and its hypocritical codes and fallouts. I'd like to think, however, that some folk who went there didn't have to put themselves together so much. (Read: it was okay to drop the façade of ableness, of competency, for a while.) I liked to think I didn't have to pretend to have a clue about anything, generate any allure, or appear as something I wasn't. I'm sure I recall it with the gloss that recollection casts over things long past. And, I don't have a clear picture of the room's furniture or décor, or of its layout within the larger, sprawling campus. I do remember though that it was in that room that I had my first conversation with C. who would become my friend.

This first conversation could only have been brief, leaning against the back of the main couch, staring towards the laminated shelving, where the tea bags, free tampons and discarded philosophy texts were scattered. It would have been in my broken, fledgling Deutsch. The conversation couldn't have been very witty or amusing from my side (I had two years of university intensive German behind me and next to zero local immersion at that stage). I'm fairly sure, though, that we didn't revert back to English. C. was one of those considerate (and patient) German people who realise a visitor to their country might want to learn the language, and thus don't bombard the person with fluent English, thereby closing down any possibility of the visitor acquiring their own fluency. She must have listened to my inelegant account of why I was there, whom I was living with, what subjects I was studying, where I came from. I must have been able to ask her some questions in a way that made sense enough.

Doing a degree in German back home. Close by with a local family I met through my German lecturer. A reading group on 'population politics', Foucault course on *The Order of Things* (with a likely very brilliant lecturer whose insistent stutter combined with my stuttering German meant I couldn't string and hold any concepts together), feminist linguistics. And – Melbourne.

I would have asked her questions along similar lines. She was not from there. She'd come to study from an area in the south of Germany. (They have a wonderful language particle, *Gell* ... It means, sort of, 'right?' or invites your listener to confirm what you're saying. Like the French *n'est-ce pas?* ... I loved hearing her use it.) She was living in a big student house. Studying Psychology.

After about ten minutes – it couldn't have been longer – we both had to go. I assumed the conversation was a once-off, since

I had no sense that I'd been conversationally charming enough for this smart person to seek a repeat.

I assumed I'd never speak to this person again. At best we might cross paths in the *Frauenraum* but, even then, she might ignore me on that second encounter – with that furtive or flustered glimpsing between people that slips away, and crumbles into non-greeting. (I've often wondered whether this Pretending You Haven't Met Syndrome is linked to people's profound lack of social skill, or to honed arrogance, or even to simple short-sightedness. For a long time, it seemed part of the wallpaper of a coldish and careless world.)

Then I heard her say: 'Are you free next week on Wednesday afternoon? I'd like to meet again.'

I knew no one in the town, had no social plans, and a minimal timetable. I had twice-weekly appointments to teach English to a friend of my host family. I was securing paid work as a casual fitness instructor. Digesting disbelief (at her invitation), I said I was, and that I would also like to.

'Good. We can meet at this café, near the main park, and we can go walking, if you want.'

I nodded, probably, while she scribbled out on a piece of paper a café name and street address, before ferrying the pen back into her canvas bag. She gave me the paper. 'Three o'clock?'

Fünfzehn Uhr.

There were no mobile phones at this moment. I don't recall that we swapped land line numbers. We simply had an appointment. I noted it and she left for her next class.

I was astonished. Germans have a way that surprises someone with a certain flavour of English as mother tongue. I think it's because they tend to use the conditional mode of verbs far less. There're fewer 'woulds', 'coulds', 'mights' and 'shoulds', and more direct verbs. Here's an example. English-y person answering the question, 'Would you like some cake?'

'Well, of course. It looks absolutely delicious. Normally I'd love to. Unfortunately, today I'm a little upset in the tummy, and am wondering whether perhaps I should have a little break from sweets ...'

A German: 'No.'

One could see this as rude – where is the fawning quibbling and voluble reassurance? But, for a German (as I read it) a piece of information was sought (about the wish for a piece of cake) and an answer was given. The answer isn't trying to coddle the relation further; it doesn't imply that the rejection is loaded in any way. Its style, tone and concision has nothing to do with how the non-cake wanter feels about you in their heart. It *isn't* a 'No' that implies other things about the wider relationship. It's an answer to a cake query. 'No – but I want some more of the salmon sandwiches, please.'

As newish to Germany, I was similarly stunned by C.'s friendly directness, at her clarity regarding wants and plans. I was more stunned again that she might seek out a further meeting with me. Weren't people likely to take an interest in me if I was nimble and amusing in language or could play with ideas? (none of which I could do at this stage with my toddler-level German). I hadn't encountered before such a crisp *and* warm way. At once: crisp and warm. It all felt very *plain*.

Also (for those of you of a certain mind) it *wasn't* a queer flirt. I wasn't being stealthily propositioned. By all accounts, she wanted to meet with me a second time. Well, to do that, we would make a plan and stick to it.

The next week we did. And the week after that. And then probably at less regular, since more frequent, intervals. I stayed with her at her student accommodation. Met her neglectful boyfriend (and the blonde pixie-headed flatmate she was in love with). We ice-skated together out on the big paddocks which the farmers skilfully flooded when February winter hit its peak. We did a theatrical student demo intervention, with costumes and face paint, that got us all in the newspaper. She became a regular feature at weekend breakfasts with my host family. We went to Christmas markets, studied together, walked often. We became friends.

(Are you waiting for a dramatic twist, a sinister-yet-drama-filled turn of events? She turns out to be 'borderline'. She kills herself. She betrays me. She is a consummate liar. She is working out a plan to nick my stuff. She gets pregnant to the person I'm pining for … You might be. A lot of writing styles prime you for that. I can tell you now, there is no such denouement …)

I don't know if such a thing would be possible, in this same way, today. Perhaps it was a meeting for its time. Of its time. As new friendship, it definitely couldn't rely on a certain convenience and wasn't subject to the complications that recent technology can invite. It may simply have taken a different shape, but still a good one, had it had access to messenger platforms, had it been able to plan (and change) its meetings minutes in advance.

I suspect clear wanting and affinity looks the same no matter what historical moment one finds oneself in. No matter the technological, historical, economic backdrop, when we want things, we pursue them, working around the obstacles and with the affordances of our times. Or eventually … we learn to do this, right?

To want things and pursue them, I mean.

C. seemed early on to know how to do this. Or to have an idea of how this would work. She managed to pull it off with me.

She didn't do it in some heavy 'go-getter' way. (This ability to feel-and-do wanting isn't – I don't think – another phrasing for 'ambitious'.) It wasn't some slick effort at extending her circles, 'building her network'. *Blah*. No. Her ability to initiate a plan, to invite me respectfully to be part of it, to stick to it … in other words to *show up*, in that metaphorical sense of the term … I'd now put this under the category of *good character*. Good character is an old-fashioned notion that a therapist re-introduced me to (probably when I was struggling to find words for a way of being I may have wanted from others and in myself). Sometimes it's a useful expression to have. It hints towards a register of quality that some more fleetingly current categories don't accommodate so well.

C. and I are still friends. She has posted me stuff I request from Germany, and I've transferred her the money. We meet, if itineraries allow, in hotels midway between the places we respectively find ourselves. (Once we met up in the hotel that Rachel Cusk set her novel, *Kudos*, in, with our room in the circular architecture of an old water tower. I struggled to find the bathroom behind the strange sliding panel, and got dizzy in the Escheresque halls; it was long before the novel existed); we phone sometimes; we send long essay-like texts or rambling voice memos. I tell her, as one of my closest people, my closest things. I helped with the flowers for her wedding.

You are wondering why this is the story about deciding – it is. And, more interesting again, it's a story about learning a *principle* of deciding.

It was from C. (who was merely beginning her psychology studies, but has subsequently become an established therapist) that I first heard a most straightforward and non-resentful framing about people *and deciding in relation to people*, that has stayed with me. It struck me like a bright lamp turning on in my brain, lighting up a corner of life and how to relate to others that, until then, I hadn't done so well with.

It has to do not with deciding things about people, but rather: deciding about your own behaviour in relation to people. (C. may have used this logic when deciding to invite me to meet her that first *next* time; I flatter myself she might have.)

Now, there is a certain reading of the seventeenth-century thinker Baruch Spinoza that comes via the twentieth-century philosopher Gilles Deleuze, which in those days I definitely hadn't heard of, and I doubt C. had heard of it either. It concerns our *capacity* and how we tend to it. Look after it. Care for it. Cultivate it. How we might *resist* the very-human impulse to squander it.

Deleuze's reading is about noticing, too, what happens to capacity. By the term 'capacity', we can simply understand it as *what we can do*. Sometimes, I would also read it as being able to change, to become something else, should we feel a bit sick of ourselves. Deleuze, at times, frames it as a kind of 'health', something that doesn't wreck the life we have.

Now, you might think I'm about to lurch into a lecture about maximising your efficiency, productivity, satisfaction or self-worth, but obviously, *no*. If you've gotten this far (having traversed the eponymous first chapter), you will have noticed that this is not my interest at all. So, what does Spinoza, as read by Deleuze, possibly tell us about capacity and feeling? How did C. somehow have a version of this at the young age of 21?

∝

BETWEEN NOVEMBER 1980 AND MARCH 1981, DELEUZE gave a series of lectures called 'The Velocities of Thought'.[2] He had already given a lecture on Spinoza in 1978, which sketches some of the concepts I re-invoke here below.

Deleuze, already in the late 70s, reads Spinoza as suggesting that we have at least two basic affects (which envelop further ones). These two basic ones do not correspond to any particular state; they are not descriptions that match a *static* state. Rather they occur when we're in the process of *changing* states. Deleuze calls them *slides*. According to this reading, we have the basic affects of joy and sadness, corresponding to two directions of sliding. Affect equals 'slide' equals 'change of mode/state'.

Here's the concept: joy is the affect that accompanies an *increase* in our capacity; sadness is the affect we have when our *capacity* is going down.

Pause a moment. (If you already know this idea, you can go make yourself a hot drink.) If you don't know this idea, you might let its originality reverberate in you for a moment.

Think of how often you can feel 'sad', or 'flat' for seemingly no reason, and then a day later get a cold, or come down with the flu. *Affect* here names a process and is given the nickname 'sadness'. It correlates with an experience which approximates this 'feeling' but not because this feeling is connected to any narrative events in life (I'm not sad *because* I lost something; I'm not sad *because* a friend was unkind).

I know, after Deleuze's Spinoza, not to invent a story about 'why' this tone of experience ... my 'sadness' here is blatantly *not* psychological. 'Psychologising' would be when I invest in the sad feeling imprecisely by upholstering it with confused associations and possible interpersonal 'reasons'... Thanks to a Spinozan take, when I experience 'sadness' of this kind, I tend to wait. I remain internally quiet: *let's see what the reason might be.* What's the process generating this atmosphere in my organism that we can shorthand as 'sad'?

If sickness comes along, I can see that, at least part of why I've felt bodily 'sad' (translation: a downward slide of my capacity), might be due to something in my organism that is making me sick – in other words, less vital. Sickness is my body's encountering of another body that isn't good for me.[3] Spinoza might call it a *bad mixture* for me. I might find myself calling the lurgy 'evil', too. That lurgy-constellation, splattered out by a very sweet, but unmasked, sneezer on my morning tram! The lurgy that's hitchhiked on a cuddle with my neighbour's toddler ... Spinoza wouldn't disagree with saying it was evil, as long as I only meant evil-for-me. For him, this word only works for describing encounters that make *me* sadder. I can't generalise the adjective 'evil' for other mixtures, for other bodies in their own mixtures.

In that sense – and this is *so* interesting – this 'evil' isn't moral.

Better to just say that it's bad for me. It doesn't however have some *intrinsic* evil quality. This isn't how Spinoza viewed the world.

Hence, another entity – this lurgy – also with capacities, with joy and sadness of its own, has encountered my body. The point is that my body and the lurgy's body are a less-terrific mixture *for me*. For a while, my capacity plummets. Fatigue, pain, snot, bad moods, fearfulness, scattered thought, eerie whimpering from my huddled form on the bed. The name for this process of sliding down in Spinoza's terms is the affect 'sadness'. It's a name we give – not to a 'something' in the world (an *extensive* thing, a thing with extended dimensions), but – to something *intensive*, a way to name changing-ness, as such.

One of the best anecdotes that Deleuze tells about Spinoza is how the latter got on the wrong side of influential people of his day because he read the Garden of Eden story along similar lines to the theory above. Spinoza had the notion that God wasn't at all on a power trip. *Huh?* No! he wasn't trying to *boss* Adam and Eve around. There wasn't even a solid notion of good and evil ruling in the garden that could be applied universally, where God knew the secret code for the categories. Rather, God just knew a bit about Adam and Eve's bodies (he'd made them) and he knew a bit about the qualities of the plants in his garden (he'd made them as well, supposedly). His so-called 'decree', which according to Spinoza wasn't quite that at all, was more a fact-sharing session, simply saying that they might not want to eat that stuff, since it wouldn't be a good, or *vital*, mixture or encounter between bodies (humans and fruit). Deleuze says that God just knew that that fruit was – for Adam – poisonous. In that way *alone* was the fruit 'evil' – evil, or sad-making for *a human constitution*. That particular fruit wasn't going to make these two particular human bodies feel better; in fact, the fruit's qualities were such that they were likely to become quite sad.

Downward slide. And *not* like the *wheeeee* feeling on the terrifying rainbow ride at the water park.

The Edenic Fall wasn't a good time by all accounts. If it *wasn't* a 'punishment', if it wasn't an exercise in moral argy-bargy, how are we to understand what unfolded after that? Speculating with Spinoza, I'm guessing it becomes instead about a lack of intelligence, a lack of integrated knowledge (failure to heed shared knowledge) leading to unpleasant things.

As the 'first people', Adam and Eve, for Spinoza, were likely to be at a very rudimentary stage of ideas and thinking. This differs from what Deleuze calls the Adamic tradition, where the assumption is that they embodied perfection at the outset, *then* that there was a loss thereof due to an accident from the outside. For Spinoza, mostly we begin imperfectly, since we don't know much.

Adam and Eve were living solely via each encounter, each *ocursus*. (This is his word for it in Latin.) We are all like this for a long while. Adam and Eve grasped what was pertinent for them (for their bodies, for their organism's unique situation) only after undergoing the *effects* of the fruit. They made a risky experiment, even while God was *revealing*, Deleuze says, a basic fact of their physical universe. The God character, then, was giving them some insider info implying he had an understanding of the … *causes*. (This is how Spinoza arranges it: effects, causes.) God's knowledge of causes meant that he could predict (before anyone's having to undergo effects) that the ensuing mixture would be 'bad' for them specifically.

The fruit, let's reiterate, wasn't *evil*, in itself. This way of classing things isn't how Spinoza thinks. Deleuze considers this a sign of Spinoza's rare, sage-like innocence. The fruit was just bad for them, specifically.

Whenever I revise this part of Deleuze's Spinoza, I groan a little inside. How often do I still embark on things that I kinda suspect will be sad-making for me? I mean … (embarrassingly) I do this *plenty*. It goes badly, and then I might even imagine that someone is punishing me. Instead of contemplating that this thing just wasn't in advance good medicine for me, I can go off on hideously gauche tangents of *why*? Why me? Why did it faceplant? What's wrong with me, them, the world, &c.?

Now, you can see, too, why Spinoza's popularity among religious power mongers would be plummeting wildly. We can ask ourselves what the contemporary version of the good and evil binary is that *we*, now, believe without question, when we might care to be more cautious. We think we're really 'modern' and don't have these moral binds on us anymore.

For us, our consistent moral imperatives are arguably the unquestionable, nigh-religious (in their invisibility) categories of productive/unproductive, efficient/inefficient, even motivated/procrastinating. These are the poles of our new moral code, of our Set In Stone categories. I suggest strongly you consider coughing up what you've swallowed undiscerningly about them, and examine the chunky, rainbow pile more closely ... but don't tell anyone. Keep your 'Productivity or Die' t-shirt for office parties, or people get antsy. Withdrawing a little of your good-natured allegiance to these categories will soften something, give a little more breathing space. You won't even need to download a new app. You're also likely to remain quite energetic, collegial and not snowed-under.

Bad encounters, in their various shapes, perhaps are for a long while inevitable. We test the things we want to test. *Why can't I have the fruit?!* Well, have it and see. This, too, is an aspect of being alive, a slant on living. Spinoza, according to Deleuze, says that mostly we live like this endlessly, instead of developing *from* it as a basis, towards other modes of 'reason' (i.e. not squandering our life force). He sternly says that when we're stuck like this, we're spiritual automatons ... We are forever just bouncing between effects of things on us, and never leaping to the next level of ideas, where we are less prone to the passivity of the passions, less a gullible schmuck dragged up and down by randomness, and only dragged.

You can see that once you frame things (that are avoidable or repeatable, that you seek out to test) as *experiments* you are making, then a certain mode of resentful complaining eases up. You dignify yourself and your adventures. You intentionalise your own movement through the world. This doesn't apply to toddlers, nor even to those in the dimmest twilight at the end of a life, but if *you're* reading this, it probably applies to you.

Deleuze elaborates: *it's less that we have ideas, than that ideas are affirming themselves in us.* Whoah. These ideas, that provoke the slides (up or down), are having their way with us. *Ha!* Sleazy, *gell*? We are passive in relation to them. We stumble on through our encounters – with little intention, not so much dignity.

How often am I mostly a spiritual automaton? Well … mostly. I confuse principles with handed-down rules and objective consequences with punishment … the brain does this merging, but it's often not very precise.

What happens if we subtract punishment as a concept from our list of default assumptions? Leave it softly behind, as a worn-out thinking we acquired during childhood … where we may have perceived constant punishment (and circled subsequently in storms of vengefulness).

I've learned (from Spinoza, but also psychoanalysis) to hold off from assuming anyone is 'punishing' me now, even when it could seem they are (at work, in friendships, in broader circles).

Usually, people are *wildly* self-involved. They are immersed in galloping reactivity to their own internal chemistries, landscapes and fantasy narratives. They're tired. They're frightened. They're on a merry-go-round of hormones / self-medication / burnout / nostalgia … They tend to have little tenacity in these or other matters. Sometimes.

Punishment, you see, does seem like a lot of extra work for the other. They have to be at the top of an energy wave to have energy spare for punishing. Sometimes it's punishment, but more likely you're not that special and the other is not that organised. They, too, are more likely to be tumbling from encounter to encounter.

Now: back to the garden, and to what tends to go with punishment, that is: 'rules'.

I consider it a sign of my own immaturity (the immaturity that can continue deep into adulthood), when I interpret someone sharing information with me as that person telling me what I *should* do. The assumption leaps to thinking it's about *control*: they want to have power over us! We know that certain people do like to wield knowledge as power. On the other hand, giving information and trying to control shouldn't be collapsed *necessarily*. Adam and Eve might have misunderstood God's basic gesture, and then believed they were in a *rule*-scenario – they assumed that God had a rule that he was inventing and imposing. In Spinoza's reading, *there was no rule*. Maybe it was more of a fact, a *law* ('law' of physiology, 'law' of botany ...). For Spinoza, God wasn't inventing a rule and then enjoying telling A & E what to do. His God wasn't invested in power ... (If anyone is invested in power, surely it is we paltry humans ... surely God, with all that infiniteness has better things to do?)

Spinoza's God wasn't using capricious means to structure behaviours of those beneath him in the hierarchy. He was, rather, informing his nude, frolicking, fresh humans that a mixture between their being (anatomy, make-up) and the fruit's being (enzymes, G.I.) may not work out best for them. As the story of Genesis goes, it didn't.

(Now, *fantasies* of rules and of punishment are also fantasies of attention. Trying to get punished can be a scheme for getting attention, even if it comes in an unpleasant package. This is all basic stuff, right? When we are imagining punishment as the main logic, we are also often imagining a scene in which we (unhappily, painfully) are the centre of attention. It's a negative version of Being the Main Attraction. Wanting to be attended-to has sneaky ways of cropping up. Sometimes I'm slow to see my strange behaviours as also being related to that. *Oh! I just want some attention.* In adulthood, furthermore, I can now see that where I once would have imagined interdiction, being-forbidden-to-do something, I usually just have to come to terms with an objective Limit in Reality.)

I'm lobbing the concepts at you fast and furiously. Let's gather ourselves for a moment.

We're considering capacity, how it slides up and down, and its connection to affects, processes of changing. Two basic directions of affect (or in Spinoza's Latin, *affectus*): sadness and joy. We've seen that Spinoza has a different take to most on ideas of good and evil; he is not interested in this binary in the way people tend to be (with some things established in the intrinsically 'good' column, some things stranded in the 'evil' column). Deleuze says Spinoza's approach is more *innocent*, in that he considers evil as that quality which emerges due to bad mixtures *for us*, and which can't accurately be generalised.

We consider 'good', following Spinoza, things that are good *for us*.

The question is: would this lead to mayhem, to wild selfishness? To a horrible world? Some would say the world is already a Bit Horrible for quite a few people ... and has the generalised, moral notion of evil really served us well? Let's leave this open. We aren't under any obligation to be sure. We are considering ideas. *Carefully.*

Deleuze says Spinoza might view it as imprecise to extrapolate cases of bad or good mixtures outwards (to generalise and then essentialise them) *too* enthusiastically. It's like holding off on offering advice that only bases itself on what was once *good for you*. It may be relevant for the other *or* it might not be. We live through local happenings, meetings, mixtures. We try to notice.

As someone who 'looks after' some people in my world (and

same goes for any parent, a teacher, a boss, probably You, with one of your hats on ...) a real pitfall, as I've mentioned already (see previous chapter), is not to pass on your fear to those more vulnerable than you. It's super hard. The fear is in us from a bad mixture we once lived, and then we want to protect those we care for from having this same experience. But, if we don't really understand the *cause* of the bad mixture, and we only lived it as *effect* and now have the trace of its badness in our reactive bodies, then can we really offer it as a solid principle to someone else?

It always *depends*. This is why it's difficult.

I know that when I offer advice off the basis of my past fears, it tends to be useless *and* might be damaging for another (the *experience* itself, of my doing the 'Telling'). I need to come at the person's scenario while not being mired in my own past anguish. I'm likely to get seduced by the drama of my own anguish, and 'enjoy' myself and the drama-story a little too much, losing even my grip on accuracy. People can smell it too. Young people can smell it when you're masturbating via a lecture on your own Painful, Superior Experience.

They're likely to despise you a little ... or feel sorry for you.

C.'s 'advice', as you'll see shortly, was much more useful for me than if she had tried to tell me in every instance, with whom to be friends, or if she'd warned me off people *of a certain kind*. Instead, she ventured a principle, rather than advice. Principles last longer.

(A tad more theory and then we'll be back in snowy Germany. Snow, even sleet, by the way, has tended to be a great mixture for me. Sun less so. And, for you it might be the other way around ...)

For Deleuze's Spinoza, being bodies means we are kinds of 'kinetic' (moving) constellations, collections of aspects in motion. Encounters with other bodies – 'meetings', 'mixtures' – produce changes of state: increase or decrease in capacity. We're probably going through umpteen shifts like this a day, an hour, even every minute, if you think about the communities within us, subterranean communities (research has shown that this is undeniably so ... *mitochondria*!). Our bodies are working with (are workings *of*) countless internal changes, slidings of state, with these layered changes being literally ceaseless.

Deleuze lends this idea in Spinoza his own term: Continuous Variation. It is the melody we live along. A fluctuating line, a process. (Deleuze says that this is his own term; he derives it from the *Ethics*.)

What Spinoza will refer to as *affectus* (affect) is this very melody. At this *inadequate* level of ideas (as he terms it) we mostly travel the melody line *passively*. We live the effects, and our capacity goes up or down with random meetings, mixtures. Joy. Sadness. Hither. Thither. Undergoing, but not so much paying attention ...

These encounters, then, these meetings with other bodies, leave us with less capacity and some encounters leave us with more. Some modes of getting mixed up in the world enliven us, and others don't. Sometimes I walk around very disbelieving but also curious as to why we appear so interested in choosing that which *dis*-enlivens us? (This isn't a word ... but it *does* something, as word, don't you think?)

It is perhaps to do with the layers, what I called the 'umpteen layers', within the constellations that we are. One of the layers is enlivened by an encounter (or repeated encounters), but perhaps not the whole set-up. Your tastebuds love X, but your gut chemistry/blood sugar does not love X. Or a hidden, past version of yourself that you carry around, having forgotten to let it lie, loves a certain kind of buddy, but your *actual* life as you are now living it (or trying to) does not love a certain kind of buddy. Or the little repetition machines in your muscles love repeatedly touching your phone screen, and your fingertips kind of love the glass-smoothness, but your overall spiritual thriving does not love the image- and word-combos thrown back via this phone screen, and so on. Or not *all* the time. It gets complicated, of course.

Can you see how this may have serious relevance for the question of compliance with an economic order that loves us Not One Bit (it doesn't *do* love; it does auto-perpetuation)? Can you see why Spinoza injects something shining into how we might make decisions under the current socioeconomic regime? If corporate interest can capture a part of people, then it might manage to snare the whole person, who is arguably dragged along behind this captured part (taste buds, fingertips, repetition machines). This could be the heart of what we call 'convenience'.

There is, incidentally, no easy German equivalent for our term 'convenience'. They do a kind of workaround involving 'comfort', but it's not the same. I could speculate that the culture might be less ripe for absorbing convenience logics. Maybe, but no one believes a generalisation.

Let's keep going with the story ...

C. somehow, not long out of high school, had a take on this whole idea. I'm not sure if she had read it in her psychology texts, or heard a watered-down version of Spinoza, without knowing it. She may have been observing the encounters in her own life and testing ways to understand them. In any case, I must have been fretting about something or someone, and it drew out of her the theory of how she operated.

'I try not to decide what people are like,' she said. 'I don't ask myself that, or pressure myself to know that. I just see, after I've spent time with them, whether I feel more or less energised, stable, more or less alive.'

Amazing, right? Did it dawn on me then how incredible and unusual this way of thinking was? She was definitely a new and becoming-dear friend, but here! she was basically ... a sage – in her bulky jacket, and corduroy pants and cotton scarf, clasping a steaming mug of something herbal, tucked into the corner of a student café, hubbub seething all around. It would have perhaps been that excellent mixture of sunshine + below zero outside. It was the winter semester, after all.

She continued in this vein: 'If I feel shaky and more doubtful about myself and tired and short-tempered, I just notice it. And if those kinds of feelings happen consistently after I've seen that person, then I simply notice it again, keep an open mind, but I may stop going out of my way to see them too often.'

Is it just me, or is this, like, luminous? I was barely 21, on the brink of a breakdown from which I was being quasi-rescued by a steady family vibe in a big snowy town, that was neither A-May-Zing nor Dull. A place. Just a place, with bicycles, a Christmas market, bread rolls for breakfast, and somewhere to sleep that was simple and interpersonally less fraught.

If you're thinking, Incredible Privilege, you'd be right. It's the incredible privilege both of nothing special and nothing terribly awful. A plainness you can barely explain, but you know it when it goes missing. You know it, even when you don't have words.

Regarding, C. and her formula?

I'm grateful that I got to hear such steady sanity from someone so intelligent at such a relatively early moment – *afterwards, check how you feel*. I'm not saying I've managed to follow it often. I may have forgotten it soon after and begun many a misguided relation and friendship, that left me miserable, drained, self-denigrating or wobbly. Either way, in *that* moment I knew I loved it as a conceptual tool. (A conceptual tool is a shape for thinking, for filtering the world; it gives a certain shape to random knowledge that works for a while – good-enough, without being perfect. You don't convert to it; you apply it discerningly.)

Her maxim relieved me of the thing I couldn't quite get comfortable with: *deciding things about other people. Trying to work out what people intrinsically were like*. It gave me a fresh way to play with this problem.

Psychoanalysis would later help me to see that one of the reasons I'm unlikely to be able to say for sure What Others Are Like is that it's actually quite difficult to know even *what I am like*. The glittering mesh of projections and warped perceptions we cast across things makes objective statements of those kinds too random. To assess for oneself, however, whether one is more or less vital due to repeated encounters isn't the worst approach. Maybe C.'s formula helps with the 'capture' I spoke of above. If you gently inquire with yourself afterwards, then maybe in that moment you include more of yourself, and thus can ignore the singing delight in only one part of your person, to pan out and ask a bigger collectivity of yourself: *how did that go?*

(For 'women', this can also be a helpful shift, since apparently we are trained to blame whatever didn't go right in an interaction on ourselves – 'how did I not do everything I could to make that awesome?' *FFS*. It's harder for us, apparently, to be like – 'that felt bad for me afterwards, maybe I won't try for a seventy-fifth date ...' *Bitte sehr*.)

Deciding something essential and fixed about yourself? It's barely achievable. Highly inaccurate. Mostly, only very shoddy approximations emerge. Mostly deciding things about myself is a time-squandering exercise. I prefer to do other things. With almost no idea of what I'm like, I'm hardly going to make claims of knowing anything too certain *about you*. That's the point of C.'s method. Don't ask about them ('what they're like'), ask about some version of Spinoza's Body Mixture.

Is it a good mixture – this 15:00 rendezvous at the park café during a German winter? Joyous slide? Sad slide?

It was a softly joyous slide, I think. Plain enough. Not evil-for-me.

If you have a model that asks: 'Is this a good or interesting person?' 'Is this a person you should spend time with?'... well, you're already required to have information you don't have, to make judgements you simply aren't equipped for. How could you know *how* someone, anyone truly, or deeply *is*? This information is not for any of us, since, as Spinoza makes clear, bodies anyway, people-in-bodies, are always in flux and changing. So, this imprecise question is to be avoided. This is a wobbly way of trying to make a decision.

The decision – as C. demonstrated for me – doesn't need to ground itself on *what they are like*. Rather, it is about *what you want to do*. If they are a person, a live creature, a life that is changing and growing, then you can't (i.e. it isn't ever possible, it doesn't have to do with your insight, &c.) sum them up with any easy accuracy or foresight. But you can decide if you want to spend time with them, based somewhat on a small sample of times of being with them. Arguably imprecise, *at least* it places the imprecision somewhere other than ad hoc, shonky character judgement.

I *know*: we tend still to make the judgements. We are not very good at not putting labels on things, whereas Spinoza is trying to lead us towards observing processes. Holding off on the fixed label for even a tiny moment ... His is a very high-level kind of noticing.

We make them, these sketchy summaries – she tends to be short-tempered, but funny; they are generous but can turn a little mean when nervous; he can lurch from dark moods into boundless affection ... Sometimes these attempts are a guide of sorts, but I'd suggest we cultivate the art of only lightly believing any takes we cook up. They often are not complex enough to capture a living creature. We may form them, only to let them go later. If you haven't seen someone in a long while, there's a chance you know very little of what they are like, of how they have become.

When I used the clumsier model of trying to decide 'how people were' (read: *knowing what they 'were' intrinsically*), I just ended up feeling bad for picking on, criticising, sledging, paying out on ... I didn't want to do any of that. *Grimy*. Or I could idealise people, also inaccurately, polishing them up with words and descriptions that also missed the mark.

This model of C.'s, then, is helpful if you tend regularly to 'find' new, exciting friends and admire them blindly, or wallow in being impressed by them, or enthusiastically line up your opinions with theirs, when they are also likely to be a complex mixture – schmucky, saint-like, unreliable, generous, oblivious – that many of us are. A certain style of attachment (here: too fast, too shiny) might get some needed modulation, if you were to use C.'s 'how is my capacity after' method.

If someone makes you exhausted, short-tempered and dislike yourself a little more after you hang out at the shops, at school, in the staffroom, in your shared kitchen at home, &c., and if this *reliably* repeats, then C.'s model says: don't speculate about them, don't soul seek too much (you might just be seeking a way to blame yourself ...). *Just consider that together-with-them might be not the best mixture. Maybe don't jump at the next chance to see them.*

It's possible you could blame the bad feelings on the withdrawal from them. (As in, I only feel really bad and frightened tonight alone, because I *need* them ...) Oooo. Tricky. But we tend to suffer from 'withdrawal' in relation to addictive things. Usually withdrawal signals not a very sustainable mixture, for me anyway. Good mixtures *for me* tend to feel plain or good at the time, and they leave me steadily feeling plain and good after.

Now, (I can hear the cogs grinding ...) you might counter that we also need to include here the fact that, for some folk, being made to feel *less* alive, more *in*capable, *less* dignified and somewhat *un*settled, could – if you have that kind of psyche – be precisely the *lure* for wanting to see someone and have that very mixture again.

Humans are wild creatures. We want wildly, strangely. This is okay. If you can bear to look at your own way of wanting even sideways, that's something.

The test – so far – has slightly *smeared* two aspects together. These *are* (you're right!):

- How they impact your capacity and
- How you respond to how they impact your capacity.

Four combos (let's get faux-mathematical now):

i) Joyous, want a repeat
ii) Joyous, want to flee
iii) Sadder, want a repeat
iv) Sadder, avoid a second round.

And none of us is categorically ever in one of these options. We wriggle about. But who knows! Maybe you do tend to lurk in one of these. If it's no. ii) or no. iii) then that's interesting. Don't panic. Just notice more. Notice repeatedly (it may take *a lot* of repetitions ...).

If you watch without fiddling, do as little as possible, shifts occur (of themselves). I know this for a fact from yoga. It's not an *improvement* model; it's a *transformation* model. And ... transformations of any real kind tend to happen behind your own back and aren't foreseeable. Transformation is less defined by moral categories, a telos of 'better', and it involves something both riskier and *plainer*. It just gives you a chance to differ from yourself, which makes a life feel like one.

A person may leave you feeling happy and energised, *and* your sincere want is to run a mile. This may be because your hard-wired experience of relating has mostly equated to 'feeling a bit sexy-scared, unhinged and high'. Well, good. Linger with that style in yourself for a while. For a month or so. For a long decade or three.

Someone may make you feel appallingly average – wan, tired, full of doubt and blossoming symptoms. *And* ... you might sincerely want to call them up as soon as you can (because we can have these trained tendencies of attaching to certain vibes, even so-called negative ones). Also, well and good. We have to ride along with how-we-are usually before we can intervene. We can seldom jump cold (as a 'doing') to being entirely someone else.[4] We have the patterns of reacting that we have, and we often lose these slowly. When we get defensive and rush, this is impeded further.

To put this into Spinoza-ese: we aren't typically very *reasonable*. Reason, less boring than it sounds, is *rare*. Our tendency to repeat and repeat and want to repeat again isn't very reasonable, right? And it is very human. Our intelligence is emergent, *and* promising.

This two-step enhancement above (i-iv) does offer clarity. With it, you are more privy to your own process. We've separated out the strands somewhat. Our model de-sediments, at the very least, what would otherwise be a quick succession of reactions, smoodged together. Mysterious and imprecise.

It's a power to know that you prefer (or one part of you prefers) to feel deflated and self-denigrating. Okay. Good. And to know that things sit more comfortably when you have people around who facilitate that outcome. Also, good. Fine. If you can survive it, and leave room for a sneaky transformation in there, you can work with that. There's fallout when you're edging towards newness.

I'd like to think that C. applied this test to our first fifteen-minute chat in the *Frauenraum*. And that her preferences align with i) – 'spend more time with someone if after seeing them capacity slides up'. Maybe she didn't feel worse after that short meeting, and this explains her proposed follow-up.

I didn't feel worse either. And maybe both of us didn't mind floating on a joy-slide that felt plainly sweet, the expanded capacity that the encounter seemed to bring. We risked a repeat encounter, and since then, (to use a nice litotes) we haven't made each other's lives any worse in any way.

*Think of the infinite ways – cleverer, kinder –
that could organise how we might live together.*

On Love and Making Ones
the non-satisfaction of 'reasonably happy'

I had a small break for a bit there, to go sort my laundry. (How do humans wear so many clothes!) While I noticed how *un-*ergonomically I was heaving the clumps of clothing from their deep basket, a further thought occurred to me about deciding.

I want to sketch it out here before the washing cycle finishes.

∝

THERE'S A PARTICULAR MOMENT WHEN PEOPLE GET tied in knots about deciding, and it has to do with partners. For good reason, we're likely to invest a lot in deciding with whom we might spend loads of future time, with whom we might sort laundry, arrange holidays, live through illness, or to whom we might confess our resentments. I don't think there is a principle for making that go away.

I know from my own life that I've spent a panoramic number of years pretty confused. Do you see the vista: wide horizons of bumbling about, Instagrammable scenes of me, groping blindly with sunhat and insect repellent in hand, crashing around in the undergrowth of misconception?

People would say: 'relationships are hard'. And I was, like, *okay ... they're hard.* So, when I was gruellingly unhappy, definitely disenlivened, I'd hang in there for years, seriously, because someone had said they were 'hard', and I imagined I must not *yet* be giving it a good-enough go.

I've had friends tell me (after the fact!) that I can persevere romantically for ridiculously long times. No one mentioned anything during those long times – but what *can* we say? It's the bind of courtesy to which we're often, as decent friends, reciprocally doomed. Friends might be frank at times, but often we're unhelpfully diplomatic. This is because there's nothing worse than offering some frankness following a break-up – *you did never seem yourself with Y* – only to hear later that your friend and Y are back together! Subsequent foursome dinner dates are likely to be tense at best, if they even happen.

Foreseeing such clangers, most friends tend to say *less*.

If I give myself some credit, I also stayed because I *loved ... sincerely*. At the same time, the situations at too many levels didn't work. What does this mean? A therapist implied (as I understood it) that it means we spend the majority of our time and energy trying to Make/Maintain the Relationship (it becomes the dominant focus of our efforts), rather than the relationship serving as a base, a steady platform from which we then lead a good (a plain?) life – alongside, in parallel, together.

Relationship pushing Life out of frame ... that was this therapist's take. Takes are words, and words are always only a part of it.

We also might stay because we aren't flighty, and because we're really checking before squandering a Good Love (more on this below). There's no drone you can send up above a current relationship to reach an altitude from where you'd be able to encompass past, present and future, and fetch down images offering hindsight and a generous, accurate perspective. It's easy to parody one's efforts after the fact (as I have above), but those efforts were also my life during those years, working it out the best way I could with people I always deeply loved, was in-love-with – even if, in the end, those lived Love Scenarios were too awkward a fit for the long run. That means: exhausting too often, not just uneasy sometimes.

My heart-brain was mostly taken up with *how* to make it work, rather than with life-ier questions. *Do you have any whites for this* load? *The Wimmera? Why can't I stop bitching about Z. and let it go? Do you think that chicken was off?*

I was often confused and at sea, and these Advice Sources – good friends, books, hearsay, &c. – didn't seem explicitly to say, or I didn't listen if they did say, many *further* things that (at that time) might have cast fresh light on my dilemmas, might have nuanced this adage: 'relationships are hard'.

Things such as: relationships are bumpy but should regularly be at least a bit lovely; or humans tend to like company when it's kind-enough and non-toxic; or sleeping with another body that's like home is really *good*; or living on the impossible threshold (where it doesn't resolve, its lack of resolution being its definition) between fucking and tenderness is a good-enough place to teeter in life; or it's humbling to witness up-close how a person can be really admirable, can surprise you with gestures and follow-through over and over; or time with another person that's quasi-boring, quasi-frothy is worthwhile in a basic, simple way; or being with a creature who is Infinite *and* Repetitive is very interesting. Such things. They didn't say such things to me.

Partner Choice, which sounds like a brand of frozen peas, is artless shorthand for the more-dignified sounding Decisions about Love – when the brand of Love we're talking about *also* has Something-of-Sex involved in it (translation: attraction across a difference). There is the debate about friends being arguably the same as lovers (naturally I've experimented with this argument in one of my decades …), and this is not the moment to delve, but let's run now with the idea *that they aren't*. Friends vs lovers/partners. One can move inside these silos, move between them, but often one is not quite in both at once. We *can* have sex with friends – of course we can (it's the risk-free way) – but I'm talking about Big-L love.

In Alain Badiou's take, what constitutes the sexy bit is an 'x', a factor that is not calculable, and which involves a *wanting* beyond meek and tidy *preference*. This factor is a site where vulnerability and a kind of selfishness collide. I have to want *from* myself. It's my want. *I* want something *from* the other (and might dare to want that they want something from me), and this is soooooo scary. Practised coldness, honed hostility between 'the sexes' is often an avoidance of straying into this rawer feeling. My *friends* don't make me feel like that. I don't have *that* with friends, by definition, hence it's cosier and less laden with risk. Pants on or off, they would remain *friends* without this 'x' that defines Love.[1]

(It's okay if you want sex with no risk. Fair enough. We have to be quite daring for love. And in some phases we don't have the verve. We put our bits among other people's bits, and this passes the time.)

This x, however, is a real thing. We could argue about it, but I think, in our psyches (since we do have them – *psyches*), there is usually a difference, whether we're in a moment of facing that or not. Like a dappled smattering of light against a painted wall in late afternoon – the difference between a friend and a lover-love is subtle, but it *exists*. As I said to someone recently, who seemed to be wandering listlessly in the swamps of politically-well-meaning polyamorous hell: 'You have to leave room for the Catastrophe of Love.' What I meant was: it's all very well living in pods where there's lots of sprawling desire (or not much) swilling around, as long as when Love's Rare Catastrophe (its ability to transform your life) comes along, your so-called political commitments don't leave you paralysed or structurally locked out of *doing what you deeply want*. Again, I guess I was cautioning them about squandering, about hiding inside an ideology, as a way to evade the serious velvet wallop that love is.

You could be loved! I wanted to blurt to this gorgeous young creature ... since it seemed clear that all of the polyamorous kerfuffle could also operate as a genius strategy to ensure that *this* could never be proved or disproved.

Me, back then? I was using a creaky conceptual model (one I couldn't see) to approach Decisions about Love, and for a long time nothing was really helping me. One doesn't usually know that one is using any kind of 'model' at all. One just *does* things, responds to and from feelings, imagining that this one way is the typical way.

I had scenes from cool European novels. I had my own ornate, quite clever but untested ideas. I had what I'd observed of my own parents' relationship (that prime example which imprints us all strongly and indelibly and which we also might both forget somewhat *and* covertly mimic, even in our concerted rebellions against this model). There was good and terrible poetry. There were friends and gossip and logics gleaned from partial, vicarious understanding.

Maybe these Advice Sources didn't think to say these other basic things to me, assuming I'd already worked it out. I really hadn't. Not for years and years. Probably still not, but I think it's a little clearer.

Sometimes I did have a good hunch about these Basic Things (on Love), but I might have been with a partner who – for whatever reasons of their own, be it family history, preference, style, character, whatevs – was unable, unwilling, to commune with the nice time on offer. This can happen too. Oh, it's not fun, people. Sometimes the love object loves you undoubtedly, but they can't do love, per se. They can't meet it grown-up style and with some pragmatic manoeuvres to foster a context for it, a liveable container. And that's a very sad thing.

You just have to get through those phases with strength and good humour. Don't saunter too quickly down Bitterness Ave. Not if you can shiver off those Awful Feelings and revive your Pluck. Things await you, more surely than you know. People can and continue to love. They're about, and often they aren't shouting about it.

Okay, so assuming sometimes we don't really know about partners, being with them and so on, or how to work it out ... (and this chapter is clearly not trying to give you any shortcuts, no ...)

how does anything in the last chapter – C.'s method, Spinoza's melody, joy and sadness and withdrawing energy from certain Sad Compliances with an Order that Doesn't Love Us ... how can any of this cast light on the partner question?

I guess one thing has been bugging me or nagging me to be explored.

I'll preface it by saying that the reason it seems worth exploring this question about how we approach Deciding on Love, is that how we spend our most intimate time and energy probably does matter, in the scheme of things. Neoliberalism might want us fucking triumphantly and getting the news out on your favourite platform, but it doesn't want the revolution that being in love invites. Love upends your whole world, via a collision with the world of another. Pornography, which keeps the risk at bay, is dandy for our current life-dulling regime. Whereas messier eros, more startled, courageous and stumbling Love... well, this threatens to create waves, to make us uninterested in what we are told to be like, what we are told to like.

Thus, being captured economically or ideologically obviously interacts in some way with how we make choices about our Heart. Yes, our Heart! Our heart and loins together – in impossible, clunky cadence (as Badiou would say). True love is inconvenient, and we wouldn't want it any other way.

Tenderness. Devotion. Canoodling. Snoozing. Hilarity. Companionship. Unknownness. Exasperated Fondness. Gratitude to drown in.

This is Badiou's Communism of the Two. Or minimal communism. At the very least can we be, desirously, justly, audaciously, with one other person – as a newly invented Two? Maintaining a Two-ness. As a modest beginning ...

I was once walking at a city protest alongside a serious thinker and practitioner. It wasn't the protest where people in the high-rise apartments were throwing eggs down on us, that was another one.

We were walking along, and he was gazing up at all the apartments. (This city has recently leapt up into the skies, the latter's blue lavishly upholstered with glass, steel and vertical lines.) The apartments were slightly fewer then, but still a lot. In the absence of egg yolk, the gentle sun tippled down on us.

I asked him how his cohabiting with his then-girlfriend was going.

'Badly', he said. 'Badly.'

I laughed, because of the frankness.

'I see.'

'What I mean', he continued, 'is that it's not easy for me. But I'm sticking with it a little longer. The system would love for me to end up living alone, in one of those …' he pointed to the apartments above. 'They'd love it if I was a single, autonomous ever-consuming unit, needing my own dishwasher, my own couch, my own game console, for myself, my own internet subscription, my own everything. They'd love that. The more we are isolated,' he said, 'the more we need to buy. Do the maths. When you don't share stuff with at least one other person, profits must double … right?'

There are two strands here, and they're awkward bedfellows. The first is that perhaps, like I'd been known to do, he was trying to stay somewhere that was not so great for him. Maybe this relationship he was in was a bad mixture, after Spinoza. A fruit that he couldn't tolerate too much of. He might have been having a Sad Time because that encounter did not increase his aliveness (or it was a complicated mixture, all at once …). Due to his own difficult emotional history, he might have been blaming himself, when really it was simply a person-combination worth taking space from. His political thinking, too (as astute as it was), might have been scrambling his ability to take another path.

The thing is, however, that we have to live things out. We have to live and see. There is real risk here; we do 'waste' time, but so it is!

Sometimes, we can see things faster than at other moments. I'm personally a fan of dignifying these efforts, not to the point of blithe self-congratulation, but just giving ourselves less stick for not being clairvoyant. Persecuting ourselves about things we, in hindsight, might have done differently had we have known some detail or had a bird's eye view of patterns, can be a pervasive style of unkindness that we all peddle. Why didn't I do [x & y]? Because we don't know things until we know them! This is not the same as excusing Bad Stuff, or shirking responsibility. There are nuances here that I'd like to pursue, but we need to press on.

The other strand, of my friend's cohabiting dilemma, is a little more subtle to draw out. I want to recall Springer's words ... and think about C.'s method ('how do you feel after'). How and why do we return too often, too willingly, to scenes that aren't very great for us (what Spinoza would term examples of unreason)? I remain very curious – politically on high alert – about what might conspire to have us mess up conveniently our close and crucial relations (or even fail to recognise these relations as such at all) such that we end up lonely machines, scary Prosuming Units, buff and solo. What slithering factors might lead to potential cherish-able loves getting mangled, mistreated by the neoliberal lobe of our psyche; via what subterranean influences and pressures do we conspire to losing what will turn out to have mattered?

I refer you to Byung-Chul Han here, the Berlin-based Korean thinker. He has a searing analysis of how we have lost a sensibility for atopia ... This term refers to the unknown space that the other (person) opens for us. In its unknowing (the a- of the topos, the place), it hints at a particular mode of powerlessness, possibly lostness, that love requires. French psychoanalyst Jacques Lacan is known for saying that in love we give what we don't have. We offer our ontological lack, not our fucking CVs.

We are, as Han tracks it, drowning miserably in trying to match ourselves up in an 'inferno of the same'. Same schooling, same (or complimentary) sex styles, same class sensibility, same politics, same smoking preferences. Same stance on collagen drinks, jeans brands, number of piercings, niche tunes, and so on. Is what we're really seeking just a clone of ourselves, so that we aren't technically 'alone' but we are also not confronted by anything that doesn't cosily confirm, mirror and indulge us?

These are the dating-app inventories via which we classify ourselves and organise tawdry meetings with strangers who aren't strange enough. For Han, there can be no eros there – there, where we think we can sculpt our encounters the way an algorithm pre-programs our emaciated taste. With this misunderstanding of the stakes of love and eros – which are about sidling up to what we don't know, at some level – we're doomed to circle in the fiery furnace of reiterative, predictive pornography.[2]

(It was due to C. that I came across my first Byung-Chul Han book. Through luck and timing, we'd found ourselves within a rare four hours of each other. C. took a train from her home base; I travelled from a conference I was attending in Belgium. We had a tiny window of 36 hours to see each other. Wandering around the river and cathedral in Köln, we went into the art gallery shop. There, I spied a narrow purple spine among the volumes on offer. Sporting a curious title, the book was Han's *Exhaustion Society, Burnout Society, High Time*, published as a trilogy. Without a second thought, I bought it. This was some years before his books began appearing in translation. It felt like finding a tiny but important treasure – an apt souvenir for a visit with C. Han's book on eros came much later, but the sensibility, the spotting and saying of the motor of some of our troubles was there in those earliest works.)

Another possible scenario, even a likely scenario if you don't take care of your digital practices ... we squander a Real Love, because we're reading TOTAL BULLSHIT on the internet! (Antonia, so much shouty font!) My preferred term here is 'squander', or sometimes I rant to friends about 'bad thinking'.

How do we end up squandering things of potential beauty, closeness, thrill and substance? A smart person said to me recently: 'Humans are squandering machines' – and I don't disagree, but I get no pleasure in saying it out loud. Sometimes, however, a few techno-enhancements can really dial up our capacity for life-wreckery. We can have some bro' on the podcasts convincing us to join him in some appalling Bad Thinking and then, feeling smug, we trundle off to damage our futures irreparably. Well done, lads.

What is it, on the other hand, that might attenuate, mute, reduce, temper our penchant for exploding our chances of being together (naked, making toast, patting the cat, washing dishes, talking theory, putting in new seedlings, &c.)? Since, as my demo friend stated, if we do that too consistently, we're also gonna need to spend a great great deal of money on Being Very Independent.

Hey ... friends, readers, comrades out there who feel allergic to the other, or are quaking from unsavoury experiences ... it's hardly comfortable, and Han's atopia isn't a suggestion to open yourself undiscerningly to some dodgy pas-de-deux (if you already have a history with that). It's more an invitation to pry oneself off those programs of living that our devotion to efficiency, strategy and streamlining lure us into. What might be a great approach to household budgeting might not be something to apply to Love. The very precious otherness of our others fits poorly into the columns of a spreadsheet, and can't really be captured well by generic interview questions. I recall the question about pineapple on a pizza that Hinge threw at me. As if that filter of humanity was going to help shuffle a Wondrous Version of Human into my app feed ...

There can be bad mixtures, and we might care to leave them behind in a timely way. However, I'm not talking those; I'm talking the lovely-enough mixtures that we trash. Those are love-chances lost when we activate ornate modes of nasty compliance, bad thinking and thereby fuck ourselves rightly over. The Us. The minimal communism. To grind good meetings into the blistering bitumen.

In the current mash of technocapitalism, habits of device engagement, personal histories of untended-to (intergenerational) trauma, poorly digested thinking, undigestible edible non-food products, diligently-digested ideology, rampant competitiveness, models of masculinity, models of femininity, genres of conversations, instrumentalised rationality, &c., are there ways that these things conspire to make us misrecognise love when we're in it, send us off to seek worse mixtures or yet another opportunity, or to use up too much of our hearts? The latter are robust, but we shouldn't hammer them too flagrantly ... They get scars; they get a little petrified and tough around the edges.

People are falling in love all the time, and many are sticking with it. We aren't as shoddy as we like to think.

I would translate one strand of this meandering, CBD demo conversation as pointing to the fact that our modes of experimental, very human unhappiness with each other (which are unlikely to go away, by the way) can be exacerbated by certain dysfunctions woven into our systemic existence which mean that we may end up more alone, bitter and heart-gutted than we need to be. Sometimes we do need to be more solo, for our own reasons. For some people, the number Two is not their bag. Very good. Then My Dishwasher/PlayStation/Toilet Brush it is, and this is nothing to be ashamed of. It's more in those cases where you inadvertently comply with modes, imaginaries and practices that might mangle a Two-ness that you're longing for (or just curious about).

All of these complications with love that I've been exploring can be grouped together under the column: Unhappiness Added On. It's *this* that I'm taking issue with – the extra, non-essential misery that we are not in fact ontologically signed up for. Neoliberalisation tends to make us both hardened and spineless at once, tangling our capacity for plain thought, for fierce, good love, for making our own dinner and own decisions. It schools us in bloated expectations, all the while hiding inside these a core of terrible, know-it-all, pouty-mouthed Despair.

Now, I'm going to give you a little section break, so you can fetch a feta and tomato sandwich, or a late day Hojicha. Or, yes – because it is heavy – have a little weep on the toilet. Off you go.

I hope it was a spacious break, because now we're going to discuss something slightly sobering. It's the very human progression wherein unnecessary unhappinesses (pl.) get 'added on'.

Let's spell out the cascade ... there is a progression we can track.

Ontologically-Given Non-Satisfaction sliding into Extra Unhappiness ramped up to Neoliberal Optimised Misery.

Consider this three-stage exacerbation. The first two moments are not unusual or atypical, in any way. They are stock-standard fare of any wisdom tradition with any credibility. Life is reliably unsatisfying (by nature!) and humans are pretty deft at resisting this and creating a bit of additional unhappiness in the very manoeuvre of insisting there *should* be less.

The third leg, however, is the open question for me.

We know we are inclined to turn the volume up on the Non-satisfaction-That-Is-Being-Alive to err towards an extra layer of unhappiness. This is 101 Buddhism, and even Yoga Samkhya, and surely other savvy traditions. Already this is something to work with in a life. However, does our current order have the means to ramp this typical unhappiness we make for ourselves (being ignorant of How Life Is) to *new* levels of intensity, so we end up in what I'm irreverently calling Optimised Misery.

Because everything is *optimised* in a Neoliberal, Competition Is my Mother's Milk, Does my Spiritual Destitution Look Good in This, My Glow is More Winning Than Your Glow, Military

Instagram Complex ... *Hahahahahah* ... why aren't you laughing?

Are you already familiar with the difference between the first two?

It involves the distinction between the non-satisfaction (let's call it 'unease'), the woven-in discomfort of being alive (as creatures), that we need to get on with having (*yep*), and the next level of unhappiness which sort of has to do with *appearances* and the ignorance they incite in us. It *appears* the world hangs around reliably, so we err towards thinking things are primarily permanent, rather than appearing solid-ish, but being basically impermanent. We have habitual mechanisms for stringing instants together, and due to this we come to imagine, to assume that we have kind of autonomous permanency *as selves*, whereas *we* (as entities) are also in flux, divided, undecidable, flickering. We believe in the 'I' as a thing, rather than it being more of a function, a phenomenon.

And, I suspect, there is a further mode of extra, ramped-up almost-misery ... that we get lured into cultivating for ourselves under transactional regimes like our neoliberal theme park. The first two – the way we interact with and understand them – impact on each other. If the second one is not seen through, we are more likely to be dragged towards the third one.

If we don't 'get' the workings of the first kind, we're anyway likely to escalate the built-in minor unhappiness towards the Extra Unhappiness. This is what the Buddhists know (have known for centuries): without a bit of ontological insight, we are doomed to *cultivate* the second kind.

So, already hard-wired to cultivate the second kind (due to innocent ontological ignorance), we are *then* more vulnerable to technocapitalism's definite interest in getting us even *more* optimistic about 'satisfaction' and thus primed for the next layer of misery.

Call me snobby, but I reckon we are far too good-natured about what we are being sold. We set out most obligingly, taking steps that *dig in* the misery, or its conditions, which turn the misery clods over, prepped for more misery seedlings.

You're like, *Go easy, Antonia, I don't think I chase after unhappiness. Really. I'm all for having Maxxx Happiness. That's all the internet is doing, that's all everyone is on about. We're all about Optimising Good Feelings all round. 4EVA. We're consistent working on Feeling Great. Living our Best Life. We're conscientious about it. When we wobble we declare to ourselves (and others) 'You've got this' … Efficient, Best Practice Happiness is the mantra of the Civilised Connected World. You must be mistaken. You're implying we're running at misery with open arms. No way. You need to spend more time on social media and get back in touch.*

Hmmm. I'll press on, shall I?

The three, you see, are embroiled … they do not unfold in an unrelated way. It is *this* little combo that the plainness query orbits around. Like a kitten sniffing the edge of a semi-closed paper bag.

Now, I need a sandwich. Or a nap. Take a moment if you want, to let all this settle in. I'm sure you've read it all before, because these days the internet contains all the answers to Happiness, except that this alone doesn't necessarily help us. *À bientôt.*

∝

DO YOU REMEMBER THE SERENITY PRAYER? *GOD, GRANT me the serenity to accept the things I cannot change, courage to change the things I can, and wisdom to know the difference.* In my childhood, our house had a brass, engraved thing with this prayer on it, an image of two hands pressed together … Do I misremember?

I've just gone looking to learn about it, and I find that it's less ancient than I would've thought. Its author was a twentieth-century American theologian, Reinhold Niebuhr (1892–1971). These lines are an excerpt of a longer poem from 1926. It wasn't quite yet the Great Depression. It was still in the heady moment of the 1920s.

Beaded dresses. Flattened boobs. That coy, fetching dance craze. Promiscuity.

A suspicious reading of the poem might pigeonhole it as some kind of Tool of Compliance. That reading would evoke a squashing, behave-yourself kind of slant. *I* had furthermore assumed a Catholic source (it was on our walls, and my mother's side is Irish Catholic). In fact, Niebuhr was Protestant. One could read the prayer tightly, too-knowingly, along the lines of: the Church is too big to fight; be sensible and settle for your measly lot; don't resist structural oppressions or name them; learn to relinquish hopes of widespread political change, and just change the colour of your bedsheets and stay polite ... *That* kind of tone. This would be a suspicious way to read the prayer, and I'm less convinced by Flourishes of Suspecting these days. (Being ever-suspecting is a sloppy habit.)

The prayer seems to be used in AA a lot, as part of the suite of Skilful Means on the way to getting sober. The info I found was on an AA site for therapists maybe, listed under other menu tabs, like Twelve Steps, and Alternative Twelve Steps. (It seems there is a Normal Twelve Steps, and then a Secular Version. One includes the divine, and the other includes a more psychology-icky language.)

AA really *gets* something. They. Know. Stuff. The AA people. Maybe because they have tested at the darkest coalfaces some serious experiments about how the human can roll, what can happen in a body, how certain dire combos of thought, practice and chemistry can run an armoured tank through your life, obliterating everything, and finally killing you. People go to AA (NA, &c.) only when they've worked out that they don't really want *certainly* to die.

Anyway, that prayer. Interestingly, in the longer original poem, you also get these words:

'That I may be reasonably happy in this life.'

And there it is. The luminous, vast-minded measuredness of what we sometimes call wisdom. *Reasonably*.

Niebuhr knew it. It's right there in his use of this word. I doubt even Lacan would argue here. What you get in life, in this creaturely life – if you're quite fortunate (right? actually *quite* fortunate) – is a rare chance to be *reasonably* happy. It's *so* much. Many may not be in a structural situation which permits this *at all*. This is the plight, as Badiou makes clear, of literally millions of people on this planet and, I'd add, gazillions of other sentient sorts (creatures, plants, lichens, rocks). Let's keep this in mind, if our situation is *not* this. If we are within reach of some steady possibility of reasonable happiness, we can consider ourselves in a blessed minority.

Reasonably? This is old-fashioned language because this is not how we talk now. We are not encouraged towards the 'reasonably'. We could replace this word with *mostly, fairly, pretty much, quite*.

To be mostly happy.

To be quite happy.

To be fairly happy.

To be pretty much happy.

Happyish! (It's already a lot.)

We, in our sloshy, screedsy historical moment, are encouraged not to settle for *reasonably*.

'Reasonably happy' is not clickable. We won't click it. It doesn't have the fake frothy provocative vibe that hooks into us at multiple levels and makes us Daft Puppets of Optimisation. More on this below.

Niebuhr is on to something. I would reiterate it like this:

There is a non-negotiable Human 'Unhappiness'. It's the low buzz in your day that won't go away. Or if it does, it's not the beginning of Your Perfection-Dream Finally Happening – *no*. It's just a rare trick of the light, don't get insistent about its staying. Bewonder it, move on. If you try to eradicate (note the pushiness of this verb …) the low buzz, then *lo!* you dig yourself into a world of Properly Unhappy.

This inkling of dissatisfaction, this incomplete vibe in your days is not going anywhere. Most of the hubbub around you (that wants your cash, that would not be ruffled by your self-sabotage), however, knows to leverage you at your weakest link – this secret hope that your life will be an exception to the rule of Low Creaturely Buzz. We don't love the buzz. We can't wax lyrical about the buzz. It's the being alive, being not (at one's core) stable or permanent. Having entered this raucous stream of living-for-a-bit, we get the buzz as part of the package: you get this not-horrendous, but definitely uneasy, non-negotiable non-satisfaction that the Buddhists have a name for.

You *won't* be an exception to its necessity. Within the realm of what the yogis call 'prakriti', the phenomenal world ... you *can't* be.

Do you suddenly break off your reading here? Do you feel the need to pee, to make a beverage, to call your mum? If so, that could be called the Unconscious. A part of you doesn't care to hear this declaration: *You Won't be The Exception* (to the low buzz).

You won't be.

Even if you pose on your feed as having already managed this. 'This is bullshit!' (channel Tommy Wiseau to perform this out loud) and you do *know* it, even if you resist recalling it.

As well as having a nearly built-in impulse to pursue an eradication of the buzz, you'll be wooed into believing it can be eradicated, that you can *hack* the buzz. As mentioned above, with the triad of moments, this last moment is where capitalism works. And I'm not saying we're leaving it imminently (and I'm not saying we aren't ...) but capitalism simply ramps up this inherent fact, works it, massages it, twists your nipple a bit, to keep you kinda hoping that the buzz can go away, and this new power tool, cedar decking, French cookware, is the pathway. I think there is an ideology no one really believes (but longs to) and then a reality which delivers, if I borrow from Lacan, *morsels* of the satisfaction.

I love that. It's like we're following the crumbs – the satisfaction morsels – to the candy house of the witch who plans to bake us in her delicious Persagne. *Hahaha.*

Maybe 'buzz' isn't helping, since you might think of that as the 'buzz' you get from your coffee, or cocaine, your 3pm donut, or your doom-scrolling. It's related, but different. The buzz the Buddhists help us to tolerate (even chuckle *with*) is the shred of 'not quite right', not quite *there* yet. Or if you 'have it' now, this 'it' will and must change. That feeling. Dancing with that feeling is the art of being alive in a way that might not entirely depress, oppress, or undo you (or others).

The shreddy, incomplete feeling? Most likely, you'll be complicit in encouraging others to believe it can be eradicated, too. Acting as if you live a (charmed and exceptional) life that has slipped its binds. This is a lot what social media is.

In our recently emerged digital lives (recent in the grand scale, I mean), this is often how it goes.

I pretend to *you* that I've maxed out my Life Efficiency with a Flawless Colour Palette and Burgeoning Income sources from a lazy start-up, photographed on a pricey couch with a luscious, dishevelled but *very* well-dressed toddler scampering about. I'm lean, but don't appear deprived. *You* get an unprocessable rush of mixed feelings that you don't have time to untangle, so it just turns into that Generic Feeling which now, as shorthand, is commonly termed 'anxiety' (on the street, if you haven't noticed). *You*, then, return the favour, doing a special photo shoot, or languid post, which emphasises what *I* Don't Have or Can't Ever Get. And then *I* get a rush of feelings I can't process. It's very compelling. On and on, the next episode, with seemingly very different (but exactly the same) content, cued reliably.

We feel very bad (or just jangled), while our feeds look Very Good. (Good enough to peddle the no-buzz-to-see-here myth.) By God, they – the feeds – should look good, for all the energy the Prosumers, I mean people, give them.

Even without the socials, this You Can Pretend to Have Eradicated It, but You Can't Actually Eradicate It, is what Niebuhr's 'reasonably' was alerting his 1926 reader to. And people would have had their own versions of this for that time. Wearing fancy clothes to church? Having a nicer front garden than others? Whatever. His meme, furthermore, has hardly gone stale. You can be *reasonably* happy since you won't ever be (not possible!!!!!!) entirely happy. In this life, in the form we know ourselves in.

So, am I saying stop shopping and riot? Well, *naturally* this is the message [side splitting emoji].

Other aspects of our swiftly changing digital worlds also take the buzz from being low level – *fine* – to being somewhat more hyperbolic. 'Unsatisfactory' here shifts into Ferocious Anxiety. On our daily remote meeting/workplace platform, the buzz (which is a little quirk in my face) is amplified. Young, wondrous, unique people attest to getting Lip Flips just so they can look better in their Accountancy101 lectures.

Foster Wallace foresaw all of this. In *Infinite Jest* there is a chillingly prescient section where people buy whole costumes to wear on 'videophony' calls, since they feel so exhausted by being seen. Then he writes (a prediction! a prediction! this was *decades* before Zoom ... before you could Uber in a thread-lift ...) that they stop going out, since the real version of themselves isn't as beautiful or sincere-looking or attentive as the mask-costume they invested in, and so they can't risk exposing the difference! I believe I gave myself a small injury from laughing too much while reading it.

And, ah, also Not Funny.

The video platform (no longer fiction, now as normal as a single-origin strong almond latté) *itself* turns the buzz bigger than it needs to be – not intentionally. It's just simply that we may not have evolved yet to be suited to being constantly *filmed*. Our recent tech worlds both have means for making perfection seem likely, and also tend to make the small inconveniences of life appear more damning, more intolerable. When unfilmed, people's raw faces look loveable, memorable and alive. People's *filmed* faces (or our perceiving of our own filmed faces) risk looking like sad, sickly AI Picassos which unmoor us entirely.

That's interesting, *gell*?

Lucky, we all have a special savings account stash for humdrum, ego-ergonomic cosmetic adjustments. One of those pie sections in your banking ap Spending Tracker. *Phew*. Lucky.

This existential remainder, this shred of uneasiness, has been called many things, but one of them, to borrow from our pals in the East is *Dukkha*. I believe that it translates well to dissatisfaction, though you may know its translation as 'suffering', even 'anguish'. To my English mother-tongue sensibility, the latter are a bit much; they sound too flashy. They mislead us so that we miss the genius at the heart of this concept. When we encounter Pop Buddhism on the radio, or a proper practitioner, or another source, we might hear that one Noble Truth is 'Life is Suffering'. The inflection of this *Dukkha*, however, as a given and not always dramatic, points to something more inclusive and persistent than only overblown, acute suffering.

Dukkha – as unease, non-satisfaction – is evocative in a more precise way.

It's a very good word for indicating what I've been circling here.

Dukkha is less inflated than its translation as 'anguish' implies. *Dukkha* is just the grit in your shoe. It's a clean sink, with another spoon or dish appearing in it. It's a great day, with a little spat of bickering that marred it. It's the special event you hosted where someone also said something mean to you. It's your face, often, that is quite glorious and adorable, but with this or that which catches your eye. It's getting sick sometimes. It's wasting a bit of money due to a mistake. It's letting your favourite coat slip off your elbow crook while you're running to the tram, never to be recovered. It's a parking ticket (that you *can* otherwise afford). It's a bit of slowness at the checkout. It's someone in front of you who doesn't know how to advance into the intersection on a green light for a right turn. It's the sexual time with someone that's pretty good and a bit awkward, and never your fantasy exactly. It's your partner being a bit preoccupied or overtired. *Ja.* All of those. (And the amplitude of the 'uneasy' *can* get more intense – these are the milder examples – we're starting off gently.)

Then, on top of this inherent aspect of being alive (yes, *inherent* – you *cannot* get out of it) there are plenty of extra globs of something much more problematic, and which are *not inherent*. I don't mean real lurches into misfortune. These are out of our hands, often ('to accept the things I cannot change'). The Globs, I mean, these Extra Lashings of Unhappiness, which you don't need, are not inherent in a kind of essential way. So, *yeah*, you don't have to chase after them quite so desperately. Sorry.

This is my obnoxious provocation: we ignorantly chase after the Extra Misery Globs, and we fight the inherent but innocent-enough aspects. The two, as mentioned, have a connection. Actions that try to eradicate one (the buzz, the *Dukkha*) effectively leave you wide open, prone to (what the theorist William Bogard has, in the wake of Deleuze and Guattari, called) 'capture' by various forces, and likely to embark on courses of action that leave you vulnerable to (even embracing of) the other more exaggerated forms.

The Optimised Misery. We collude with its conditions. We live it. We're embroiled in it. I wish I could botox that into paralysis ...

For example, I keep seeing aspects of the gig economy making everybody's lives worse, even if the 'worse' takes a while to blossom. Take the attempt to make restaurants, for example, feel they have to go with a delivery service. This service ostensibsly gives consumers access to the restaurant's products and thus might also 'increase' business, *but* it is likely to make certain conditions under which the business has to operate become much harsher. The service 'added on' has to siphon off profits or add an expense somewhere. The slice of pie for the so-called middle man. This doesn't magically appear like a blessing from the Gig Gods. No. The convenience *costs*, even if the cost gets hidden, or passed on to the most vulnerable link in the nasty chain. Someone has to pay: it's either the person who orders, or the workers (the riders), or it's the restaurant (the density and pressure of tasks they need to do; the effective hourly rate; the vibe between people all working for a little less, and angry about it somewhere). The gig mogul doesn't *pay*. It's their business model, after all. Ditto the tradie app, ditto the exercise class app, ditto the transport services apps. You *love* them? Well, they don't love at all a world that would otherwise perhaps sustain a liveable life for you and yours and ours.

And *some* restaurants (hooray, hooray) simply say, *Nah. We're fine thanks*. They don't buy into the sunny ads, the celebrities wearing zany food costumes. They know it isn't very sunny, not very flavoursome, at all. This *not*-participating is risky, though, and it takes some business confidence, some political insight, to dare to enact that critical No (more on this 'No' in Chapter 8, up ahead).[3]

I assume I'm going on about something we already *know*. Yes? As my example parodically hints, that we open ourselves to this capture? Sometimes collectively. Sometimes on our lonesomes.

Probably, but I can't know for sure. I don't know you, though I'm guessing you read stuff, contemplate often, have a healthy caution in relation to the Shiny Things the world puts in front of you, that you don't imagine the internet loves you, and so on. I suspect you already have very creative, quite subtle ways of navigating existence, at this time, in this dimension ...

To reiterate: there is a fundamental unease built into the world, built into being a living creature or, as Lacan might say, a speaking-being. Dancing around, and finally *with*, this unease is perhaps what I mean when I say *plain*. Or, plainness can emerge

– rich, interesting and *enough* – when we work something out about this unease. The working out involves understanding deeply (over and over) that life *by definition* feels a bit bitsy, a bit shreddy, incomplete, sometimes disheartening, sometimes inconvenient.

In rare moments, in a minibus at an outdoor art event, or for a filament of untimed time during meditation, we stop tantrumming that this shred could go away, and we learn to love it, and this opens a new dimension in the world. *Plain*.

These shreds stop being a sign that you're failing. Life just *has* remainders. Things don't square. Time is always too little or too much. We never attain 'Just So'. We are (must be!) inefficient often, *and* we can at times be graced with little splurges of Smooth. We feel 'seen' sometimes, but mostly not. We don't really get to see what we look like, know if we are loved, gauge how we are received and whether we matter. Not really. This is how it is. Plainness emerges, as a kind of strange quiet superpower, when this settles in, and you run at *it* with open arms.

I was teaching a yoga retreat some years ago, and a very sweet person was along for it. They were energetic, super smart, eager to learn and, at times, a wild card in the space. Basically, they were *young*; and all this was absolutely appropriate for their moment, even pretty impressive. A good heart, a pleasant vibe to be around. I had admiration and affection for them. At some point we discussed the idea of *Ananda*, bliss, from the *Yoga Sutras*. It was a passing moment, but the word snagged for this person. In a discussion later on, they declared that they *loved* this bit of the retreat, since that's how they wanted their life to be: blissful, perfect, amazing, always beautiful, in every moment to be in touch with this pleasure.

Egad! Did I go into fervent panic? Well, no. The concept is both *horribly* flawed (and a path to some operatic sufferings and disappointment getting cued up in the wings), *and* also the reason people begin the slog of practising. Both both.

You want constant bliss. Okay then … the work begins now.

And via this work, your quest will change entirely its nature.

Going by the tone and vocab of this aspirational declaration, it was also straight out of the bowels of the internet, straight out of the furnaces of The Socials. It was already prepped on her lips and in her brain by the very context she's striving to find a foothold in. Someone said it in an online yoga class. Someone used these same series of words in a seductive TikTok. Not just someone, so many people using this language. Life under late Neolib Capitalism ... it's got a very narrow vocabulary, don't you find? It whispers to you (or bludgeons you with its unforgiving repetitions): don't put up with second best; that's what losers do. You can eradicate the dissatisfaction; you can make the Best Life Ever. It can be yours, why wait!

This is the Capture, but it also needs for us to be trying to *escape* from something. (For Bogard, the two go hand in hand ...)

This marks one moment (of many) in our Capitulation. Our resistance, not that my student could know this, isn't achieved by insisting on (my right to) Wholeness. Such insistence amounts to a mere powerless and background mumbling as we get captured over and over. Resistance isn't activated inside these kinds of claims ('my right to'); it has a non-relation to this kind of Groomed Optimism. Rather, our entitled neolib insistences ('I insist on bliss alone') are the creakings of the binds tightening, and squeezing a pseudo-smile onto our soon-to-be-eaten-off faces.

It's not that this young yoga student won't hopefully make a very decent life, quite a thrilling life in moments, a life with big love, whimsical, rude sex, rambling friendships, trips, some years of feeling gorgeous and irresistible, intellectual nourishment, professional leaps into competency, phases of deep joy and other passages of transformation, change, surprise and interpersonal grace. I wish that for her, sincerely.

And this, if she's *that* lucky. A plain life is hardly on sale in the middle aisle of ALDI.

Everything in that paragraph just now (about a thrumming plain life) has nothing to do with the previous insistent Fantasy of Bliss that her language was peddling, for which she has been given (by the current moment) some swollen, sickly aspirational language. The paragraph just now is one version of a plain life, not a perfect life. It's a shreddy life, with a lot of weird dropouts and confusion, run-of-the-mill misfortune, bumbling around often, clunky and unnoticed transitions, both forwards, back and sideways. The self that lives this paragraph above is rarely stable, often in flux. It doesn't know itself and experiences a lot of doubt.

This self is *neither* a smug adept of technocapital, nor are they hunched over the conspiracies squinting into revelation's glinting iris.

I'm connecting this Aspirational Thinking/talking style to the extra Globs of '(Un)happiness'. While this attitude (which we are fed in obscene mouthfuls) *thinks* that it's evading, slipping the binds of, the fake shame-binary one side of which is To Settle for Less ... the other is to get a doctorate in Taylor Swiftness, it paves the path for potentially more serious Globs of Unhappiness. It guarantees our participation in a system that would steer us clear of joy that might be steady and feasible.

Sound boring? Well, deal with it, and it also *isn't*. I won't use narrow vocab choices to sell it to you in the way you're used to being talked at. To say 'joy' is a placeholder. You have to supplement it by living through it.

Glob isn't the only word, maybe 'tendrils' is better. These misery tendrils, that look shiny and lithe, but which are conniving, winding mechanisms that wrap us into serious unhappiness, find their way into our lives, and gain ground, proliferating like ginger roots. They are silent and obvious, and I continue to be stunned at how often we good-naturedly seem to give them the benefit of the doubt ...

How can we think well, or *plainly*, this more generalised,

sleekly designed Unhappiness that is *not* inherent, but which is hard to tell apart from the basic, wholemeal kind, the kind called *Dukkha* by the Buddhists, and assumed by a certain psychoanalysis, maybe ...

In short: you don't get to be satisfied (for long, or *ever*, it's always 'just been' or potentially 'up ahead') ... and if you want to call this not-getting a name, we can call it *Dukkha*. The little itch. The feeling that something is Not Quite So. The lack of Completeness. We can let it be, or we can squirm, impatient with it, and in the squirming get ourselves tangled in all manner of Bad Business.

Does it sound as if I'm advocating for quietism? Does it sound as if I'm saying to settle for the world as it is? If it does, you have misunderstood me entirely. I'm saying you need to settle for the details of what is inherent in being a creature. Alive? Creature? Speaking-being? Then Inherent Low Buzz of Unease. Because you'll never have room for revolution if you're busy chasing the shreds that promise you an exit from that which is going nowhere.

Now, I need to go see if – in fact – I might have left a tissue in the load of black laundry ... *hahaha*. After that, we'll get back to where we started ... decisions about love.

∝

NO TISSUE! BUT SOME DAYS, THERE'LL BE A TISSUE, and white flecks everywhere, and I might slide into dismay. *Sheesh* – all that lost time picking off the white bits. Other people might go into a Life-always-fucks-me-over kind of headspace. It depends on your style. Since I'm quite *trained*, since I've worked on myself over the years (accumulating a noticing of one's aptitude for sulking, moods, &c., applying oneself in particular directions), there's a good chance I'll find the Great Tissue Debacle mildly *funny*. Tissue, everywhere! Ha! Life asserting again and gently that it is not able to be tidied up, domesticated, planned or perfected. I take reassurance in this. In any case – I tend to say – it's happened, so dodge both the outrage and magical thinking ... slip through into ... comedy. (Neither outrage nor magical thinking is interesting in the longer term.)

Tissue is just one example. Please extrapolate with your own. Sick again! Burnt rice saucepan! Car trouble! Period comes early and now some days to wait before getting busy with your partner won't be a huge mess on the sheets! Or, no partner, or a date planned, while a luscious pimple surfaces! Inconveniences, all! Bring on the inconvenience. All manner of Mild Debacles. If you're lucky If your quite lucky, safe-ish, and plainly privileged life has room for such inconveniences that harm you not one real bit. Read the news. This is not how it is mostly ... there are other degrees of harm, we know. We had, however, another focus.

Love.

How to decide about it.

I've really come the long way round to say something very simple. It's this:

The question of whether someone is The One is not a good, not a reliable filtering principle, for deciding about love. This 'poetry' (tired, old-fashioned, tainted) isn't IMO a steady place on which to set going your heart's decision-making practices.

You might want to argue with this. (You've seen Julia Roberts. You've understood the plot of *Love Actually* (plots, actually ...). Surely the Ollywoods have all the love answers. Well, they might. They've got agendas – explicit and implicit – and I don't know what they are.) I guess, you just hear this memey-fragment floating around – *I'm looking for the One* – this framing for how to decide. You get it at the end of schmaltzy weddings. I love a schmaltzy wedding – the big hair, nail art, woodland-drag eyelash extensions – but you can have one without uttering, 'I realised [name] was the One.' You hear it bandied around a lot. And I'm not wanting to defend its ostensible opposite, which might be 'anyone will do with legs and a pulse'. There's a middle ground, people. Not even middle, just off *to the side*, round the back of the bike sheds. We'll get to it.

Now, you perhaps aren't vulnerable to the Siren Song of someone being The (assigned for you) One. You might have had more workable role models. If so, head off to book that dinner for your 34th anniversary, or something. Keep yourself entertained.

But, if you haven't quite wriggled free of this classic way to talk about big love *when you're looking for it*, then bear with me.

The person you are with isn't The One. The person you are not yet with, but with whom you fantasise being, is also not going to be The One. The person who left you, whom you left, or who is otherwise indisposed, is not The One you missed out on. They are people who matter to you – yes – and this has nothing to do with being The One, as a kind of destined category.

I still need more words, since it's very subtle. It's not that you don't make someone Your One. This is entirely possible. This is decision. Years of work. Tiny risks taken; enormous risks taken. Daring gestures, declarations, late-night last-minute zinging car trips with sheer hope and no toothbrush, potentially embarrassing bouquets sent, some further years of gentle drudge, glorious repetition, broken sleep, decent sleep, talks about money, patches of being long-distance, doubt, doubt, moments of certainty and good fortune, décor fights, bickering at the Stupidmarket, criminally good orgasms, someone who has your back like you didn't believe possible, &c. You can *create* a scene in which a person who matters might well-enough be described as Your One. It's just that this isn't decided in advance *for* you, by some outside force. It's not written in *the* big book of Love (unless it's the book mentioned by The Magnetic Fields, which is apparently long and fairly boring – yes!).

The point being that it's entirely up to you. And to the other. Your want, their want. Horrendous odds, and *also* okay odds. Because you mustn't try to predict what the other wants, must hold off being sure the other wants or doesn't want you. You *will* predict (this is having a brain prone to temporal presumption), but you *can* be sure that you *can't* be sure. So, leave a little chink of unknowing in there, through which the blinding, breathtaking grace of desire's unfathomability can get in.

You think you know *why* someone wants you? Well, they do, they might – and you're wrong about the *why*.

We're contra here the speech of Aristophanes in Plato's *Symposium*, where Aristophanes recounts the Lost Half love theory of Greek myth. No lost halves. It's far more interesting, or as Alain Badiou might say, *mathematical*, than that. There is a deadness to perfect halves, to perfect matches (to anything 'perfect', in fact). We think we want this deadening, but it would – were it achieved – feel horrifying, less a feeling than a howling void. The non-matching 'match', the edges that don't map, the almost-fitting that has wriggle room to invite movement, change ... life, that's where we approach a kinder theory on love.

There. *Couldn't I have opened this chapter with this paragraph?* Well, maybe. I'll discuss with my editor.

This framing (of looking for The One) is really worth setting aside. We can leave it kerbside with the broken roll-top desk, and unused breadmaker. I'm not even inclined to argue with it. I just want to suggest that we leave it be.

The One – against whose notion you measure all your quirky, interesting encounters – hides within its folds the notion that somewhere your Love Happiness has been decided, and this kind of *excludes* you. It *excuses* you from having to make a decision, and it *excludes* you from your own ability to make a decision. Where decided? In the sky? In God's book of romance possibilities? In a profound and destined organic and spiritual suitedness? I dunno. You might be drawn to this idea if you enjoy the experience of being bossed around. It's a way of saying that life *knows* things for you already.

We can play at enjoying that. I get it.

Still, you make Ones. They aren't handed down. This is actually a massive idea in the history of philosophy ... from Plato, through Heidegger, up to Badiou, via Lacan, who says it beautifully. When trying to provide an accessible gloss on Lacan's notoriously difficult work 'L'Étourdit', Badiou reminds us of Lacan's phrasing: 'There is something of (the) One...' [*il y a de l'Un*] which, he says, is an entirely different matter to claiming that 'The One is'.[4]

Our lives together may display something of a Oneness. Or: we make of each other cherished Ones. This status isn't declared for us.

Being (if we're gonna get technical) also isn't One. *However*, once Ones are made, we forget that we made them, and it seems retroactively as if they were always there, or we read them as destined *after the fact*. Thus, we end up with a slippage in thought, that assumes Oneness as originary. And it makes trouble. For philosophy, yes! But, for our purposes, it makes trouble for love.

Can you see how this ties into the incompleteness, the non-bliss, the mismatched Enoughness I was going on about above? They are ideas totally in parallel with each other. (Antonia goes into weirdo flushed-cheek conceptual enthusiasm mode ... sorry, eek. So *gauche*, but so fun!) We think there can be no *Dukkha* in a way analogous to how we are prone to retroactively see Oneness as something that was always waiting for us and predetermined, where in fact we made it. Like in love, there is no completeness written into life. But when we live well, towards Niebuhr's reasonable happiness, plainness is not shut out. In plainness, it can feel as if an existential tantrum calms down, or has finally got sick of itself, but the reason for this calming isn't that one's 'needs' have been satisfied, or that everything is in its fantasised place. It's almost a new kind of sensibility, a new taste.

This same plainness, as you could imagine, could *retroactively* be read akin to Wholeness – a space free of the usual hum of high *Dukkha*. One could imagine, too, that it was *there*, was lost and then recovered. But this is a trick of the light and crucial at this juncture is to maintain for precision's sake that satisfaction *still* isn't enduringly possible. Plainness isn't (thank goodness) satisfaction as-such. It's a flavour of another order.

And – joy? Yes, whereas satisfaction, per se, contains no joy and is more aligned with an illusion of completion that could be sustained. Plainness – Niebuhr's reasonable happiness – also tends to carry on its thermals little flecks, or quiet swoons, of joy.

I'm unsure if satisfaction and joy appear very often together. It's a question. You could go test it.

So, how does all this link back to how love decisions can get derailed?

I have some friends. They met on the internet and started dating. The sex was pretty hot (or so one guessed), or hot enough, which is what matters, *and* alongside the sex, they seemed to have a really good time together. I don't know if it was THE BEST TIME YOU CAN HAVE … not sure. It was just a really good time together. Reasonably good. They seemed to like trying out the different things the other did. They travelled. Camping. Music gigs. Day trips to markets somewhere. Sometimes when they were together, we'd joke that they looked like a condom ad. They looked *so* happy, at ease, that they would have been perfect for a family-friendly (no pun intended) condom ad. They could be childlike together, unabashed. They would forget that others were there. It took my male friend, K., a while to admit they were going out. Caution is fine, right? It's fine and honest. Finally, he admitted that they *were* going out. An item. They lived separately the whole time. World events rolled on.

Something must have happened, because one week, out of the blue, K. was spooked. He stalled and then he bailed. Like, seriously. It was over. Everyone was super sad, shocked. L., his now-ex, stayed around, disbelieving, and then finally moved cities. Who wouldn't? We texted a bit. It was awkward … what to *say*? K. would come over for dinner and look haunted. Hollowed out. Life was now hard, empty and monotonous, whereas with L. it had been normal (hard enough) but not empty, and still monotonous, still a normal life, but *good*. I tried to press him, as to why the bailing. Desire is not easy to grasp. How to discuss it? He was pallid, lost weight, trudged to work. Bought musical instruments he didn't need. Exercised diligently, could mostly only converse on the topic of Netflix series.

We never asked directly, or maybe we did. We wanted to ask: 'You're not asking whether she is The One, are you?' Dear God, don't ask that! The two of you are making of each other new Ones (which add to a clear Two, as Badiou insists). To ask if someone is The One usually involves asking (checking, filtering via the idea of) whether they will ...

... eliminate the Buzz. Resolve the *Dukkha*. Whether they'll be able to eradicate the shreddy feeling life can have. That a post-coital moment can still have. This is like asking if someone (to whom you haven't committed) was determined in the sky, in the book of destiny, whatever, as The One. In that big ledger that apparently contains the names of all future partnerships. *Preserve* me.

But (you're saying), Antonia, in love something wild *does* happen. Isn't it normal that we would explain the Big Feeling with mystical justification? Yes, but you just need to read Alain Badiou on love. You are right that there is an event. And you are right that it feels 'true'. For Badiou, we don't need any meant-to-be-ness, we need transfinite mathematics. *In Praise of Love* will sort it out for you.

Under my breath, as I watched True Love dwindle and go belly up, I whispered, 'surely he is not asking *that*?' You only know *not* to ask that when you've perhaps asked it a few times, waved goodbye to a few possible Happinesses, and felt the loss it brings tumbling down on your life, on your ditzy little head. It is a recipe for Squandering.

250g Magical Thinking (whole)
6 Fantasies (shop bought is fine)

3 tbsp Consumerist Ideology
12 leaves (freshly picked) Imprecise Extrapolation
2 tsp toasted Bitterness
1/2 tsp ground Denial

I've squandered things. I've had my own Loves squandered by artless counterparts. We know it. It's not going anywhere. Invoking the One-that-Pre-exists-Formula (whether you do it, or whether they do it) aims at the wrong things. It's a bad logic.

What we need now is a nice herbal tea with C. in a snowy café, in a German deep winter. C. needs to take K. aside, listen for a while (she is very well trained, after all those good *Geisteswissenschaft* study years …), let him thrash it out, and then give him the formula.

'Well, we don't know if she is the One. Perhaps put that aside. The question is: how do you feel after you've spent time with her? Do you feel more alive – more *sweetly* alive – or less so?'

Well, we know the answer, even if we can't hear it above the roar of the demo songs getting practised in the corner, and even if we can't see my friend's face in the low light of the back of the café, lit only by weak fairy lights, strung from the beams. We've seen them together. Think condom ad. Think spontaneously bursting into a harmonised tune at the outdoor concert that day. *FFS*. (He's Swedish, so they are very good with singing; she's a music grad.) If you get spontaneous song effortlessly in your next romance, just clock it, kids. Take note.

We know the answer K. would have given C. as he blew dejectedly on the surface of his hot tea.

'She lives in another city now. Yeah, I don't know if she's The One. You say this isn't knowable. When she's around I sing more. And since she's been gone I look like *this* [points to his wan complexion, and hollow cheeks]. But maybe she isn't *The One*.'

Eek. I'm afraid now. He might get a dose of German What's-Whatness. But no, C. is very gentle. Stern but gentle.

Like me, she might be wishing, hoping that he won't squander this. Why do we care? I mean, it's none of our business, and people like to suffer (I mistyped 'duffer', haha!) many times before they don't. It's just a lot of pain. Well, *okay*.

Anyway, C. has to go. Sharehouse dinner. And my friend needs to take his time machine back to the future, to *now* – the 'future' for this speculative conversation. It's icy out, so C. will need to put the bike seat low, and ride very carefully in the slippery bike lanes. She's gone. (She even paid for his tea on the way.) He's got all he needs now.

What's he gonna *do*?

This question of The One is an old one (Aristophanes was caught in its lure), but it is also activated anew by the machinations of Technocapitalism. It's porn – training you to not to settle for awkward normal person sex. It's *that* coupled with High Cheesy Faux Romance vibes – a mix of factors insisting that you *can* have the feeling of Completeness. Look around – don't others have Their Destined Ones posted up everywhere on every platform? *No*, it's just good use of concealer, a trick of selection and what's out of frame.

(They might have *made* of each other some Ones … that's all.)

I suspect only some of you, Readers, will suffer with this. And as I said, *if you don't*, then skip ahead to the next chapter. People can also have this *thought* (as in, they'll spruik it, say the *One* thing because it's woven into our cultural vocabs), and yet manage to *act* aslant to its poisonous influence. They probably have better role models for relating, or they just got lucky with themselves and managed to keep on where the feeling was Pretty Nice. Their behaviour avoids the squandering recipe above and opens them onto the sparkling Ordinariness.

I can't remember how it finally unfolded. Months (and months!) went on. My friend, K. remained lengthily a mess (but people are smart; they work things out).

One day we got a dinner invitation. To *their* place. He'd nabbed the big room in the sharehouse lottery, and she could fit. A story of a last-minute fifteen-hour drive to her adopted city. Declarations of the overdue kind. Or perhaps perfectly timed. Same same. We went around, took flowers and ate something from the fancy recipe book. It felt very normal. Some laughing. I probably said sweetly obnoxious things. Like old times, but actually very *new* times. We talked about their getting a cockatiel, calling it Bjorn.

There's this funny thing that happens when people (probably) let fall the insistence on Satisfaction, the whole, the One, all of that. It's that it happens very *quietly*. They may have words. Maybe they could put it in a story. Often they don't, and the next thing just happens. They find that they haven't smashed their own life up, and that abstaining (from smashing) looks like nothing special. It is something they *didn't* do. Thus, it doesn't *appear*, and there's nothing to look at. Even less to tell.

Don't let the not-telling fool you ...

Being Bothered

a question of metabolism

Once I booked a cosmetic consultation about a facial matter. As I lay there, on the table, under the bright lights, my nurse – relaxed, personable, planning to ski Aspen with her fiancé next break – phrased her opening question like this:

'So, what is bothering you?'

I noted the wording: no hint of disapproval, knowingness or any pre-empting of my answer. She didn't start by assuming what I might've been there for. *Genius. This is how they train them*, I thought, surprised to be impressed by the artful courtesy of an industry I knew little about.

We are, indeed, bothered by many things; often these are not obvious to anyone else.

These things aren't *objectively* a bother. They are *our* particular bother. Other people, assumedly, are busy jousting and bickering with their own personal botherments. The latter, given our usual state of fretful self-preoccupation, escape us in turn.

This nurse, who was neither snobby nor casual, and vivacious rather than strictly 'stunning', had probably seen *thousands* of cases. Versions of me on her table. People visiting for things no one else would think twice about, about which no one else might be *bothered*. Scars, splotches, pits, inflammations, discolorations, burns, bumps, freckles, spots ... Traces of a history ... (sometimes it's the history that bothers, and we'd like its trace not to keep reminding us).

This woman was smart enough, experienced enough, to know that what brought a person to a consultation was not predictable from a cursory glance. The mistake of the unskilled is to put a hasty name to what – from their perspective – might be bothering you. (Note to recent neoliberal dentist: this will only make me despise you and never return.)

Our troubles, or how they live *in* us, are unique *to* us.

I, you, they, we have specific troubles, and for these apparently disparate troubles, there are arguably some less disparate root causes. One thing we can surely cultivate, if we want to, is a clarity around *register*.

Does it help if we can spot the *kind* of trouble we're dealing with, to spot on what *level* of our existence it is occurring?

This deemphasises the *content* of the Botherment (mine, yours) and turns attention to the general engines for Being Bothered *in principle*. We don't share specifics necessarily (my left eyelid, your right nostril, my feeling of inadequacy in this kind of scene, your hating when someone says your name that way) … Details! I want to explore the meta-fact of Being Bothered, as something we collectively endure, as well as ways we could disambiguate the levels on which this being-bothered is occurring.

My further curiosity is whether these two words – 'being' and 'bothered' – when lined up like this, generate a kind of shimmer in meaning. Together, in this order, they could mean several things; their sense flickers like those optical puzzles that are sometimes vases, sometimes faces. They can't be every sense at once, *and* you can't quite make one version be the dominant one.

Being Bothered.
Being Bothered.
Being Bothered.

An additional preposition (by, by and to) might give the game away, to clarify intention. Context is required to stabilise this wobbling meaning, its steady meaningfulness (which in a pithy chapter title, we don't have …). For now, let's press on with a clear-enough question:

What is bothering you?

I pose this seriously. Imagine you are lying comfortably on a consulting table. The voice above you is calm and non-judgemental. You've just used the scented hand crème in the blinding bathrooms ...

Can you tell me what is bothering you? If anything is.

Not being a cosmetic nurse, I cannot help with the welt you got from a fall onto a barbed-wire fence at three. I can't assist with the dappling of acne scars near your temple. I can't help with small spider veins that are skittering lightly near your nose. There is an industry for all of that, and they help a little, and sometimes, even if they don't objectively help, they just let you lie on their tables, taking your botherment seriously-enough. No mockery. No sarcasm. Their business relies on exercising a studied respectfulness.

I'm not that kind of nurse, so my engagement with the matter of your botherment will be of a different order.

It isn't a bad filter, though, is it? What is the *register* of your botherment and can you work out its nature and what category best reflects it? A kind friend or therapist (or a patient notebook) might allow us to lay it out ploddingly, to get a better sense of it.

Is my bother pragmatic, architectural, emotional, spiritual, geographical, historical, alimentary, energetic?

Sometimes you reckon you've got a 'mental' problem, but actually, you live on sugarless energy drinks, have never been supported in doing small amounts of regular, pleasurable movement, barely eat actual food not from a franchise, and your partner is a narcissist. My point: I don't know if the adjective 'mental' (while it might describe the way it shows up) will assist you to account for where this constellation of unease comes from.

Pull a few threads and see what happens.

Whence does the itch stem? is how we can frame the question. Sometimes, we're just bothered by our flyaway hair, by our piles of dirty dishes, by our stutter. So, we could just buy a hair oil and get on with things. Consider a dishwasher and save for it. Or try to get assistance from a speech pathologist. If funds allow. If funds allow ...

The serious person, the sincere person, can still get a bit tangled in misreading the register of what bothers them. Or, god forbid, lurch into futile 'guilt' about too-promptly solving the easier things. We needn't be pious. We ought to save our 'serious' energy for problems that really are intractable. Hair and dishes are surely not so complicated. Stutters might be more complicated ... then, our inability to feel connected to life, to others, to a future ... more complicated again.

Yes – so, first up, it helps to sort out the simple things. Find the places where one can apply oneself and get some leverage. Some things that bother us are both insistent and relatively *finite*. A certain bother can eat into my brain over days, and dealing with it can finally involve quite a small and harmless action. *There*.

This is true up until a certain point that we each must derive for ourselves. We might pause when, after solving one 'finite' thing, another thing quickly leaps up as if you're playing a repetitive video game. The things in themselves are finite, it seems, but they appear in a series that is uncannily endless. In other words, the set of examples I gave might easily turn into myriads (as the Buddhists say), into the 10,000 things, and then ... you'd never reach their end. Sound familiar? You'd never reach beyond the botherments linked to conveniently available consumables. God knows, too, our moment has skills in monetising the wildest servicesthingsexperiencesatmospheres.

There are different registers of botheredness (surface, structural, spiritual) and the art is to distinguish them. Two initial and practical questions might be: i) which register? ii) what next action (or ceasing of action)?

Maybe it's *not* really 'mental'. Maybe press pause on the Red Bull, the sequential visits to toxic relatives, the work email before bed, doomscrolling the news ... for a week or so and *see*. Sometimes it's embarrassingly easy to get a bit happier. We're almost enraged at how easy it is. We'd like to have Grander, Graver Problems. We want to be troubled, moody, broody and complex. Fine. And, if 'happy' is not your current aesthetic, not on your palette of states you're wanting to experience, then go forth and feel the *things*.

(The field of experimenting is vast and full of odd smelling flowers, eerie carparks, the entrails of abandoned dishwashers, and discarded cosmetic packaging.)

For low-level botherments, there are books and podcasts in abundance. You can web search some stuff. You can even chat with an AI bot and see what tumbles out. What interests me are the ways in which our botherments surface, the ways we read them, and the fuel that powers them. As we know, it doesn't tend to unfold so simply, and we have blind spots. We are hyper-logical on the whole, with glaring blanks in reason that only a frank, rambling conversation with an old and trusted friend might bring to light.

Or ... visits to your therapist. Or some lengthy bouts of *unguided* meditation (as in: intentional lostness that isn't read as 'a problem' or 'lack of focus').

Sometimes the botherment lies elsewhere (or draws its energy from somewhere off stage), but we *read it* as attaching to a mere pragmatic thing. If only the floor stayed clean after earnest mopping, I'd be able to feel peaceful and organised. If only my coffee were always well made, I wouldn't get impatient on my commute. If only I had a series of matchable outfits that I didn't need to think about, then I'd have more time, be less terse. We go at *that* 'problem' for a while. We focus ourselves there and prod, massage and stretch the issue. The only way to work this out – often – is to test things in action. We implement better house rules. We find a new café. We invent a whacky but workable wardrobe strategy. *Okay*. This uses up a bit of time, even a bit of money, but hopefully not inordinate amounts. It can feel thrilling and frustrating. You can feel a bit silly, after, since ... *ping*, a tender shoot of another botherment varietal reliably sprouts.

We churn through the *apparent* reasons for our botherment. Domestic order. Beverage consistency. Clothing crisis. And we add more and more categories. More sites of botherments to potentially 'solve'. *Hmmm.*

Many contemporary folk hope that one move ('hack') will resolve a large part of our botherment. You see those sidebar ads: *put toothpaste on your fingernails* (you have to click to know why, and I don't). But, I guess, people want there to be a trick, a shortcut, so they click the small, blurred photo, of a hand piled with ten little meringue-like blobs.

Sometimes, you think you're uneasy because of Y, and there *is* a practical item you can purchase which might treat, allay, resolve Y (hair oil, dishwasher, &c.). Say, you're constantly getting sick, but you don't take vitamin C, zinc, D and K, whatever. I'm no naturopath. And sometimes this combo of things works. It actually just works. You feel sick less often, and *you forget even that you once had this problem!* End of discussion. (Of course, you'll still get sick – or have to deal with your corporeality – in other ways. Bodies are, after all, like that.) Sometimes the 'solution' works for a short while. Sometimes it becomes part of your suite of Arts for Living. Older people – though we can fail to acknowledge this enough as a society – often have learned many beautiful Arts for Living. *Ask 'em.*

My provocation about register is that this kind of 'fix' (these Arts) will work with certain kinds of botherment. Thus, it's a wise person who can distinguish botherments you can fix (with a servicethingexperienceatmosphere) or which transform through cultivating artful capacities, *from other kinds*. With the latter, no matter how many fixes one tries to purchase, skills one tries to cultivate, the Being Bothered persists, insists and shapeshifts; it crops up again, wearing different trackpants and another flavour of nail polish. We can keep trying to hack these registers pointlessly (*would Spinoza say unreasonably?*) or we can sit tight and watch them. We can watch how they endure, displace, become 'new' things that're really not so new. We might then – just *might* – consider a different approach.

Can you see how capitalism *is* the shadow that falls into stealthy step when we can't do this distinguishing operation? Only mildly brilliant, it has a plodding, dogged way, that really gains ground after a few centuries. It's ever-ready to put a 'thing' or 'service' in the path of your botherment and get *you* to draw a line between them, apparently of your own accord, but also not only.

Aphorism for you? *Retail Therapy resolves things that are susceptible to being resolved or allayed or accompanied by Retail Therapy.* There.

When algorithms fill your sidebar with targeted ads (from eavesdropping your search engine, messenger, transcript service), then the 'accident' looks a lot more sinister.

The answer to the question of whether technocapitalism *feeds* you the unsettledness, and then primes you for the superegoic tang, then turns up the volume on how rubbish everything feels ... is surely yes. Isn't this what marketing *is*? Equal portions of indulgence and uneasy-making – a *most* unsavoury parenting style.

Still, and I'll repeat myself, perhaps none of this bothers you. You are Bother-Free.

If you have no bothers, no botherment, and registers thereof, then No. This chapter has no point for you. Go out and play some tennis against a brick wall. Or cradle lovingly your share portfolio. Or learn a new poem off by heart. *Vielen Dank.*

Capitalism, in its most-hopeful guise, probably *wants* to believe a purchasable solution can allay every botherment. Cute, hey? As I am trying to imply, sometimes stuff we buy *does* help. Me? I can dawdle too much on purchasing discrete, considered objects, which would (if I stopped dawdling) be quite brilliant for my life. I really *could* invest in a stand mixer, since I make plenty of cakes, quite competently, and beating butter and sugar is always needed for good cakes, and my hand mixer just sprays gritty butter clumps all over my kitchen. Daft? Definitely.

The butter clumps, however, don't really qualify as a bother. They're just fatty and sticky. Cakes have been made for centuries without stand mixers ...

A therapist once gave me a wonderful riposte to my description of purchasing something that was helpful to me. They said: 'You know how to take care of your own narcissism.' Wow, yes! *Yes*, I probably do. A *part* of us, they were implying, is benignly narcissistic; we are invested in a degree of sane self-care – within reason and *fairly unproblematically*. The person who *never* inconveniences anyone ever, never 'lets you down', never thinks of themselves, never buys themselves a 'nice' or useful or comforting thing, becomes an oddly shrill creature. Flowers for the bathroom, anyone? Some shoes that don't leave you limping? A raincoat you'll own for decades? Sometimes, we just choose our own mild self-interest – not always, not adamantly, not without also knowing the steady pleasures of service, care and realising that you need less than you feared.

I do know that people can take their politics somewhere very far in the direction of deprivation. They neglect their narcissism entirely. Sometimes, one wonders if they could solve *some* bothers in a nonplussed and non-ranty manner, to relieve certain strains that aren't particularly revolutionary or relevant. These strains might just be strainful, making us less buoyant and a bit smug or disapproving.[1]

It's plausible that, for our current economic model, it's convenient if we remain persuaded that the *majority* of our botherments align with a solution we can *buy*. Due to this presumption (which multiplies stress rather than allays it, I daresay), those with a critical bent can grow wary of such a blithe equation. Stuff = Fulfilment. *No, Siree*, they say. This caution *is* a sure bulwark against rampant conspicuous consumption, and planetary pillaging.

At the same time, we can acknowledge that *in some cases*, for some botherments, having Useful Stuff *helps*. And this is not a very interesting thought, or idea. Just a plain thing. We have relations with the objects of this world. Caring for them, appreciating them, sharing them, passing them on, rather than mocking them, might actually *deflate* the beast we call consumerism. Or the speed at which we 'need' new things.

(When self-proclaimed pseudo-anarchists break, then lose, the bicycle I entrust them with in Berlin, they defend their poor behaviour with: 'Don't be so materialistic', I say, 'Objects are our fellows; don't be careless, and follow through on your commitments.' *Gell?*)

The wariness (of the idea that we can buy our way out of botherment) is hardly silly, and not just prim, however. When this caution is drowned out entirely, capitalism's capture becomes more saturating, less wry, and its bravado-logic ploughs on with breathtaking and icy circularity, solving-and-worsening its own constellation, as well as injuring our capacity to distinguish *well*.

So ... access to resources of all kinds can relieve many struggles and sufferings. What, however, would there remain for us to do, when we have cycled through (enough of) the purchasable solutions, only to find that the niggle persists, or if we haven't got the funds to embark on this existential experiment thoroughly, or at all? It is never complete; you will never reach its end. Rather than wholly devoting ourselves to a life of only getting more money (how dull), we have the option to recast the question. A measured combo of sufficient means with all that these provide a ground for would be more possible under non-neoliberalised conditions. Just sayin'.

We know those studies that show that happiness doesn't increase after a certain level of income is reached. And also, that below a certain level of income, life is just really hard, and maybe happiness will elude many in that situation. Universal basic income then becomes a topic and isn't my topic. We can, however, follow these studies; we can take note. We may even riot. *Pack a thermos and some little-lunch.*

There aren't any spoilers to this chapter. It becomes, upon minimal reflection, quickly obvious that a swathe of what bothers us, in our soul, is not simplistically linked to stuff and the getting-of-it, but rather to our relation to objects, to people, and the big one: *our relation to the conditions of being alive.*

The wisdom traditions give us plenty to chew on in this regard. It's the esoteric knowledge that is now an open book – hardly *eso-* at all since available to a very large 'circle' and no longer very secret. Perhaps it *is* secret only insofar as: you can 'have' the knowledge ('information') but its content won't be easy to activate in any powerful way. We *know*, nowadays, plenty about how to be less bothered. We don't, however, as often have *exposure to those who have worked out something about botherment*, in their fibres, in their sustained practice. Information without relation counts for little.

The 'methods' read well or less well, depending on who says them, and while supposedly amendable to dot-pointing, they are in fact *resistant to summary*. It all hangs on the degree to which the knowing is carried in someone's organism and history of actual grappling. People call it learning-by-doing. I call it durational practice alongside established practitioners.

The things that the Buddhist say 'bother' us are greed, hatred and ignorance. *Hmmm*. It could almost cover it, *really*. For greed and hatred, I find myself abbreviating it to 'awful' – the Awful. Alongside this, ignorance amounts to a kind of bad thinking, a misconception about the nature of reality. They go together as a thorough triad, which covers more bases than you might at first think. Ignorance is about how we don't really 'get' the ontological facts of our fleshy situation and thus bang our heads against how things *aren't*. (The previous chapter made a start on exploring this.)

Things aren't permanent (but they also have *some* staying power, depending).

You aren't therefore permanent (*and* you have a kind of workable, while also changing, sense of being a person). It takes some embodied training to learn how to live an elasticity around this in a sane way. The elasticity often relies on some early life phases whereby this mutable self was established *enough*.

And finally, there is emptiness ('vastness', if you prefer) ... this is the hardest. Let's leave it aside for now.

The other open secret of the wisdom traditions is that they often end up saying that the best training we can embrace involves *Samtosha* (in the Sanskrit). Contentment. The highest practice. It doesn't imply being a martyr, tolerating violence, grovelling to power, standing by and letting bad shit go on, or never pursuing stuff sincerely and steadily. It merely intervenes on the madly insistent tendency of us, humans, while possessing or being in shining relation to Plenty of Stuff (material and immaterial), to continue to fixate on and dig into what we *don't* have. Most astonishing and off-colour when encountered among the Privileged (who seem to *have* so much), it is anyway widespread across the classes and categories. The fact that its habit is so difficult (even for The Havers to avoid/lose/forget) tends to uncouple contentment from being conditioned by objective 'having' per se.

Contentment is a mode of relating. It's available as psychic jungle gym any time you want. It might have plenty to with non-squandering (but I would say that).

Thought experiment: we could have *everything* and still might (and probably would) remain discontented without applying ourselves. Contentment, if I channel a Buddhist's stance, can be said to bear a *subtractive relation to circumstance*. They only *seem* causally and plausibly connected.

∝

THIS CHAPTER IS GOING TO ADDRESS THREE MODES OF Being Bothered, with three prepositions, as mentioned. We've explored Being Bothered *by* stuff we don't have. Now I want to consider the second inflection of Being Bothered *by* – where this state gets raised to a higher power. As you'll see, this next BBb turns out to be a kind of suffering that I'm going to class as ... fortunate. Ready?

We might find ourselves – if we're lucky, very lucky – being somewhat bothered *by* our humdrum and non-sparkly capacity to be a bit average. We may find ourselves bothered *by* how awful, or shabby, or routinely unkind *we ourselves* can be. Awful, if you recall, is the umbrella term I'm using for our hateful and greedy ways.

Strong language you say. *Can't you water it down a bit, Antonia?* Yet, these words are accurate, if hard to hear. On top of that, there's our (entitled) obliviousness. As Nick Carraway in *The Great Gatsby* says of Daisy and Tom Buchanan: 'They were careless people.'

I think we are all often quite careless people. We indeed often don't 'care' enough about what we do, since unaware of doing it. Even so, the consequences (which our lack of care unleashes) come back – sometimes – to *bother* us.

Let's say I don't know that I've behaved in some unfortunate way. *I missed its happening*. Whatever it was couldn't be integrated into my self-image, so my brain glances off it, and I conveniently omit to recall it. My hunch is that I may (if I'm lucky) still feel uneasy at some level of myself.

I'm calling 'being oblivious' *less* lucky. If I don't notice the action, the awful, the fallout and plunder onwards, I'm not bothered. Well, this is common. It's *around*.

I wouldn't want to propose some *theory* that bad things haunt people necessarily. Because I'm not other people. I dunno what they/

you experience ... Some stuff *I do* can bother me. (One could say 'haunt' but I prefer a plainer verb, to keep it less Bonnie Tyler, less choir-boy gothic.) I can feel *bothered* and be unable to locate the feeling's source. It would be easy for this bothered-feeling to get swept up into discussions of mental health, and this might be fruitful. The point is: I'm bothered by something, and noting my Relations within a suite of Awfuls might unpack part of the problem.

To feel explicitly uneasy – which I'm saying is 'lucky' – is a *new* phase of the 'suffering', a *desirable* form, arguably. It's the beginning of waking up. I can face it, or I can bury it. Being bothered, in *this* way, isn't a sign things are going wrong; it's a metabolisable discomfort that offers a gracious alarm system. I'm classing this as a new mode of Being Bothered *by* – I've gone from being bothered by tangible things or lack of things, to being bothered by my modes, habits, or inherited ways of relating to the world, to others, to my own actions. (This, as we'll get to later, might then lead me towards Being Bothered ... *to*. But we're not there yet.)

I first want to explore this next inflection of Being Bothered *by*, which has shifted from being about stuff, to being about relations.

It might involve aspects of my own mediocre awfulness that I am able to catch. Awkward, sure. There! Just then, I made a resentful remark about someone because they had a success I would have liked. Ooooo. Interesting. It was jokey, but it wasn't mostly funny. Or I'm afraid I'm losing your attention, so I might do something to make you feel insecure ... (This *isn't* a strategy I tend to use, but we know it as one, yes? It's a common example, of Awful-Lite.)

There would be plenty of moments when I catch nothing, when I can plough on, oblivious. It's hard even to acknowledge this. I must do plenty of grimy things and not really clock them *enough*.

When I can spot the awfulness operating, I have no great affection for the way it feels, for the taste of its unfolding, and

I 'suffer' from the botherment of *how I can be*. However, my provocation here is that I am glad to be bothered on this matter. I want to remain a person bothered by their own human, run-of-the-mill, unimpressive Awful. If I can manage to suffer at this arguably next register, by facing myself, I may become curious about attenuating this mode of botherment.

How could I behave in a less awful way next time? What determines how awful? When does the Awful crest and ebb away? What is this all connected to?

Do you ever think like this? I'm curious about the internal experience that other people have of it. I'm quite aware that I can be as awful as anyone. I have a lot of force, which suggests that, unchecked, my awful behaviours would also have a lot of force … This fact doesn't flatter or set me apart in any way. Awful is pretty widespread, pretty normal. And there are plenty of vivacious arseholes. *Hahahaha*.

I might align this second-level of Being Bothered *by* – where unease crops up in the wake of something awful which I (or even someone else) did – with the old-fashioned mechanism of *conscience*.[2] Some people like to explain the popularised notion of the Super Ego by using the easier, more widespread, older idea of conscience. The Super Ego, they say, is just the psychoanalytic name for the (religious) idea of the conscience. The moral agency in us. It's definitely more complicated than that.

I have an experience of arguably *two* different mechanisms, which I can't collapse into being the same. The first, what I'm calling a 'conscience' – as I've known it – is quite *kind*. Kind but quietly unflinching. It speaks but not with an imperative, demeaning or despotic tone.

'You know, that thing you said/did/orchestrated wasn't wonderful. I reckon he/she/they is pretty hurt. Have you been feeling troubled in a vague way? Well, consider joining the dots. You can't accept that thing you were part of. And now you can see it, you can do something, or just know it happened – no fudging.' (This will depend on the 'thing'.) Saying 'sorry' is an option, sometimes. Making amends. Sometimes there is just biting regret, and no nice feelings or actions to soften the fact.

&c. &c. Is this a tone you know?

The Super Ego, on the other hand, is officially nastier. It's locked in a dysfunctional relationship with us. The Super Ego tends to the extreme; psychoanalyst Jacques Lacan has called it 'obscene'. It's forever running you down, running down the company you're keeping, warning you, frightening you. *Don't do that, or go with them, I'm the only one who can keep you safe. If you do that you'll come off as a loser.*

When you meet someone nice, but who doesn't stack up to the Super Ego's plans for your conjugal future, it whispers: 'Look, how they eat their toast! You can't stay with them!' Or ... 'They dress like *that?*' (I think someone Super Ego'ed me on that basis once, which turned out to be sad for them, but splendid for their Inner Tyrant.) The Super Ego can really fuck your romantic life and send you off to be with someone it approves of, but who oddly replicates all the unhappiest and worst features of your approbated, earlier relationships. (You're left dazed, 'enjoying' your life that never changes, and the Super Ego preens like a satisfied cane toad.) The Super Ego dictates what you 'will enjoy'; it has been described as an anti-legal morality.[3]

The high theorist in me remains unconvinced (theory can be its own Super-Egoic force); at the same time, the practitioner in me (of yoga, of decades of sitting practice) remains more willing to consider this two-fold possibility.

Conscience *could be* something else. (In psychoanalysis, there *is* the notion of the Ego-ideal, which has scope to sublimate ...) Hold it open, just hold it open ... and if so, would a conscience 'bother' us, more akin to a little kid pulling quietly on our sleeve. We find it irritating, tedious, until we look down to see what we had been ignoring. The conscience might – unlike the Super Ego's more sadistic operations – function to protect our *heart*. To fiercely guard our Spiritual Metabolism: what we can't and don't even wish to become capable of digesting.

I had a yoga teacher in my twenties who worked in the Japanese tradition of Okido. She knew a lot about the body and was also a long-time Shiatsu practitioner. One time, she gave our class the example of someone eating some spoiled (toxic) food. She gave three scenarios, asking which was the 'healthiest' response. One person spews immediately. One person is okay, then gets sick in the night. A third person feels under the weather but then is okay. Various answers were given, but the answer is (you guessed it) the *first* one: immediately spewing.

Health could be the ability, the inclination, in this system anyway, to spit out what for the long term would not be good for you (foul oyster; industrial milk that's rancid; slimy raw chicken, five-day-old rice in the plastic container). Thus, I'm asking: is this next inflection of Being Bothered *by* (which can lead to Being Bothered *to*) a *sign of life*?

∝

FOR DELEUZE, RECALL THAT IT'S NOT SO MUCH *WHAT I am* (each of us is infinite, and not predictable, so the 'what' never grasps the moving phenomenon) – it's *how I can*. This is to be watched, learned about, plainly. What kinds of mean things might I be capable of? What levels of neglect? What styles of almost-invisible lack of concern and abandoning? If I ask these questions with sober observing grit – neither embracing my Awful, nor pretending 'I don't/wouldn't do that' – this is the beginning of other things being possible. What's possible first up is sheer *spacing* – to pause, simply, our 'Behaving' for the slimmest instant.

I might be *able to be* awful. And you! Yes – you, too, have potential to be awful. This doesn't make either of us worthless, not even undignified, not unloveable, not demeaned. Just able to be a bit awful, and the Being Bothered response suggests to me I'd like to stop it, or 'attenuate' it (as the *Yoga Sutras* say). My heart would like me to stop it.

Could we risk considering that being in the vicinity of awfulness and, either being subjected to it, or colluding with its logics more generally, really does us over? This is a further notch up on the Botheredness scale. It's beyond a bit of sleeve-tugging – and no product, service, subscription or internet order will really fill the breach, or allay the unsettled feeling.

So, where are we?

There is Being Bothered by an objective thing. Can you buy your way out of it? Maybe. This may include the state of *feeling* Bothered, stemming from typical (but not shiny) habits of ungratitude (when *Samtosha* goes missing); and we can't find any contentment.

Then, there's the bother of waking up to Perhaps Being Awful. Lite or otherwise. The wonderful ability to be bothered enough by it. To be itching from Awful, and curious to intervene.

Then … to be Bothered to …

A conscience, perhaps.

If we are drowning in our too-relaxed manner with Awful (one of the audition numbers for a well-adjusted neoliberal subject), and if we don't have a way to observe coolly our own Awful habits and modes – to let the conscience level of Botherment in – then I reckon we just self-medicate to the Maxxx.

(Lunching recently with work colleagues, one of them talked about stopping drinking, after having drunk a lot. I said, 'Well, people are under huge pressure and it's painful. That's why the drinking, yes.' She responded, 'Yes, but it also doesn't work.')

There's much to suggest that what we conveniently call 'mental health' – as fine as this expression is – merits a parallel framing as that which we cannot metabolise, at various levels of our organisms, although it would be convenient to be able to do so. We'd like to orbit easily near Awful and without the niggling. We'd like certain edible substances marketed as food to go down better (or not make us have systemic malfunctions). We'd like to feel peaceful, expansive, wide-eyed and blissed out, even when we are enmeshed with behaviours, Ways, notions and practices that are ... Awful. Greed, hatred and some structural indifference thrown in for good measure.

Would we? Would we like it? To be able increasingly to not be Bothered by this?

Perhaps you are entirely Unbothered (at all the levels), and you let it roll off your oily feathers even when someone splashes you with a decent douse of Awful. I don't quite believe you, but I do know how much armature we can cultivate when exposed to the current moment. And you might have lifetimes of such exposure and negotiation ... I get it, if you are behind a wall of cynical protection, if your unfelt grief has harried you into a corner, if humdrum brutality has bruised you beyond the reach of tenderness. When you want to risk poking an eyelash out, I'll be here.

Let me channel another more common angle on this. People hate other people being awful, and show close to zero interest in noticing – in some other moment – their own participation in comparable modes of Awful. If we only take offence for one side of this, our suffering's got low chances of ever resolving. This is why (perhaps) the Tibetan Buddhists train an emphasis in focusing more on others. Focus on how mediocre you are towards others, and things will shift. You'll wake up with different kinds of complaints to before. Even ... (gasp!) fewer overall.

If, when people are horrible to you or to those you love, your genuine response is: Fine, I'm down with Awful; I don't mind it, I realistically accept it as the best we can manage ... then, well, the next bit won't interest you. Except, check your metabolism (at every level). How's it really going?

To join the logic of someone who harms you is the deepest triumph of their harming. They've managed to influence how you are. In the storm of reacting, we often think we are 'getting back at them on their own terms'. Well ... we might read it like that, but this reading would leave a lot out. They have arguably brought us to the point where our actions now betray an admiration, our behaviour attests to our impulsive mimicry. (We *do* mostly retaliate, and we *do* mostly join in. These are bleak facts. And to hold open that this cascade might not always eventuate; something else sometimes does happen ...)

Reading this chapter, I questioned how precise I was about the Awful. Are people regularly Awful, or do they perceive they are? Aren't we often quite *fine*? Maybe a good example, of how widespread Humdrum High Awful is, can be seen in domestic relationships that aren't working. Holy moly.

The stories you hear. Your own stories (hopefully past). The things that go on. The storms of mutual Awful that people enact, survive and emerge from confused, dazed and complicit. Our capacity for Awful goes sky-high when we are enmeshed intimately and dysfunctionally. We can even use the closeness as justification for the spontaneity of the horribleness.

This is why another dear friend – who's a counsellor (a genius, truly) – tells people to stop obsessing about the 'communication' in their relationship. She suggests they focus for a while on the more pressing combo of Sex+Manners. Hahaha. I love this so much. Fucking and tenderness, remember.

'Communication' could justify anything. Often, it's a pleasant-sounding name for verbal incontinence (see earlier chapters). Under the guise of 'communicating', we can simply indulge our leakiness. Leaking resentment ... Closeness, especially over the longer term, is never for me a justification for being less considerate, less kind, less cuddly.

Now, where were we?

If you're in a horrid close space of dysfunction, try to shelter somewhere. Shelter from your own impulse. Select the situation otherwise as soon as that is workable. Keep steady, loving company elsewhere. Know you might be Addicted to Awful (in the form of an interaction). I, too, have been Awful in those contexts, and it rocks the heart, world and sense of self like nothing else. We amass regrets. We feel remorseful and wounded. These all bother us greatly. And if we can stop the noisy distraction of blaming (the other/ourselves) and notice how we've learned to join in with Awful, we might come around to seeing our heart tugging forlornly on our ragged, snotty cuff.

∝

IN THE LAST CHAPTER, I TRIED TO TALK ABOUT THE uncomfortable buzz – *Dukkha*. The low-level feeling of non-satisfaction that accompanies being alive in most of its moments (apart from a few, which are to be viewed as the exception). The buzz is ontological, or *built in* to how things are. Without training, our reaction to the buzz is likely to be on autopilot, ergo we'll *resist* it. Our reactive impulse to resist the buzz tends to exacerbate the buzz – taking it from low-level to something more intense, more substantial. The provocation would read: the more we resist or disavow the non-satisfactoriness of life, the more we expose ourselves to grander degrees of serious suffering.

These are the terms of the capture by our current moment's less endearing personality traits.

Derrida's work could be said overall to orbit this observable phenomenon. It considers how the inconsistency, or undecidabilty, originary 'brokenness', or built-in 'loss', can't be eliminated from a system – even a system that prides itself on completeness like Western Metaphysics. I read him to imply that if we skip over these facts and forms of incompleteness, impasse and loss ... then we don't reduce their future likelihood; instead, counter-intuitively, we almost guarantee them. (It's our ignorance! – in the Buddhist sense.) It leads us further into suffering – and at a new, magnified register. More dug in. Reinforced now.

I once had a lover who was a bit older than me. He was not entirely pleasant to be around, as it turned out, but he was a practitioner of various arts (health-related, artistic) and shared the odd wise thing with me. One that made the slightly uneasy passage worth it in the end was when he said: 'You think that I'm stable and calm, but I only appear that way because I accept to some degree how not stable and not calm I mostly am.'

Subtle, right? He didn't speak often, but this rare confiding left an impression. His equation implied that he simply didn't carry the dissatisfaction into its second register. He left the loss, incompleteness, uncertainty, non-knowing be. This, in turn, gave off the impression of being 'fulfilled', 'complete', 'certain', 'knowing'.

Are you revising your coolness strategies? Well, why not?

This could be the concluding paragraph of the last chapter. Something happens when you settle down with, even ... forgive, the unfightable fact of the unease: by making sure to resist the urge to 'drive the car off the bridge', aka going into the dead end of resignation. No!

Rather, take a bright-eyed interest in its mechanism. The Buddhists train this practically – into our little reactive systems – via meditation on the ontological givens known as the Three Marks of Existence – or the Three Seals (in Zen). Firstly, everything is impermanent; secondly, *Dukkha* is built in; thirdly, you, yourself, are never a graspable, stable entity, with any enduring identity.

It's funny. I never think of myself as a Buddhist. (What would that identity mean anyway?) But I've spent a lot of time doing something which aligns closely to what Buddhists (who practise) do. This is the sitting. Most people call it 'meditating', but sitting doesn't even have an object. (To put this grammatically: 'meditate' is a transitive verb; 'to sit' is an intransitive one.) One doesn't meditate on anything in sitting. One just sits, and the whole circus of being a creature unfolds in the private cinema of the practice. It has no expressible aim or end. It involves a frame (setting one up). This is the methodology for its experiment, that's all. Straight(ish) spine. Stay still(ish). Do it for a length of time. That's it. That's the frame. There isn't a specifiable end for its activity (though we are forever trying to impose one). It's an 'activity' which is barely one at all.

The evanescent threshold between doing and non-doing. Hang out there for a bit.

The Buddhists have a take on Botherment, per se. When we come face to face with a non-magical thinking about existence, we might find ourselves bumping into these three modes of misconception. Permanency, satisfaction and self are each notions which don't hold water in any lived life that isn't wholly deluded.

(And, part of letting go of all these spurious fancies is also letting go of thinking you can escape delusion in any thoroughgoing way. That's the Zen full-stop, right there. They're super clear on holding off on that unwise direction.)

There would be many Buddhist things to say about what is bothering me, you, us, them. Is one register at which I'm Bothered also (collectively) Bothering us? I've hinted at it already, and the next chapter will get more explicit. It takes further the Bothered bys, towards a Bothered to (and what conditions this possibility).

We've got so many theories about our closer miseries. Not only the grand planetary ones, though they are related, of course. I'm curious about the details of how we are personally so beleaguered ... together and sometimes similarly, in ways our good brains have the capacity to look at.

Unwisdom is nothing new – those pathways that lead us to squander life and amplify its built-in suffering in knowing and less knowing ways. Spinoza might call it unreason. Deleuze notes that Spinoza, too, was preoccupied with the strange fact that people like to cultivate their own incapacity, their own slavishness. He found it odd. It is very odd, and old, this problem. Each new context, moment, historical phase, activates the basic ingredients in new ways. I find myself being bothered to approach the typical forms of unwisdom in our current moment – how we run (have been running) with open arms into emergent modes of slavery, collective and personal.

So! Our collective strains of botherment are bothering me. Tug tug. Despite the time on the cosmetic massage table being pleasant-enough, and despite my knowing how to steer clear of piety when it comes to being practical about Stuff, I still suspect the deepest Botherments won't tend to be resolved there or like that. And I'm keen to shield myself somewhat from the modes of capture that can really sweep up the Bothered person.

Not being a card-carrying Buddhist, I want now to think this further with help from a few other paradigms, with help from other sages. If the last chapter considered falling in love, this next chapter considers what we might want to fall out of love with.

*Unlearning our fanaticism for 'optimised', 'excellent'
and 'maximal' might also ease our complicity
in many needless, everyday persecutions.*

Virtue: falling out of love with Awful

From my stack of second-hand books that I collect about the place, I grabbed a little commentary on Plato. Slim volume. Bright aqua cover.

Sometimes I need a lighter read: alongside a cup of tea; on the tram; on the loo; before bed to rest the blue-lit eyeballs. A ratty, analogue book of commentary, with some fifth-century BCE vase-detail on the cover, fits the bill.

There's a nice bit at the start where the author, philosopher Guy C. Field[1], highlights a confusion in modern readers about the Greek notion of *arete*, virtue. Virtue, he says, tends to be viewed in contemporary life as related to something that you *aren't supposed to do*. Virtue can be misread as only ever being a kind of restriction, a behavioural constraint.

Virtue, as we tend to view it (probably unsure even of what might be in a list of virtues) leans towards sounding a bit ... *dull*. Who'd want a virtuous person at a party, we ask? That's not the first quality we think of when selecting guests, right? Wouldn't we prefer some kind of unpredictable, fact-smearing, gaslighting, passive-aggressive, binge-consuming heart-throb? *Hmmm*.

Virtue, Field emphasises, can actually be understood to reflect *a* capacity, or *capacity* generally. We could render this with some consistency as: *a virtuous person is someone with a lot of capacity*. (We see this implied in the *Yoga Sutras*, too.) For now, stated in this order, I think this is accurate enough to run with. (If you *flip* it into: 'a person with a lot of capacity is reliably virtuous', it's *not* the case; the logic no longer holds.)

The cardinal virtues in classical thought include prudence (choosing a wise course of action), justice (or capacity to be fair), courage or mettle (bravery, tenacity ...) and temperance (ability to restrain oneself).[2] I think it's okay to add to this list, to consider other things one might put on it, mess around with one's own constellation of virtues. Already this is a sound way to activate Deleuze's provocation to experiment.

And what about capacity and virtue? There are a few ways one could think around this.

1. The virtues take a little bit of effort, and so you need to have some energy for them.
2. Virtues aren't what you're *meant* to do (who is this entity who would 'mean' for you to 'should' do them?). Rather, at the peak of your 'capacity' – when capacity equals joy (not surges of aggression, revenge, 'I'll show them', &c.) – virtue has a chance. Virtue becomes more accessible, becoming *how* you might be, what shape your decisions and behaviours might take, when you have more steady stretch.
3. In moments of being in relatively 'greater' capacity for myself, rather than a relatively 'depleted' capacity for myself, my behaviours might align better with a set of tendencies that have been called virtues.

Another way to say it is that, with capacity available, I might find myself operating at a greater distance from Awful, or even from Disappointing, especially from Retaliatory (noting we can retaliate outwards or inwards – same same).

The first thing to remember is that 'capacity' needn't be read in line with current cultural cliché. Reconceptualising what you want capacity to mean *for you* is a good beginning. Clarifying your own concept here is almost as fun as … say, decorating your new sharehouse with milk crates and fabric offcuts, or cleaning out the baking cupboard. Or, packing a hiking pack for a long walk. There's some joy to the benign deciding.

What are you going to put in this category – *capacity* – and what are you going to leave out?

It's an amusing and not unimportant exercise to consider what might count as 'capacity'. I am cautious now to read every instance of frenetic doing, of incessant activity, or uninterrupted inertias of soldiering on, of being eternally 'available' ... as functional 'capacity'. Nietzsche has framed such stuff as herdlike. He can read as a bit snobby at times, but (reading him generously) he's also alerting us to the fact that joining in with the frenetic might just be a way to avoid asking ourselves: *what do we want to be doing?* It can be a way for everything to stay the same, with no creativity, since the inertia of 'doing' rolls along and changes nothing.[3]

There *are* (of course) gender questions here. Sometimes women have traditionally been 'busy' because they don't wish to drown, to have their families drown, in the errata of unhygiene that accrue if you simply don't do boring tasks. Right? The lack of sharing out these tasks is the history of less sex and grumpy home life. Just sayin'. My sister has been known to say that nothing's more of a turn-on than a man doing jobs he hasn't been asked to do. Bins out. Hard rubbish dealt with. Shelf repaired and lunch boxes washed and ready to go ... Who doesn't want to get their pants off immediately?

It's *so* contextually dependent. How about the capacity to leave the party? How about the capacity to lie down on the bed for twenty minutes before you actually injure your vitality for the day, or the capacity to contain oneself (a positive action, not a repression) in order to avert a reactive disaster?

Not speaking.

Not reacting.

Not having a quippish comeback.

Not taking subtle revenge on autopilot.

Hold this notion open, as we proceed below, and read 'capacity' with your preferred (and evolving) take in mind. 'What capacity means?' can operate as a very good question in itself.

Domestic life.

When a person in a closed space – me, you, your lover – isn't coping so well, then, they are usually a less pleasant version of themselves. With less energy, less bounce, they might be snappier, tetchy, even meaner than normal. They probably don't *want* to be like this. This might not make for a particularly *just*, or I like the word 'magnanimous', way to be. They'd prefer to be another way, but capacity isn't available. Or they haven't decided to cultivate the capacity, or haven't had persuasive human examples to model it.

Here can lie the resentment swirling in a lot of relationships ... One thinks: they *could* decide to sleep. To go for a walk. They could make more of an effort to be less of a difficult unit to be with. Yeah, but they *aren't* – doing, deciding. And that also has to do with capacity.

Take patience – example #1. Most of us frequently experience a state one might call 'impatience'. Examples like this are best when confined to *yourself* – not comparing your levels of patience with another person's, okay? We can read these levels as being in flux for *ourselves*. I kind of *know* when my own capacity (with which I am somewhat familiar) is up or down. I know the shapes that will manifest as I slide into lower capacity. I'm rarely mean, for example, and if meanness slips out, I know I'm exhausted, worn thin, overwhelmed. So, I watch these slides ... for precision, not for the sicklier love of self-judgement.

It's *really* less convivial to make these calls for others ... have I already said this? People *really* stop liking you if you do it a lot.

What about commuter patience? When I'm having nicer times, when there is a bit of joy in my heart, I care less when I'll reach my destination. This looks like patience but, in a way, it involves losing interest in a certain modality of time. This mode, after Deleuze, might be called 'the living present'. It's our habitual, instrumentalist mode; it's very ends-focused. Patience happens when I can expand my palette of curiosity beyond the tunnel vision of the tasks and expectations pressing me. These instances aren't rare, but they can become hard to access. It's like walking with your face way ahead of your pelvis. Off-centre. Already inching into an anticipated future. Regarding capacity, then, impatience tells me I don't have enough. I'm in surviving mode. I'm working off scant verve.

In case you're already grinding your teeth, neoliberal working conditions tend to dovetail such that one is slowly divorced from one's capacity in multiple facets of being a person. A lot is conspiring for this to be the case under these conditions, conditions we're slowly learning to suspect and to disdain. There is a kindness to noting how one's capacity is impacted when it comes to eviscerating work conditions. At the same time, as as a result, we can struggle to remain steady, to curb our resentful tendencies (which harm us, which we don't want to become) in relation to these modes of meanness, to the current fashions in filthiness. There are no easy answers. And any such answer would be glib and fatuous. We might want to maintain a stubbornness regarding how we comport ourselves, for ourselves. And we might consider breaking up with this system (offering any casual approval regarding its 'givens'), because it hampers our capacity, while at the same time giving us poor and perverse definitions *of* capacity.

We can disrupt these definitions; we are disrupting them.

When I'm less depleted, less pressed by what tasks I have to 'get through', my interest can dreamily involve itself in *what is around*. This is a sideways expansion, out of that tunnel vision, bringing into focus things that are more *beautiful* and arguably less *useful*. I see the geometric scales of bark on those towering pine trees near my house; or, while sitting in a line of idling cars at the blocked intersection, I can see the vine, creeping up the painted wall, leaves as brilliant as cherry juice. Sometimes, the petrichor overwhelms me and – contra-utilitarian-logic and the state of the world – one finds oneself swooning, spawning associations, lurching into memory, glad for no good reason.

(Mostly, we feel in a hurry to get home and touch – again, again – one of the glass screens we own, to be told tedious things, to be told nothing, to be given our daily dose of envy, strain, fear or confusion. It's boring to speak of addiction. To leave it out, however, might also be negligent ...)

Impatient feelings could signal for me that I'm a bit exhausted, that it's been a tough day, that I haven't eaten or drunk enough. When my capacity is greater (after meditating, after doing even a small bout of one's practice) then the usual knee-jerk impulse – which demands that time adhere to my calculated anticipations about how it would go – simply doesn't rise up. I'm not even in that landscape of calculating at all, really. Time is functioning otherwise. It has passed beyond the atmosphere of neoliberal efficiency and gone fully *intergalactic*.

Is this still an irritating paragraph? Well, it probably depends what kind of capacity you're in while you read it.

I think it's clearly irritating if we're in a moralising brain, rather than an experimental brain. (I'm borrowing from Deleuze on Spinoza here ...[4]) If you want to read patience as a moral value, then you are at risk of judging yourself for not having capacity (judging yourself for something that is hampering your capacity), or for thinking that I'm implying that we should judge this fact. (Judgement, too, is a particular kind of activity. There are other kinds of things you can do with your mind, as Deleuze points out.)

If we are in an experimental brain, then we're not in this landscape at all. We're in a more curious landscape, where we wonder about the ups and downs of the melody of our bodily constellations. How interesting that when I'm low in capacity (fact, not judgement) I find myself positioned in relation to time in a certain way, where I have to propel myself through it, and it feels only like an obstacle rather than a luscious medium. And how interesting that time itself feels different when I've got more capacity (fact, not judgement), how my habits of anticipation (patience/impatience) then operate in more pleasant and stretchy ways.

Another way to say it: *I'm less anticipatory.* If anticipation is a practical narrowing of focus, a kind of survival stress response, then – when my capacity is greater – my field of perception is more expansive. Less a tunnel than a panorama. When in more abundant capacity, I don't zero in so desperately and, as a result, I get a wider (and often more accurate) view of things.

When I have more capacity, it can feel as if things take an apt amount of time. Just the time they take. With time itself feeling elastic, gentler, a medium that's a pleasure not a hindrance.

How it can flip, though! We all know it.

So, some days this luxuriating isn't what's *factually* happening. This is the melody I'm in. Choppier. Pressing. Snaggy. We can learn to steer clear of magical thinking. Assess your capacity with precision! This is the art. How much capacity do I actually have? Don't let yourself lurch towards self-flattery, denigration, or faux modesty. Be precise.

And if you assess with clear eyes, and it's low? There are more days ahead. More encounters, maybe some decisions I can make about my encounters. (If this is not 'moral', would it be ... *aesthetic*?)

This would be the Vast Experimental viewpoint that won't disappoint. *Yes*: it's calling on the frame of an experiment which I can take or leave. For me at least, it makes things spacious. Pushiness is subtracted.

Now, you might be wondering where this is going. I seem to be talking about capacity, with the implication that capacity is interesting because it has to do with *virtue* (odd topic, but hey). Why, you ask, would we be interested in virtue, Antonia? (We're not in church. It sounds vaguely passé.) Is this a religious chapter, somehow? Virtue may not even be a category anyone cares about anymore. Can you tell me if this will make me more productive and get me more followers?

Because virtue has to do with Awful. No, we're not. It's not a religious chapter, but it might be a chapter that acknowledges something that exceeds the regime Badiou calls 'bodies and languages' – democratic materialism. No, it probably bears no relation to productivity or followers.

There. Let's press on.

If I'm curious about virtue, and patience is one of them, and I don't want to lurch constantly into operatics of impatience, what options do I have? Well, there is also a sterner version, which sits alongside the Vast Experimental mindset. This other one might be of use, depending on the moment. And it will depend on one's constitution; I might be able to use it without damaging my capacity too much, but we're all unique in this respect.

Some friends, who admit to high couture-levels of jumpier neurosis, might say that this take for them is a bit dis-enabling … For *you*, I couldn't say, about this sterner approach. (Even this light talk of virtue might already be shrinking your oomph.) You might have a history where you became allergic to certain kinds of structuring, to cool reasoning of a particular tone. For you, like my friends, this sternness vibe might *gut* your capacity – it could just be a bad encounter with an idea, a framing. In which case, use the experimental mindset, or invent another one. *Notice*, again, what helps your capacity. Out of curiosity, not out of moral duty, right?

Sometimes I do use a stern logic, followed up swiftly by some necessary humour: 'nothing told you, Antonia, that this car journey would reliably take X amount of time. You don't let Google Maps *decide your behaviour* and sway more genuine temporal insight, do you?' ['Yes, I often do and I've never been more regularly late in my long life' – hahaha.] The humour itself, if I can find its thread, might be the thing that increases my capacity to tolerate a long time sitting still in the car, with a few too many brake lights in my eyes. Maybe I'd like to be somewhere else right now, straightaway. But I'm not. And it definitely isn't the fault of the guy indicating beside me to merge lanes. He's just another element, hardly the mastermind of my malaise.

I could be really awful (to myself, to him), or I could seek a thread of my own capacity, somehow, and stay idling closer to patience. This may avert fully-fledged road rage meltdown, and my own post hoc confused feelings afterwards.

How lightly do you need to communicate with yourself to slip clear of your shut-down capacities? Some framings will create more reactivity than space for us. It depends on what your body works best with as an encounter. Hard logic + kind humour? Experimental openness?

Thoughts are a body, you see. You encounter the thickness, the *stuff* of your own thinking, and this is a mixture which might – for you – be joyous or saddening.

So, I give myself a varied diet, of sorts. If I'm needing to pull my own head in a little (because the topple of resentment and blamey feeling won't take me anywhere I care for), then I can mobilise a reasoned set of thoughts, such as: 'No one has personally wronged me'; 'I'm safe in a car, which is a workable temperature and I'm likely to get home anyway (*haha*) to find something else to be upset about'.

The *Yoga Sutras* of Patañjali call this method – where you counter a feeling/image slide with concrete measured thoughts – 'contemplating the opposite'.[5] Commentators have noted that it's more a band-aid solution than anything very long-term. Maybe it's a version of CBT in earthy-toned scarves, and billows of sandalwood ... I've understood this approach to be about *interrupting* (only) a dire cascade of bad thinking. If your brain is about to grip hard onto a series of thoughts that go nowhere pleasant, and have a kind of momentum that settles in, then you can artificially summon some counter-thoughts to slow you up. There's a bit of artful timing needed.

Another reading, as Orit Sen-Gupta has identified in the fifth-century commentator, Vyasa,[6] goes like this: *observing* oneself having the cascade is actually the 'opposite' of *being activated* by it. By decelerating the cascade, via a practice of observation, the activation that was going to wrap some icky binds more tightly around my thinking can be offset, diverted, distracted from setting in too earnestly. A further interpretation is that the 'opposite' that one contemplates is to recall how badly these things have turned out before. The hate and fury can feel 'good' in the moment – tasty, necessary, right(eous) – but actually every other time, these led later to a terrible feeling, unplanned outcome, or damage to relations, &c. To recall this, too, is arguably the 'opposite' of running wildly into the eye of the thought-storm.

I have a further suggestion – and it draws us hard into the pit of how politics also involves how much we comply with things that deplete and incapacitate us. How much we let the current, grimy regime determine our subjective tonalities, our interpersonal practices, the flavour of *this brief life*.

Ready?

One way to rely less on this band-aid method is *not to make* screeds of decisions to do things that you have already experimented with, which you know gut your capacity. This is to observe the *conditions* of the botherments, the very roots of our trouble.

I'm trying to explain that giving *logical* reasons (philosophical CBT) for why there are no grounds for getting impatient mostly won't really impact your capacity for patience, our example of virtue, of non-Awful. It might, like the last paragraph, just make you feel a bit more defensive, or criticised, since it seems there are plenty of 'reasons', but you still 'can't'. I suspect most people find this makes them more paralysed, or even more enraged.

If this is the case, this style of thinking (the reasoning, stern kind) won't cultivate your capacity for patience. Do you see? – we are watching for Spinoza's slides in relation to many things, including *how we think*.

The joy angle makes more sense, has more flow-on: when

you have joy in your heart, when your capacity has slid upwards, your capacity for patience (or anything else) will be greater. Exert pressure: make your experiments *less* at the level of 'shoulds', and *more* in the realm of noticing a non-commodified liveliness. How wide does your creaturely scope become? More ability to play, giggle, stumble, drift, gobble, doze, careen, stall, bounce or associate.

We know this is not the same as 'living my best life' (a recent slogan which naturally I refrain from uttering ...) because that so-called 'best life' is a bit generically determined, its shape already a bit coloured-in. (Or, as Wendy Brown might say, it is part of shunting all our language creepily towards economically rational, fake-nice expression.) This 'best life' seems already curated by so many images that reflect back to us what a best life is ... and often these images don't include us, our oddities and situations, very well. This apparently unique best life *is* on sale in the centre aisle of ALDI, and everyone seems to be 'uniquely' going after the same one. Too shaped by market expectations and logics of the market, not enough by our own unwieldy, odd, untaggable inventions.

More capacity for patience, you say, but also for bank robbery. Well, perhaps. Perhaps!

Some mixtures or meetings (if you recall the method of C., my friend in snowy northern Germany) *are* likely to increase your capacity overall and, given that patience or any virtue might be something that thrives more when you have capacity than when you have none, then as you become less cavalier about mixtures, cultivating ones that work better for you (when *possible*, it won't be constant) then you may end up more likely to operate more patiently.

Or more lovingly.
Or more generously.
Or more kindly.
Less punishing.
More able to forgive.

Playful.

Hotter? (Haha!)

My provocation is: someone able to dwell in this kind of capacity, to exist among these virtues, might be less a patsy for neoliberal lures. Just *less* of (we aren't aiming for purity) ... less interested, a little bit bored by, less willing to play along compliantly.

Virtue. Capacity. *Arete*. This discussion probably doesn't correspond to a stereotyped image of virtue – as someone who is dour, long-suffering, doing-the-right-thing always, restricting themselves miserably &c. This idea of virtue (as a kind of sadness, a dutiful suffering ...) might be more the contemporary version, but not so much Plato's. My hunch would be that this was not what *arete* was about.

If we keep playing around with the concept, we get:

When I have less capacity, I'm less able to exercise virtue. Non-virtuousness would then have to with being *unable* to do certain things, in a specific moment. Sometimes when we're very low in capacity we are genuinely Awful.

We have these lapses in verve, in oomph. Deleuze's framing doesn't use *essence* at all. It's not to do with essence; it's not about making claims about 'who-you-really-are'.

'You' is an Unknown Quantity. Your capacity is a moving line of melody that you haven't got to the end of yet.

Virtue, furthermore, has little to do with being *nice*. Virtue becomes a 'capacity', not any ingrained quality or essence of a being.

∝

NOW, ONE MODE OF CAPACITY THAT ONE COULD HAVE would be *knowing* – being able to sense – those moments *when one has less capacity*!

[Re-read that paragraph. It's quite important, overall.]

A capacity that one comes to cultivate is simply an ability to clock, to notice, to twig onto the fact of ... *having less capacity*. If one knows a little more about some of the movements of one's melody line of intensive living, then one starts to notice ups and downs of capacity, and at least one can work with that. One doesn't pretend that things are GRRREAYT.

Imprecision; tendencies to exaggerate; ultimatum thinking ... these drop away, I believe, when I have slightly more robust capacity. And, as I mentioned earlier, if you normally aren't mean/mocking/quippy/monosyllabic/shouty &c. and you find yourself behaving like this, then you can deduce perhaps that your capacity is indeed a bit lower than usual.

Better still, rather than seeing these pieces of evidence for my low capacity play out on others, I could seek ways to become canny to the low capacity *before I have to behave it*!

Sure, in our fantasy worlds, our capacities are infinite. But in fact, we do have edges. (Run-of-the-mill, very human fatigue, is one.) For Spinoza, according to Deleuze, if we live *within* this limit, just to the brink of it, we exist *beautifully*. Ugliness is when we keep not noticing our edge, and we live *just* or far beyond it. Deleuze says this is what the overdose is.[7] *Ouch*. It's what burnout might be, these days. (If you've had one, I'm sorry; and also, it may have made you an expert in exactly what I'm talking about.) If you've burnt out? Well, cool! You made the experiment. Next time, you'll see sooner, and you'll feel the edge of beautiful.

Think of the *beautiful* elderly person. They impress since they live their factual capacity with so much elegance. They don't try to move the fridge alone. And they *do* ask you very interesting questions about your life so far. They listen with incredible aplomb. They give away the lovely things they own, since they have adequately already lived their era of material accumulation. They accept help, and let you enjoy being in intergenerational relation. They make everyone's life richer, but not because they are trying to live in a way that their 34-year-old self would have lived. They demonstrate a beautiful life in one of its phases.

If we follow Deleuze, in these Spinozan lectures, 'what one can' becomes Spinoza's way to define beings, creatures. This is very different, as Deleuze is at pains to explain, from philosophical approaches that define things on the basis of what they are.

I don't really know 'what I'm like'. I can't tell you for sure about my is-ness. What becomes clear is how I can. (Expand what you think goes in this category of 'can' ... (see below) and 'can't' also goes in there ...) The constellations that make me up have capacity of certain kinds, and this distinguishes me from every other being. It is an infinite difference.

I'm being specific about the 'how' here (and this is not quite Deleuze's formulation). He says, *ce qu'on peut*; that which one can. But he wrote this prior to our current moment, and the moment requires that we remain very specific about our words. In the next chapters, I'm going to tell you why.

Recapping virtue, I find it enthralling. It's a concept we could give more time to, especially if it's part of an experimental ethic, rather than a place to drum up some self-loathing. Accuracy about how I can, about how much I can right now, might lead me to the dull-sounding, but sweet-tasting wisdom that Spinoza was so keen on. Both because it relates to our ability to side-step the capture on offer all around, and also because – in his unusual framing – it's on the way to steering clear of an ugliness that only (in its despair) believes daftly in excess as *the* path to feeling alive. To palpate limits with the deft tentacles of our intelligence, plain enough, and differently gorgeous – this is Spinozan beauty. It's when we live closer to the rare line of melody that we are. Here, awful appears less as something to avoid, and more like something which ceases to make any sense. Awful is always a little bit absurd; a squandering mode, yawnfully uninteresting. It's just the worn-out shape of our habitual impoverishments. It's really possible to do, feel and participate elsewise.

A little detour now, via a stickier medium.

Envy: a case study

I got some news from a friend that gave me a massive bout of envy.

One of the things that I think is genuinely challenging about contemporary communication media (texts, group chats, and the like) is that you can receive a vast amount of news in quick succession, all while ostensibly doing something else, and thus the time to chew – to notice that some part of that news has struck the body, the organism – goes missing for a little while. Only for a little while, however, since it rises up again (inevitably *must* return) at some point, with or without its original content or cause.

Sometimes, for me, this can make me feel 'mysteriously' sad/edgy/wired/freaked out/troubled/irritable … and, and, and.

In any case, I heard via the device, from a friend about something going on for them that I felt envious of. I may not have noticed straightaway – the envy – and I found myself walking to the kitchen. There, at the fridge and then bench, I chopped some watermelon, and speared off big, bright chunks and ate them. Some level of me was watching what was happening and luckily twigged that – of course – hearing news like that, I was quite a bit envious.

I use the word 'envy' here, and not the word 'jealous'. The latter has become synonymous with 'envy' in current parlance, since they do seem similar, but I maintain that the words are different. *I* may be the one who's confused, but 'jealous' for me is interpersonal and about people. A person feels 'jealous' if their partner seems to look sideways in a very interested way towards another love object. That is jealousy, in my opinion. I use 'envy' when I think about someone *having* something – an experience, a chance, a piece of fortune, a situation – which I would like for myself. This I call envy. Envy is about stuff, and stuff other people have which you don't. Jealousy is about and between people.

In any case, you are perfectly clear on what I mean when I say that I hear some news from a friend about something good going on for them, and then I feel a particular feeling which is unmistakable, and unmistakably unpleasant in first instance. Unpleasant, or a little off-putting. Because usually the envy is ahead of me. Envy has already arrived there, to signal where I will finally reach, when I catch up. Envy tells me about the stuff I want. Or wouldn't mind. Or could see working for me, too. Envy, I think, despite its icky flavour, does let me know what kinds of things I want, but of which I wasn't aware.

The problem with envy, and with the way in which it often reaches us, is that I get *saturated* with that person's way or mode of engaging or doing or receiving that kind of thing, and my own way *couldn't* look similar. It would be a) a different thing that I'd do; and b) I would do it in my own way, which wouldn't be their way. Another way to say it: we have our own melodies. Thus, envy arguably incites imprecision.

But – yes! Envy can also snap us out of certain denials we have. If it does this, I think it plays a crucial role. The feeling is rugged enough, though, that I don't want it every minute. I don't want an overload of daily envy (and depending on the structural inequalities I need to navigate, this want may be hard to wrangle, to sculpt easily).

What I further mean by 'snap us out of denial' is that often I have envy around something that I had *pretended I didn't really want anyway* (try to say that with a whiny, defensive voice on). Envy can be preceded by an earlier process where you weren't able to have something, and so you dealt with that by pretending you didn't want it (– that this thing was 'stupid', 'dumb', 'wrong', &c.). You tuck this away and it waits. Then you see someone who knew their want, or got lucky, or pursued the want over a long period, or got it delivered through privilege (we'll explore this more shortly), or got the thing by strange chance, and you realise – Lo! – maybe you did really want that thing (or a thing a bit like it). You'd just done a little number on your clarity, by pretending in the face of its being a bit out of reach, that you didn't.

Envy, in this case, lets you know that you abandoned your want, longing or whim. Or, because the world is chronically unfair, you took a break from it, and envy whips you back around to the objective fact of the imbalance. Sometimes we have to abandon it. Life is hard. By the time I am more ancient, I will have pursued *and abandoned* so many wants. We are constantly thwarted and disappointed. 'Tis so.

One knee-jerk way to deal with loss, with finitude, with only having one life and not seven or 50 lives, is that we can disavow whatever it is that we can't have or keep, or which we've lost. Or even something we just never had a shot at, ever. We prefer to smear the story, rather than sit in the more honest position, which is: *I want this (I really do) and I can't have it. I want to be x, and I'm y and perhaps there's absolutely nothing to be done for that. I had [...] once, and now I've lost that.*

Envy comes along and snaps us back to shimmering clarity, back to earth. (It's a rough landing, but hopefully we emerge only with surface scratches.) Presumably, we'd sold out on our accuracy, on our self-knowledge (which must endlessly evade us – of course, *of course*!) and we took the resentful way out, which is to pretend *we didn't want it*. We probably mocked it a little for good measure. Here's the smudge. Here's the book-cooking. We juggle the totals. We fiddle with the facts. Want is never (at all) negotiable. This is why we can never say about someone: they *won't* love me. We can only say that they *don't*. And also ... when someone wants you, you won't be able to square this with any plausible reason. Want is want is want is want.

And thus it goes for envy. We are simple humans. We cannot bear all that we have lost, and all that we will not live, experience, have or keep. These totals are overwhelming. Our systems bug out fast, when we start to contemplate all of that (sitting meditation is a place where I start to contemplate that). So, envy comes along, and it jolts everything towards some kind of accurate middle. Back to where you are, since you are also, in large part, your Wanting.

You feel it – envy – guzzling the cold watermelon, and you realise: *Whoah, hey, there was another thing I wanted, and which I pretended I didn't really mind not having.* The envy is like Windex on your view of the world and of yourself and all the wanting that goes on in between.

I managed to say the words in my head, and thus hopefully intervening before I did some kind of translated, fucked-up action. I mean, I *could* have sent a reply message later with a little barb. I could have bad-mouthed the person sneakily to release some of the pressure of that envy. (Usually when we pressure-release like this, we don't clock that we are doing it, since we are muddled by the storm of difficult feelings.)

I didn't do these things, because (luckily!) the sentence came through:

I think I feel a bit envious that x has y, that the nice thing w happened to z.

It's still a slithery, murky, chest-creepy little feeling. And then you say the sentence again. *I feel a bit envious of y. I feel envious. I feel envious!* The last bit suddenly comes through like a mild euphoria. (That, or the watermelon sugar ...) I reckon there really is something elating about coinciding with, or clocking starkly, your 'negative' emotion, irrespective of what it is.

Hating more, hating more precisely. Being sadder, feeling the sadness right in its centre. It's a trick of physics, or something. You intentionalise, artificially, exactly that which can never be intentional. *Feeling.* The thing you have least control over.

When I'm coinciding with my feeling, I must emphasise that often: *I won't be behaving it.* The feeling of it, in an intense way, staying with it can make your exact feeling somehow take the place of action, turns the action away from any exterior. It makes feeling stay pure feeling and not tilt into being a motor for doing on autopilot. (There may be actions you *do* wish to take; but these aren't reactivity per se. They are your decision.)

That's what I reckon. I wandered through the house and felt the odd euphoria of being in the middle of my icky, embarrassing feeling – envy – the feeling that, in this instance, shows that I avoided this content once, and brushed it off, to do other things.[1] Something I wanted (it may not have fitted with the self-image I was posturing about in at that time ...), which I skipped over. I may have resentfully decided it was a 'dumb/unrealistic thing to want anyway' (kind of response). Well, it doesn't matter. It's triggered a bit of envy and that probably means I wanted it.

And, the good news is that wanting is blessedly endless. It has this vivacious abundance. I did want that (hence the envy surge), *and* I want so many further and different things – things beside *that*, unrelated to that, even the opposite of that. Our wants teem. They teem, like a good rainstorm.

Noticing *is* the Dutch Raincoat (designed for downpours), which lets you go bravely into your storm of wants without getting too drenched, and then too sick afterwards.

It's said that we are mostly envious of people to whom we can relate, or with whom we identify. This may be true. I'm less likely to be envious of those far removed from my interests and my sphere of 'normality'. I think this points to how we mostly want what we can imagine ... usually. Hence, when envy surfaces, it is in relation to those wants. I don't know. I'll get back to you. (Am I envious of aliens who have transparent bodies made of plasmic-stuff, and who can stretch themselves in any direction, with a dual sensation of extension and coherence, and who produce perfumed ideas, which float like bubbles from their membranes and other people can smell these ideas and understand them? I don't know if I could be 'envious' as such ...)

Sometimes, my envy must arrive with grief on its heels. There are things I don't have because of things I have never had. We may not have received the support, the care, the breaks that another person received. To stare at the heart of this is no mild matter. From there, however, I still suspect one can be more ferocious and more magnanimous towards one's next decision, maybe …

Somewhere, someone could be mildly envying me. It's possible and I don't wish that feeling on them. I hope they can stand in the centre of it and meet up with the original want that spurred the feeling. Then they are *with* themselves, and not with any image of me. (Their image is incomplete, anyway. Vastly imprecise. I'm not that thing. I don't have the 'it' they are fantasising. Nobody does.)

I wish them this: that they might feel at ease in their middle a bit more, and from there feel their capacity. This notion of 'middle' lies in a chapter up ahead, but before we reach there, we need to spend some time nuancing our take on capacity.

Homeopathic doses of inconvenience, inefficiency, inability and insubordination won't ruin your life.

Four Nuances of 'Can'

including negativities

In 1981, on 20 January, in 'The Velocities of Thought' lecture series, Deleuze reminds his audience of the important distinction between two ways of understanding what, in English, tends to get collapsed into one word: power. The French have two words to indicate a crucial difference: *puissance* and *pouvoir*. For now, we can think of *puissance* as 'power of acting'. It's a lot like what we've been discussing as capacity. In the next chapter, we'll revisit what Deleuze intends by *pouvoir*. Following Spinoza, he uses *pouvoir* as something akin to power-over, and he will say that it is dependent on the sadness of others.

In the last chapter, we explored the notion of envy, which is generally framed as a negative emotion. The theorist, Sianne Ngai, has called it, an 'ugly' or 'minor' feeling.[1] It can be an unpleasant feeling to be awash with, however it does offer some information in real time, or even – as Ngai implies – constitute an *action* (or a non-passive response) in itself. Ngai offers the helpful observation that while envy might be framed as something that an apparently lacking subject undergoes, it is more than this. As my example above explored, dancing with an envious moment does not have to resemble a persecution or even a moment of petty resentment; it may have capacity folded into its bleary, toothy pleats.

Ngai, if I've understood her, suggests that I might become envious as a way *not* to *only* admire someone (to avoid becoming all fawning and impressed). My envy here can allow for some resistant argy-bargy within myself to help me stake out my own space. My 'middle', as I called it. Ngai says that if we don't acknowledge the agency contained in the so-called negativity, we also miss something *politically* crucial. Here she is, on page 129:

> Moralized and uglified to such an extent that it becomes shameful to the subject who experiences it, envy also becomes stripped of its potential critical agency – as an ability to recognize, and antagonistically respond to, potentially real and institutionalized forms of inequality.

What she is saying is that, speaking frankly, some forms of envy awaken us out of our slumber which might accept, say, that someone in Australia has taken-for-granted access to Medicare, and another perfectly lovely, deserving person residing in Australia, doesn't have access to Medicare. There's a blatant, thundering inequality for you, and why wouldn't envy be one emotion in a cocktail of many, that a parent might feel who can't get their child into hospital when they are wracked with croup? To follow Ngai, then, envy isn't always just the subject (the person) having a little complicated time within themselves, or a sign of someone's intrinsically 'lacking' status. Envy might wake us up to something objective and unjust happening in the world.

To give our so-called 'negative' emotions just a little more breathing space – without always reactively cascading behaviours *from* them – is a form of intelligence, surely.

I've given this example because this chapter, overall, wants to bring into focus the idea of negativity in relation to capacity – that which we also *can't*. It wants to argue for the capacity that is the *including* of certain negativities, noticing their happening, reading them for what they can tell us, and how they can inform our decisions or recast our situations. Envy could be one, and there are others. In what follows, we'll traverse four spaces where we can reconsider the contribution that something called *negativity* makes in its relation to what we're capable *and* incapable of.

Noticing Can't is a Can

Here's an idea from earlier: to know what you *can't* do is also a *puissance*. It's a power in the sense of a capacity. It's a power [*puissance*] to have a take on your current level of capacity. This mobile knowing requires accuracy and it's difficult to do. We tend to inflate or deflate ourselves. We have habits of self-aggrandisement or learned modesty. (Gendered? *Sure!* Socialised, in other words.) Where lie the contours of your Can? To have some inkling of things we *cannot* do keeps us factually in touch with the *reach* of our 'power of action'.

We'd do well to deem this knowledge potentially temporary, as being subject to certain shifts, *and* worth revising from time to time. Perhaps, we can save ourselves some labour by not testing it each and every time, by not ignoring entirely the wisdom gleaned from past experiments. At the same time, our sense of How We Can can get too fixated and lose its accuracy.

Yoga, as an example I know closely – you'll have your own examples – is a place where one reassesses *what one can* quite often. Without presuming how limits might shift, one checks these gently, repeatedly, and with keen attention. The body changes itself behind the practitioner's own back. These limits move, my teacher says, precisely because we aren't forcing them. We sit close to them. Invite them in for tea. Get cosy with our-powers-of-acting, which means reserving judgement about what we think we 'know' about the latter. These capacities show themselves as astonishingly elastic. Our 'can', in other words, grows, shrinks, reverses direction, stalls, snoozes, soars, transforms, regresses, leaps and lags.

There is a double *puissance* that I'm sketching here. It is both to have a take on the things that one *can't*, as well as remaining a little open to the possibility that this knowledge isn't absolute or fixed for forever. Thus, we have something beyond a watertight 'knowing', but not only a habit of always re-experimenting without drawing some cautious fresh conclusions, suited to our new contexts.

In yoga, repeatedly experimenting with pain, for example, is usually not very wise. Change goes via other pathways. Pain? We learn to find it less interesting, to ignore its empty promise. At a very technical level, pain is usually excess heat or an inflaming that we created in an artless moment or many in succession.

To paraphrase: there's wisdom when we tiptoe gently away from the stuff that reliably trashes us.

In his 16 December 1980 lecture on Spinoza, Deleuze makes a digression into the works of eighteenth-century French philosopher Jean-Jacques Rousseau. Drawing an unexpected parallel between the two thinkers, Deleuze argues that Baruch and Jean-Jacques advocated – as ethical, as an ethical move – the decision to remove oneself from a situation in which one was likely to become nasty (*méchant*) – a nastier version of oneself.

I know someone who works in child protection in Australia. They say to me that they love their job because sometimes, because of their efforts, a child doesn't die. I blink away tears when I hear this, since I know it's the flat truth. Often, this person works with young mothers who *could* raise their children fine. These women are loving, plucky, gutsy, honest (sometimes *very* honest ...). They move, however, in circles where many are using ice. Or they have boyfriends who use, who might be the father of one of their children. My friend fights to give them chances to get into rehab, to show the magistrates that a change is possible (since sometimes it *is* possible). She's been known to say: 'Julie, I have to take your infant away from you because you go on ice benders to Adelaide and leave the child unattended for days on end. In a different set of circumstances, in the coming years, you'll be able to keep your child, but currently, things are not going well, and it wouldn't be right for me to let an infant be exposed to that level of neglect.'

'Julie' has been known to reply along the lines of: 'You're a dogcunt ... but yes, maybe you've got a point.'

This is somewhat Spinozan–Rousseauian, if we follow Deleuze. The mother isn't nasty. She isn't inherently reckless and absolutely loves her baby. She is simply in circumstances that drag her towards nastier, more careless versions of herself. If the *puissance* was there, the decision to remove oneself from this scene would, for Spinoza and Rousseau, count as an *ethical* move. Some mothers, some parents, *do* manage this; they select differently. Don't imagine there aren't these stories, too. People are astonishing. They pull off brave and difficult things despite fire-breathing, stomping obstacles.

Now before you end up at an inner-city bar with some smug friends debating disapprovingly, over four bottles of red, the troubles with rural drug culture, perhaps just note that situations *do* sway us. They influence *what* we can, *how* we can, and may indeed coax our nastier sides out into the open. Pass the wine folder.

Testing what we can and can't do, our limits, the circumstances which undermine our *puissance* – for how long? how many tests? – is a matter of style and preference. Whether I want to test constantly, or repeat already-done tests, is entirely up to me, up to my sensibility. I don't think Spinoza would say there was anything 'moral' at stake here. Naturally, our efforts of testing have their own consequences and impacts; they land on others and ourselves in various ways, and not always immediately.

Anyway, you can see that this further capacity, another *puissance*, is being able to displace an earlier conclusion – about one's capacity! – with a newer hypothesis, without too much squirming, so as to respond to changing evidence, as it evolves, emerging from your experiments, not ignoring previous evidence.

My argument is this: We may want to remain intelligently receptive about what counts as 'can' in any moment or phase. If we define 'can' or our capacities too simplistically, without critique, or with compliant hastiness, their category may turn despotic against us.

As grown-ups, we can specify, and alter, what we decide to count as a 'can'. You can decide that your ability *not* to react immediately, even when people are bullying you to make a hasty move, is a very lovely capacity. You can decide that your ability to step outside and stare at the stars and then return to finish off the dishes is a solid quality, and you don't need to abandon it, even if another person goes at tasks with *their* rhythm. You can decide that your ability to take longer with a problem (including some waves of what might appear as 'distractedness') and to finally make fewer mistakes, is a decent aspect of your personality.

The 'can', then, also might include some 'can't' (which is in flux, but not boundlessly). I'm hardly the first to propose this, but we forget it *so* easily that it's worth repeating.

This mode of 'can', which includes 'can't', then has a chance of being a broad-minded 'can', reflecting Deleuze's sensibility. An exploration into 'capacity' (and its link to virtue, to non-Awful) wonders how this reading of capacity differs (if it does) from a the kind of 'can' that gets airtime, gets approval, in our current context.

Can as *Should*: Han's Critique of 'Achievement Society'

Byung-Chul Han has critiqued a contemporary and widespread notion of 'can' brilliantly in *Burnout Society*. This recent socio-historical 'can' that looms over, behind and within us has been operating as a new imperative. (Remember the Super Ego? – it returns in its new bronze, slave-labour made, fast-fashion pantsuit ...)

This 'Can' in Han's crosshairs is more like an *order* that seeps silently from the gears of the motors of our subjugation. It disdains any limit. Limits are not part of its agenda. Its language is incessantly limit-flaunting, contemptuous of any thought that contemplates a limit intelligently. Spinoza might consider that this mode of 'can' constantly presses into ugliness. Many of our daily complaints – which upholster conversations about the tone and quality of our current lives – betray, without always being able to name it well, a clear experience of this ugliness.

A colleague of mine says that he feels more comfortable with emotional neglect and thus has chosen a partner who is good at delivering emotional neglect. His partner is a freelancer, and the situation of that mode of work can mean that one feels obliged (as Han notes) to say 'Yes' (looks like a 'can') to every job on offer (one feels frightened; one frets about future work and money, &c.). This can lead to a being-ever-available, and this willingness to overstep every organic braking mechanism and need for downtime, this ignoring of being a squishy human who needs some sleep, some Friday nights for a beach walk, and some languid naked afternoons with your hot Main Squeeze, might be an example of this Can-as-Should that Han points out. He is not blaming *us*, in our precarious work lives; he is saying that this is a systemic effect.

This kind of 'can' operates as a (silent) order, an internal bossing, that we barely ever catch. This contemporary 'can' tyrannises our inner-worlds. While it enables some things – certainly – it isn't *only* enabling; its costs lurk – implicit or explicit, immediate or delayed.

Derrida notes how things often 'wear' and 'grow' at the same time, quoting Shakespeare's of *Timon of Athens* in his own book *Specters of Marx)*. For a deconstructive sensibility, the challenge is to think *both* at once. We are enabled and disabled simultaneously by certain modes, certain ideologies around can-as-should. This complicated 'can' makes us fit for *producing* (maybe ...) but might also whittle our capacity to *live*, and to genuinely like ourselves while we go about this living.

Han explains that this contemporary 'can' has come in to intensify the 'should' of the paradigm which preceded it –

a Disciplinary Paradigm, which Michel Foucault analysed so well. Now, this modified 'can' structures how we operate in this new socioeconomic landscape that Han dubs our Achievement Society. We are, he says, constantly trying to realise ourselves as 'projects', and this internalising of the manager, the boss, the foreman, the factory overseer (who demanded productivity, demanded that we align at all times with being a Human Resource for capital) means that we produce much more efficiently than we might if we were only bullied by 'shoulds' from an outside, domineering source.

We are now trained to conjure this domineering force inside ourselves; we barely know we do it; it *is* our contemporary subjectivity very often. *Producing* becomes a pseudo-virtue ... sometimes the only virtue we appear interested in. *Egad.* Its tone approaches a religious righteousness, which I'm sure you've heard in your own head, out of your own mouth or others' mouths:

Today I was really productive.

I've found a new tool that increases my productivity.

Please take your allocated leave so that you can remain rested and productive.

Golly, this sickness has made me so unproductive.

The current productivity morality operates as a ceaseless aspirational press to maximise ourselves. If an alien listened in, they might believe the most important verb for an indoctrinated neoliberal human is 'to produce'.

Thus, we *say* our lives, *say* their preciousness and fleeting uniqueness, by using the narrow rubric, the binary code of 'productive' or 'unproductive'! It's quite shocking, or it's shocking we don't laugh at ourselves more as these kinds of sentences fall from our lips.

Many people live very diligently within this – as Han wryly notes – while believing themselves 'free'. Free to be my Best Self ('self' here means a human-as-enterprise). *Ouch.* It slips by us; we accustom ourselves to it as a ubiquitous mode of regime Speak.

Some years ago, I ceased using the word productive. Just as an experiment. To see if my world, my capacity and enthusiasm for activities, behaviour, working, &c. would evaporate. Nothing dire happened; I found other adjectives to describe my life. You could say that I wanted to select for myself some vocabulary-circumstances that made me less of a nasty (fretting, pushy, hasty, competitive, demanding, blinkered ...) version of myself.

Without good chats, good debate, good writing, and loving humour, however, it's difficult to enact a filtering mechanism that sifts out the icky bits of this saturating mindset. If this is how you've been living *and lovin' it* (while internally falling apart and miserable) then Han's writings might offer you some wriggle room in the bind.

The binary, of course, with which we're presented under this regime, is that if you're not living like this and maximising your Can, then you are a loser and that your unenthusiasm for Can is gonna bite you on the arse, sooner or later. *Okay*. But, *no*. There are *never* only two options. If two options are presented to you, assume really that they amount to One Despotic Option in a Double Bundle. A non-choice presenting you with its 'two' sides. Another *real* option, or 50, requires good thinking. Waywardness. Measure. And care. So ...

I want to know if there is a difference between Spinoza's 'can' (the variety of modes a body can do) and the current 'can' that Han has theorised, which we might choose to be wary of living too ... *earnestly*.

How Creatures Can (and Can't)

When Deleuze is teaching this section in Spinoza to his students, he gives wonderful examples of different kinds of capacity. And they are very wide. They include multitudinous ways a being can live. They aren't filtered via the lens of economic expediency or social tidiness. They are truly cacophonous, rambunctious, unruly. They are a Riot of Ways-of-Being. *Modes of Being*. They are many, and varied and strange and cast a very *wide* net.

Some beings can fly. (Deleuze says of himself: 'I cannot fly'.[2])

And in this vein: some beings can rest. Some beings can sleep standing up. Some beings can digest grass. Some beings can drink alcohol without becoming drunk. Some beings can walk miles in dry conditions without strain. Some beings can make love suspended in water. Some beings can compose music. Some beings can dream strange dreams. Some beings can sit very still and remain very alert. Some beings can do detailed repetitive tasks without sliding into inaccuracy. Some beings can suckle their young. Some beings can climb rock faces. Some beings can do philosophy. Some beings can remain very calm under strain. Some beings can lounge about languidly. Some beings can endure extremely cold conditions. Some beings can turn beaten eggs into pale yellow shapes resembling coral. Some beings clean their own face with saliva. It goes on and on. Some beings can move silently in the dark. Some beings can drink nectar hanging upside down from branches. And ... some beings can be patient; they can abide temporality's theme park without fluster.

Deleuze sketches a recipe for vast and multitudinous weirdness – *not optimisation* (which often tends to acknowledge a sole direction). This is a recipe for the wonderfully strange; it sprawls outwards, sideways, frolics and soars. If you decentre money/transactionalism as the organising principle, it becomes apparent to what extent money/transactionalism had been the central, organising principle. That list is *not* organised by such a principle.

This is why I've been taking care to write *how one can*, for Spinoza's definition of being (updating the Deleuzian formulation). I'm leaving the *what one can* specifically to describe Han's target: the current achievement society. The latter is mostly a narrow set of qualities that suits technocapitalism very nicely.

Pay attention now. It's *also* likely that *some* of How You Can will align with what this moment wants to squeeze from us predictably ... *but* hopefully a lot more of How You Can will spill out beyond this, not confined by its definition, not complying at all (and not rebelling, no) – piquing instead your verve for being alive more generally.

But still, this can sound saccharinely shiny (the frolicking, weirdo bit). There has to be room left in here for our incompetence. For the 'can' to include the 'can't'. For incapacities – for stumbling, mumbling and fumbling.

The negativity, which Han wants to explore and reconsider, isn't like 'being negative' in the way we use this word casually. It's not a personality schtick, or a slant on things. It's not your grumpy uncle, or your snappy colleague. What Han implies by negativity, a desirable, crucial negativity, is the other side of the despotism of Achievement's 'can'. This negativity, if I brainstorm, might nod at sometimes not being able to get up easily in the morning. It's not feeling gleefully enabled. It's when my capacity is wobbly on its feet; when I want to weep at the thought of a single task, not to mention the twenty I feel afraid of. It's getting sick sometimes, because bodies do get sick sometimes. It's feeling afraid, feeling distant and strange, being confused and lacking direction for a time.

Moreover, Han's 'negativity' is even more philosophically inflected than this summary. It's about leaving room for what isn't there, for what doesn't appear. For spaces. For silence. For waiting. This take on negativity is more like the photographer's. Or the person who practises line drawing. Sometimes one is drawing the 'thing', but another approach is to mark the edge of the space that isn't the 'thing'. If we remain relentlessly in positivity (the what's-there-ness) only, humans actually – take my opinionated, but experienced word for it – fare badly.

The negativity and the positivity operate in tandem. We need them both. Recall the *Tao Te Ching*: the hole in the wheel is what makes the wheel work. Figuring this out and how to live with it is a riddle. One type of explicit 'can' (being able) is easy to spot, and its inertia is likely to get going. The other – what Han calls 'being able not to be able' – slips away, quiet, and we must insist on keeping it too in the picture. This – perhaps, perhaps – is another way of understanding plain.

To include negativity (whether it means our incapacities, or spaces/pauses) dovetails with a capacity for kindness. For others. For ourselves. Kindness has a rep for being 'weak'. But we are juggling words here, juggling the way words line up in columns – where we banish one side. (Diving into this metaphysical tendency was what Derrida was up to in his project of deconstruction.)

People who are 'weak' (going via Nietzsche as well as drawing on astute live observation) are more likely to be brittle, arrogant, bossy or hardened. Kindness isn't usually in the mix.

My experience is that if a person can be kind, and if they're not disturbed or depleted by their kindness, it is a sign of immense capacity. (The next chapter extends this discussion of kindness.)

Kind is an adjective (it describes how we do things, the quality of manners, moves and decisions), but kindness here lines up with our theory of virtue and its need for capacity. It's a capacity that maps less neatly with an Achievement Society's productivity hard-on. My kindness might include the can's and can'ts that I, you, we have, as well as being enabled by an ability to clock when I can't, and without a moral or super-egoic take on the latter.

I say: be a little inefficient. Waste some time. Waste some money. Tolerate dishevelled. It won't last long, and some new capacity will shimmy out and you won't have a category for it. (If you're particularly enabled, you may not even bother seeking a category for it at all.)

Negativity that pertains to non-competence, when we live it (most days a little bit, sometimes for bigger stretches) can meet a practised kindness. Thanks to this sincere meeting, it avoids becoming so loud that it will set us on edge. It's about measured doses of negativity, if you like.

If we're able sincerely to meet our twenty minutes of vagueness with a kindly mood – with less inner reaction, muted snarky self-criticism, minimal excoriating commentary, &c. – then the vagueness is both likely to pass and is of itself important. Vagueness is not just an inconvenience. It has its own contribution. This is the broader sense of negativity. Vagueness is spending some time unfocused, which is very interesting. It can be intentionalised, as another mode of being. Then it is a ... capacity.

In her interesting book, *Semicolon* (2019), Cecelia Watson spends some time examining how the philosopher William James and his brother, Henry James, the novelist, engaged with the idea of vagueness and ambiguity. William has a passage where he explicitly includes it as important for this emergent science of psychology. I cite Watson's citation:

> It's better not to be pedantic, but to let the science be as vague as its subject [mental life], and *include* such phenomena as these if by so doing we can throw any light on the main business at hand ... At a certain stage in the development of every science a degree of vagueness *is what best consists with fertility*. (p. 141; square brackets mine, italics mine)

James is hardly a lightweight. He wrote extensively and brilliantly on habit, for example; he founded Harvard's psychology department. We see his wisdom here. He's not intimidated by those who might read a contemplation of vagueness as a cop-out, as weakness or lack of rigour. He is saying there is a timeliness to when to get tighter and when to allow for a generative vagueness. This keeps things open and, I speculate, prevents a premature filtering out.

Note his use of the word 'include'. Smart people, for a while it seems, have known to include negativities. In considered doses. These days we seem so eager to jump ourselves into pathologising (diagnosing) the very variousness of modes, which make humans so ... swell. So interesting, so themselves.

Can I tell you something ... personal?

Well, the more fragile I feel, the kinder I get with myself. I don't know if this is typical. I hear a mix of things from others, if conversations ever go so far. I say kind things to myself if I'm fumbling, forgetful or a bit scattered. Because it happens, yes? Some days the wiring is not so slick, and we short-circuit a little (a lot!). We burn our fingers on the grill; we race from, and back to, the house three times for objects and have to sweat-dash to the transport; we splash the tea milk all over the bench and down the fridge ...

This kindness, that I call up in these moments, is not a mode of indulgence, as such. It's kind, not excuse-making. It doesn't make up a story or blame some other factor. I just don't pile some self-abuse onto a morning that is already a bit under-resourced.

Kindness is how you would have wanted a parent (probably a fantasy parent, not your real one, unless you got really lucky) to meet your sincere efforts of trying and missing, as a small human. We become that influence for ourselves, since hopefully as adults the efforts of trying and missing needn't stop.

For some adults they put a stop to this whole experiment – sadly – maybe because the risk of trying out things and not being immediately competent is too great. Being squishy across our lives, knowing that some days we're scrambled, staying with our incompleteness beyond childhood is an experiment I find quite moving to be around – when you see it in people of varied ages.

We're such a bright and layered cocktail of capacity and incapacity, right? Given how indoctrinated we are about what has 'value' and what is 'useless' and how this assigning of value might merit some critique, we could hold off with our categorising frenzy before it gets going. It might be that we are categorising things as having no value, but in fact they are our capacities, our *puissances*. It's probably too soon to tell what the upshot of a certain way of being is – holding off on definitive knowing is not the daftest.

How We Say and How We Select

The words, styles of speaking, that we use to discuss how-we-can, *matter*. There are many words *I will not use*. (See 'productive' – above.) They are perfectly good words, but they've been Brandified on LinkedIn, and they now are drudges for a regime and mindset that I don't wish to inflate further. I could list them, but you can just be on the lookout for them. When we slip from crisp descriptive poetry into slogan speak, we're probably in their vicinity ... They topple from mouths all day long, on default, since it's exhausting to try to track them, to navigate bound-and-gagged 'niceness' language (which isn't deeply that nice, and is just how we fall into allegiance with various orders of dubious kindness). It's my job, not yours, to find words to step us through. Thanks for coming along.

Thus, it's difficult (my 'incapacity') to write this book you're reading, since our moment has really colonised quite a few bits of vocabulary that have meant certain things by now have a thick sheen of Neoliberal Icing on them, to turn your stomach. It can feel like moving within a resistant substance, this writing. The difficulty encourages me to meet it with kindness, a tenacious kindness. If I mock myself or give myself a hard time about my own struggle, then avoidance is likely.

Avoidance, in the *Yoga Sutras*, is probably rendered 'aversion'. And aversion can get extended to include hatred. This concerns the way we bounce off things that have been too Awful. If I harass myself internally every time I try a newish thing, it will feel horrible, and I won't try it again.

I feel often *in*capable, too small for the task (as Deleuze has also explored). I *am* too small (the current 'I' is never static, never settled). In the practice of the writing itself (the thinking itself), something weird might occur where the writing happens, and I am no longer who I was (the dissolved status of the 'I' will become apparent).

Thus, I'm regularly afraid to keep working on this manuscript. There are no guarantees that this writing might be something I will finally be able to *accept*. (This is the main question for the artist, a friend once explained to me.) I am indeed too small for its task, and with this crucial negativity, I sit down gently, to see what sentence might invite me to tinker with it. Again and again and again. It's very difficult, but it doesn't have to be undignified. I bring 'what I don't have' to it ... in this way it resembles (how psychoanalysis frames) love, far more than it resembles any production line, or program of achievement.

∝

CAN YOU SEE (CAN YOU SENSE) HERE THE DIFFERENCE between a certain negativity (that we want to include) and a trashing of capacity that larger forces (in me, out of me) are often (without declaring it) coaxing us towards? This is such a delicate difference to think!

We can think back to the opening *Plain Life* chapter; it also considered allowing for the *negativity of fear* which is so enmeshed with our experience of living under forms of Neoliberalisation (or other unpleasant orders). We are *so* often *so* very afraid. For good reason. Both forms of 'can' – the Achievement Society's, and even to some degree Spinoza's (who was long ago, so we need to cut some slack) – might forget this crucial aspect. I find that the term anxiety is *somewhat* overused. As you know, I've expressed my curiosity for what would happen if we sometimes tried out the simpler word 'fear' or 'frightened' to see if this would pry open a new space in which to encounter the difficulties of our moment.

How to allow for negativities, while also not running with open arms towards that which *undignifies* us, which guts how we can? These *necessary* negativities are different from actively pursued Capacity Trashers. The latter are usually activities encouraged slyly and perversely *by* the Achievement Society, since they make us *buy! buy! buy!*, encourage us to be slavishly cheery and amenable (which is exhausting), deplete us in the deepest caverns of our being, while *at the same* time sustaining an excruciating tension with the double-bind message of: 'why aren't you more productive?' and then showing us a picture, a story, of someone who apparently *is*.

Negativities – of the kind Han suggests we have forgotten to honour, to allow for – might be non-knowing (of ourselves, of others), non-confidence, non-capacity, definitely non-productivity, creaturely fatigue, grief, confusion, insecurity, uncertainty. An Achievement Society only wants news of the positivities (which can be cashed in for productivity), but this isn't what *being a creature is like*. So where does the other face of living go? It goes underground. It becomes our poor digestion; our insomnia; our 'anxiety'; our numbness; our cynicism; our baked-on cruelty; our casual and widely approved self-harm; our shrillest neuroses and paranoias; our so-called 'depressions', our elided aggressions, our arrogant and tragic self-sabotage.

It's good to fritter a little bit of money. It's good to while away some hours without purpose. It's lovely if you don't have a list (or don't like a list). Sometimes you let a friendship go fallow, and there isn't really a conversation that can frame its ending. Sometimes you misplace stuff. Sometimes you're not the life of the party. I like to be a bit inefficient on purpose. It's pleasant, and (before you start hyperventilating) I don't *only* do that. Mostly, I simply abstain from using that rubric to classify my life at all.

How can we think the capacity that I understand Spinoza to be gesturing towards? There's a mode of myself where I just *can't-so-much*. This is something that can be ... ah, *lucidly* assessed, and ideally not mostly in the typical terms/memes/trending words that ooze through our feeds.

Probably I can work out How-(Much)-I-Can-Today when I do sitting meditation practice. It's private. I don't discuss it. I definitely don't track it on a fucking app. I surely *do not* enter my information into platforms harvested by large language models to generate 'short stories' with the ostensible theme of 'my inner life'. Thumbs Up? Thumbs Down? *Nope.* Not yet.

If you meditate, you get a bit of lucidity about *how you can*. And then, if I know something about the way virtue links to capacity, I can make some estimates about how put-together I might be in the coming hours. Why would I care if I am likely to be put-together, or not? I guess that's a matter of style, of taste. It's a kind of risk strategy, and everyone has their preference about it.

For me, I associate it with practising; it's a yoga thing. I am curious about my capacity, my power-of-acting – *puissance* – because it dovetails with the likelihood of my Being Awful, being the nastier version of me. It maps with how I'll make decisions, with how plucky I'll feel in the face of Big Choices. This is how Nietzsche, Spinoza and Deleuze come together for me as seemingly unexpected companions to ideas that are actually quite yogic. When you look more closely, the companionship is less odd than it first appears.

Wanting, Affirmation and the Plain 'No' of Critique

Our shared curiosity might now look something like this:

We seem to accept as *fine* (to endorse and to participate in) widespread harming styles, paradigms of violence, nasty self-talk, structural viciousness. Okay. Why *then* all this bafflement about why we can't sleep at night, why we have no (sober) peace ever, why anxiety creeps up our face and blinds us regularly, why the idea of *lessening* our modes of self-medication terrifies us, why we grasp after new categories of diagnosis, and why we keep sowing catastrophe into our relations and close feeling?

There aren't any surprises here. All operates as expected.

We can stop with our wide-eyed astonishment.

A whole lot of phatic conversations can cease.

If we are going to continue with being Cool and Non-concerned about Quite Bad Shit (watching it, clicking it, talking it, resigning ourselves to it, applauding it), then we can't *not* expect it to burrow its way a lot deeper into the fabric of our lives that we thought could exist in a separate medium.

We are implicated. Things implicate themselves most ornately. The questions for me are: whether I want it; whether I like it; whether I decide for more of it; whether I want to disrupt it, or lose interest in it, whether I can avoid situations that foster it.

I can't *stop* it, because I don't control other people (they have their own desires, impulses, histories, habits and preferences), as much as I might wish to imagine I can influence them. Being subjected to Awful is ... awful. However, at least a portion of my usual distress could well be bound up with my *own* implication in this awfulness. Distress here would stem partly from my cognitive dissonance about how much I go along with it all, condone or indulge it.

Now, try to watch any resentment that billows up around this. Resentment, for me, is not the yogic way, and because I'm human, I'm *also* often resentful and I do what I can in this messiness. To consider abstaining from lots of resentment might look like 'forgetting' to complain about why the world is awful … it just truly also *is* and isn't *only* awful. This is why we struggle to think it, since it evades our binary-brains. It's both. Awful, yes, *and* not only. Bemoaning is not the destination here. We like to, of course, *bemoan*. It can pass the time. People often connect to each other via bemoan-ment rituals. Without it, there can be plenty less to say.

We have bemoanment, which I'm aligning with a certain queasy slide towards resentment. Bemoanment is a *mode* of 'No', which we tend to indulge when we feel a bit lost for ideas, impotent and fearful. It's fine. It's to be expected. Yet, other 'No's await us. They could be said to come in the shape of …

Critique. It looks similar but operates differently. Critique is less fun (if whining is fun). Less juicy (if we also enjoy a little bit the fangs of how 'terrible' things are …). With critique, I *think*, we don't dig our heels so luxuriously into its quagmire. Its work is more sober, but also a bit fresher. It is a stopover rather than a destination.

Critique is something other than the Bemoaning No of resentment. Critique is the other side of the other side of resentment.

For Nietzsche, affirmation is how we can subtract ourselves from resentment, with resentment being a tricksy way to live that says: 'That's not good; I'm not like that; therefore I'm good.' It's a kind of default being 'good' by not living, not risking, not contributing. There's a personal art to spotting what for each person is their mode of 'resentful'. Often it involves bemoaning and enjoying the bemoaning vibe, as an experience itself, almost *replacing* experience. Resentment is technically adding two 'nots' to create a pseudo-positive.

Critique, on the other hand, is the 'No' that affirmation needs in order to happen. Critique might be a steadily uttered, discrete instance of No, that puts a quiet stop to a barrage of resentful ways, a plain 'No'. Not too much enjoyment in there. Critique clears some space, allows for abstaining from an 'old' thing, and it's *on the way* to affirming something you *want* to do.

A critique doesn't necessarily come sporting a haughty voice, carrying a stack of library books. Often, I activate my attempts at critique very slyly. I do its action in a stealthy fashion. Say there's something I wish to distance myself from (usually a behaviour in myself). I know it's really hard to interrupt habits, to let a familiar way of operating fall away. I go at this fresh possibility of difference *very* minimally, as if there's no kind of flashy action in train at all. The tiniest of Nos, repeated sequentially, so gently, and barely audible. I try not to trip the wires of my habitual Self.

Losing interest in something is a gently fierce form of No, that indeed leaves fresh space for affirming something seemingly unthinkable.

Is this what you thought I meant by critique?

Is it critique to acknowledge when you've just seen a woman non-consensually groped? (Some weeks ago, I saw an egregious example of this at my local, crowded café ...) To say to the woman, 'I saw that. You are not alone in that having happened.' (The guy had slipped out too fast to confront.) This, I think, performs a genre of 'No' to a pervasive mode, where the behaviour is assumed to be irrelevant, fine, a slip in passing.

My friend's child of four years or so, in the midst of a heated family spat, where everyone's behaviour was turning horrid, managed to say the simple sentence: 'Mum, can you please be kind to me?'

Ouch.

Critique comes in inventive shapes and surprising guises. And always, always, the question remains live and hard to settle definitely: *am I being resentful here?* or *am I practising critique in the service of an (unknown and future) affirmation?*

If you're an activist, it can be salient to check one's taste for resistance tipping towards an enjoyment of something more resentful. This might involve inoculating the difficult, exhausting work of the struggle with something affirming, something that offers (even just offering back to our activist fellows themselves who can burn out from the constant work). Resentment is the way of history, as Nietzsche perceived. It's the *likely* way. It's difficult to speak of, to spot; it's hard to isolate and to observe not unkindly the way a *vibe* in acting, in our behaviours, has become habitual. To track resentment in our political efforts can mean keeping an eye on something that might install itself as habituated, an 'enjoyable' negativity[1] that (one wonders) also serves (indirectly) the oppressing agenda itself.

Bemoaning, let's face it, is a source of great comedic relief. It can provide us lush fodder for funny. It's often where we source our most hilarious, our darkest material. As a beloved party trick, it can become a tempting social strategy, but it's easy to get stuck there, without other modes.

Less cool, perhaps, is the risky wondering about what one *wants*, actually.

Wanting and affirmation sit closely together in my experience. I *like myself* most when – although trepidatious – I dare to be a Wanting Creature.

'Wanting' also has that *other* adjectival meaning. To be 'wanting' means to be lacking, and of course, this is why to enter 'wanting' as a state involves some daring. It involves encountering that one does indeed lack, is a work-in-progress, a gappy, clunky unit. If we insist on a deluded sense that we are (or could be) complete, we will sputter and finally *stall*. Also – my tip – if you act as if you 'have *everything* (sorted)', no one will find you ... well, *sexy*.

Affirming has something to do with daring to feel (what you) want, as a first thing. (It's not deriving one's wants 'second-hand' ...) 'Daring' here makes it sound as if the *content* of the want is racy. While it might sometimes be the case, this would be misleading. Wanting is daring, not because it might involve racy contents, but rather because it is a vulnerable place per se, a risky place to inhabit, and one needs a bit of pluck to be there. To be in want is very *alive*. It's daring on this ground alone, not because you want to go to a local brothel and take your pants off, or find the local BDSM group, or study the chemistry for home-made methamphetamines. *Wanting is daring without reference to content*. The content comes *after* you contact the risk of feeling it. The content might not be the most interesting thing.

In the pandemic, I signed up for an online course with a psychoanalytic theorist and practitioner from Canada, Dan Collins. Participants were discussing the Id (one of the three agencies in Freudian theory, the others being the Ego and the Super Ego). The predictable question was raised of what would happen if the Id were a bit 'freer', less constrained by Super-Egoic bullying, or by the Ego's palatable idea of itself (our self-image). Dan's response – as I recall it – was very special, even moving.

'People think', he said, 'that if the Id was less repressed, everyone would be running around on the streets, fucking and maiming ...' He paused, 'I think, instead, that a few more people might just take up painting.'

Holy moly. This is why you enrol in online courses with very serious people. I find this a very serious, important thing to say. It is a *plain* thing. It implies that we *exaggerate* what we are like, depict our own tendencies in overblown ways. We like to make ourselves out to ourselves, in our own minds, as *monstrous*, which then justifies certain techniques of repression. My best example of this is The Diet.

People often suspect that their wants are monstrous, their appetites gargantuan. If they noticed what they wanted precisely – not believing what they are *told* they probably want – they might see that they wanted, say, more broccoli with lemon tahini sauce. Some slices of apple. In season. From the fridge, cut with the sharp knife. A little nap, rather than food. Sometimes I want the whole bag of textured experience which is quality potato crisps. Some breathing, because wanting oodles of food endlessly can be a disguised mode of wanting more 'qi' (food has qi, but so does air, so does a half hour among the plants outside). Sometimes, I want a hunk of cake, like I used to have after primary school, baked by my mum, &c.

Because it feels so *unhabitual* to tune in to what one wants, one can miss ever feeling it, and in the place of this accurate checking with reality, in the place of being Variably Appetited, one conjures monsters. One conjures oneself as a homogenous monster.[2]

We can fear that if we feel the wanting, surely, we'll learn that our true want will be 50 Donuts ... So, we evade the encounter with the want's content and it remains a speculation, a terror. The wanting, in real time, is skipped over. And thus, one toggles only between, I must repress (because apparently I'm monstrous), and also behaving in accordance with what I'm told I want.

Maybe a nice question is: how monstrous am I really? And can this also, when looked at, be allowed to be a little bit humorous? Or ... one conjures a loving feeling, when asking it.

I was at a creativity workshop once and the facilitator had put some chocolates in the centre of the table, to spice up the drowsy afternoon session. A fellow participant – nice enough, but also a bit tanned, a bit curated, wealthy and entitled – said to me: 'You want it, don't you? Women can never resist chocolate.'

What the fuck! I felt in that moment exposed to an entire history of eating disorders, mental double binds and run-of-the-mill headfucking. It was insane! My family has plenty of problems, but difficult relationships with food haven't been part of them. This curly, tricksy, slimy little comment opened my eyes to what people are often exposed to. I realised that whatever I did, after that comment, would seem to be in reaction to his comment. If I took the Lindor Ball, I would be proving him right ('women can never resist chocolate'), and if I didn't take it, I was showing him that I was responding to his challenge, trying to prove him wrong, by 'resisting'. It was actually quite horrible, but also an education for me.

I understood then and there why many people, due to family, dinner table bullshit, could become entirely entangled in food confusion, and NEVER FEEL WHAT THEIR BODY WANTS.

Normally, I just decide if I feel like a chocolate. It's not complicated. But in that moment, the comment seemed to evaporate wanting as a paradigm; it squished all the freedom out, leaving me only in a weird desert of women's-lack-of-discipline (they are a block unit, obviously, one can predict in advance exactly what they want [rage emoji]), and a certain craving that must be resisted. So grimy. No way to live.

I haven't gone to further events where this guy will be, and he is probably at heart *so* sweet. Someone probably had said *that* to him, near him. Or he'd just learned it on a sleazy internet site. *Lordy*.

I'm just applying my German friend, C.'s formula: don't choose to spend too much time around this kind of business. Select your circumstances otherwise! But if I had been his daughter ... I wouldn't have had a lot of choice. Every night ... 'You want the second helping of creamy potatoes, don't you?' Eating Disorder City. *Roll up, roll up.*

If anything, this shows me that if you can stay connected to what you want, you will be in relation to your *puissance*. To your innate capacity. Our wanting is that power, really. And our own wanting is weird and interesting, but not always as monstrous as we fear. Painting, anyone? Maybe a new weird hobby that impacts no one and nothing – except your own quiet joyfulness.

My own style of wanting, therefore, is not an object or thing I can get from somewhere else. I can't accumulate it. I can only stay in live contact with its unique melody.

Is this what Dan Collins in the online course was saying? I might have a painting want, but am disconnected from it, since I grew up being told that medicine is the only career worth anything, or becoming a pilot. Whatever. Then, a therapeutic process might help me dare to feel this quiet and simple want, which is nonetheless quite a *power*.

On Leakiness, Strength and Contributing Differently

We don't – need I say it? – also have to *do* (or 'behave') what we want. No, this is a separate matter. We just might opt *to want what we want*.

To have the option to want for ourselves, within a kind of private space, that no one need see, is less scary. (The way I tell my writing students to write on paper for practice and shred it for the recycling. There is no risk here, even if the writing is 'terrible'. Just to try out being a bit less hemmed in.) To know how to separate, even by a hair's breadth, wanting from behaving holds open the potential for ethics.

The young mother might also *want* to have some ice with her buff but shambolic boyfriend. She might want it, might manage to *think it* (rather than behave it) and in the strange space that opens with this formula, she might deselect the Adelaide trip. Behind her own back even. Just accidentally forgetting to go …

Some wants we *have*, but don't *do*. (You have a want to punch lots of people in the face? Well, good. And please don't do it.) Feeling the want is a capacity, I would say (meditation is a *great* place to feel it; you might go bouldering; you might hire a Break Room, &c.), and then having a space to decide whether to do/behave the want, or to not do it, is the next level of *puissance* dovetailing with ethics.

With ... virtue!

Screaming at people when they frustrate us? Retaliating when children are a bit annoying, raucous, or when they hurt our feelings? Trying to corner someone into resolving bad feelings which are really ours, and no one else's problem?

This last one is the reason a lot of partner relationships fall apart. One or both of the people have a habit of trying to get the other to take away their bad feelings. A therapist once pointed out that I was doing that. I felt very ashamed, *and* very enlightened by the observation. It was hard to stop doing it ... but I'm less of an arsehole now. More often now I can manage to restrain myself from defaulting to this child-like (and understandable) seeking. Usually, the form my forcing would take would be to *talk*. I suspect many people bully their partner into talking when the urge, the longing pertains to wanting a bad feeling taken away. It's a *bad* feeling, so who wouldn't want that? Of course, if one experiences mostly bad feelings around a partner, and one doesn't want to, or can't, resolve these, and the feelings are reliably refreshed by the interaction, then probably one could exit the partnership. With more random, everyday bad feelings, the other usually can't take these feelings from us ... often they practically and *truly* don't have the means to. They're not just 'withholding'. At the same time, if that's your bag, and the other's bag, a cuddle, a hug, a reassuring hand well placed can often de-escalate a heady situation.

In terms of our relations – i.e. with the people involved in the circumstances we select – the art, of course, is telling the difference between a passing uneasy feeling that I can auto-manage, and a systemic bad feeling which is linked to the mixture that you and the interpersonal context *are*. I can manage a workshop with

Lindor Man, but wouldn't want a marriage. This is an art, yes. To distinguish wisely.

I was at an event recently, and everyone there was at the end of their tether. It was after some intense months, worn out, and running on adrenaline. It seemed to me (and I'm holding open the possibility of my own misperception ...) that a couple of people said sequential, quite narky, hurtful things to me. Kind of snide responses or ways of including or excluding me. There were a few of this species of retort, whispers, &c. in quick succession, and it made my heart so sore, and I felt very tired. I didn't retaliate since this is often an amplifier. Though I was really depleted from the encounters, I couldn't leave the event. I considered whether I would address it, with one person in particular. I sat on it a while. It's mostly likely that people don't know they are doing the Thing. It's happening; it's a release valve, but they really don't know it. I bring my own versions of all these to the mix, too.

So, I thought a lot about speaking to it. (As mentioned, I'm no shirker with talking.) I wondered how I could do it without layering more aggression into the mix. I wasn't sure I would succeed. So ... I had to manage a wave of unpleasant feeling (a mix of 'ugh' sadness, exhaustion and disappointment). I kept it open for myself that I *could* speak of it, if I chose. I juggled the feelings, the ongoing requirement to be among the interactions, and I kept alive the possibility that I was also reading the behaviour as louder than it was. (I was also tired; it affects our perceptions.) Maybe it *was* happening, but I decided to hold off on being too certain.

Being, dwelling, hanging together, as people, in the end, seemed to lessen whatever gripes were circulating and things worked themselves out. More warmth started to come from the person(s). They possibly relaxed a little more. I couldn't say. The bigger sadness dispersed, with the tone returning to fairly normal levels. I was glad I'd had enough stretch to see it out – without 'communicating' it (we can *communicate* too much, as my counsellor friend noted about romantic relationship styles she'd seen). Things found their way. The trouble, too, might surface anew. I'll wait and watch. Relating is complicated, histories of care and circumstance are so complicated.

∝

SOMETIMES, WE ARE LEAKY. WE CAN SPILL OUT the edges a bit. We fail to contain ourselves (see: virtue of 'temperance'). I'm linking leaking here to the way that people express their grumpiness *on* or *at* us quite often, or we do it *on* or *at* them, and for most of us human folk, we'll need substantial kinds of training, effort, gentle long-term self-reflection, to manage to leak (our stuff, our Awfuls) a little bit less.

Our desires and their content can thus turn shrill, go a bit hyperbolic. But maybe on the whole we aren't so monstrous, and thus the nature of our self-hampering, the way we prevent ourselves from living can be quietly observed, with less reactivity, and more tiny openings where we can adjust ourselves just enough.

Neoliberalisation (or late capitalism or however we conjure it – as an imprecise 'out there') has often tried to work its agendas of capture via implied accusations that suggest we are monstrous and needing particular kinds of diversions, smotherings, domestication. But if we were to reject this, more people might just take up painting.

The sites where we might leverage genuine modes of freedom are quieter. They involve, perhaps, being more decent than capitalism thinks we are capable of being. Convenience might be a sneaky way of compensating for our lack of care for ourselves and each other. If I am alone, and no one cares for me, if no one helps me when I'm a bit less in my capacity, then I will need to spend far more money. Abandoning each other tends to render us better customers. More pliable. Desperate to fill the gaping hole.

There is anyway a hole. This is affirmed by any philosophy

that isn't rubbish, and by any decent spiritual path, and by any good therapeutic model. Yes. There is a gap we cannot close (see above). However, the gap is wrenched wide open by our allowing ourselves to indulge in habitual shoddiness, poor character, routine unkindness. This is the gap into which we pour our imaginings that swell to obscene proportions.

My query is whether – in these moments of lower capacity – I might tend towards grimy behaviour that I'd prefer not to behave. I wouldn't speculate on this as a kind of self-blamey admission. If I can detect when my capacity is a bit low, I might try to shrink my likelihood of impacting on others too much. Stay home, do something contained, I say. Wait till your capacity has bounced back a little, Antonia, till virtue is not entirely unlikely, and then say more, do more.

This is why Sad Leaders are Bad Leaders. They often fail to detect their own low capacity (or fail to have any perception of how sad they are) then, there's more likelihood of their non-virtue (being dicks). Furthermore, being leaders, they do actions that have broader impact than the rest of ours do. As leaders, they can really spread around the Sadness for Others. You never want a Sad Leader. (We have so many of them …)

Nietzsche, predictably, has an aphorism I associate with this. Or, I could say, I associate an aphorism with Nietzsche …[3] It's a slippery thing to say, even a dangerous thing. He uses other words but is basically trying to flesh out a similar idea. It's the notion that the strong need to be protected from the weak. I approach this as a riddle. I'm not a groupie of Nietzsche (who tends to attract young men of a certain bent). No, I'm a slow, sometimes-reader, a reader over decades, and still trying to understand.[4]

So, what does an aphorism like 'the strong need to be protected from the weak' prompt us to consider, if we treat it like a riddle, whose meaning should not immediately be apparent? It's an invitation to think carefully – not a slogan.

The virtuous, who because they have more capacity (for love, for clarity, for doing the dishes, for kindness, for patience, for generosity, for good boundaries, for making steady decisions, whatever ...) need to be protected from the weak. The Weak: any of us in a less vital state, where we are more prone to greed, to hatred, to reactivity, to meanness, to sarcasm, to haste ... and so on. Those with less capacity, who are struggling to access their virtue, need to not be given free rein to go to town on the strong/virtuous. Because the weak will find the strong annoying. When you're in lower capacity, people's plain getting-on-with-things somehow really pisses you off. *Hahaha.*

There's an amazing depiction of this in Bulgakov's incredible 1967 novel, *The Master and Margarita*. Running parallel to the whole 'contemporary' twentieth-century bit of the story, set in Russia, is the more ancient story, where we get a fictional account of Jesus' trial with Pontius Pilate. Jesus, as I read it, is very *strong* (in his vitality, in his steadiness, his gentle frankness, his other-worldly insight) in this story; Pilate (poor fellow) is incredibly compromised. Headache. The heat. He hates the city he is overseeing. He has all the '*pouvoir*' (sad power-over) but is intensely miserable. Over the course of his chats with Jesus, who is about to be condemned by this joyless, corrupt system, we see Pilate daydream just walking calmly with this stranger and having philosophical discussions. He senses something unusual in this human, who is nevertheless almost doomed to be killed by his decree. (Read the real thing. Summaries lack the force of the art itself.)

Jesus, as strong, might need to be protected (and won't be) from Pilate, in his weakness.

It's not the worst example of the idea I'm hitching to Nietzsche, whether Nietzsche would appreciate it or not, and whether I'm reading this moment in Nietzsche too magnanimously. And it's not like this is not happening *all the time*. Impressive human people. Bumbling, stupid, exhausted processes. Protect the strength of such folk from the weakness that goes with carelessness, burnt-out decision habits, conformity, mediocre greed and poor character.

Spinoza would be another good case in point, if we are willing to believe Deleuze's description of him as quite kind, even *innocent*. Innocent and *strong*. He is, however, vulnerable to, in danger from, lots of people of his time, who did not at all like the wild (and genius) ideas he was very systematically proposing. They were quite ready to hurt him physically, to prevent his work from being published. How does our riddle feel now? Does it assist us in thinking a stranger arrangement of these categories? Usually one would call Spinoza the 'weak' element here, and those in power the 'strong', but Nietzsche's formulation at least loosens this assumption somewhat. Spinoza, rather, could be seen as quite *strong* (getting on with some fresh thinking, happily, polishing his lenses as a lens maker), while some scheming political units are hoping to knock him off. *They*, unusually, might be classed here as the 'weak' elements in our equation.

Maybe … and we should continue to remain wary, remain critical, too. Such aphorisms in a wrong sequence flip into ugly thinking. We know this, too.

Also, I always like to ask: *what is the effect of this idea?*

The effect I like to let roll from it is the one pertaining to my reading more precisely *my* strong and weaker moments. Curtailing *myself* when I'm likely to be shabby. *The stronger aspects of myself need to be protected from the weaker aspects.* There! That's clearer. Learning to have a clearer read on myself, so I don't spatter the world with my less shiny moments. That's all. Perhaps the idea works best in this form, and less well when sloppily extrapolated.

I moved into a sharehouse once. A man had been living there alone for a bit, and previously with two gay guys who, he liked to joke, used to run a lot of Compulsory Household Workshops. These workshops were only ever delivered *by* the gay guys *to* him. 'Never the other way around,' he chuckled. As you can imagine, he'd received a lot of tuition about living in a house in a civilised manner via these workshops by the time I arrived. When I was moving my stuff in, I initiated the conversation about cleaning and such. His response was surprising: 'Oh, I'll just do all the cleaning.' I did a double take. *He* would do *all* the cleaning.

I tried to intervene, since this seemed (from a typical perspective) to be 'unfair', 'not right', 'unbalanced'. He was not interested in my quibbling. When asked why, he explained: 'Well, I like the house to be a certain level of clean. I have plenty of energy, and it's no big deal for me. So, I'll do all the cleaning and then there's no complication. Easy.' I said I'd do other things, some weeknight meals, baking, taking out garbage, other contributions. He said, 'Fine', while seeming unfussed either way.

I've pondered and admired this little scenario ever since. Can you see that it demonstrates something perhaps at once Spinozan and Nietzschean? He had plenty of energy. He had capacity and thus he didn't – aslant to stereotyped gender dynamics – try to shunt tasks onto me, and get into a pathetic avoidance pattern, or dole out the tasks to us both with scrupulous *fairness* with a resentful spreadsheet. He was basically saying: *I have energy. I can do this and will. Do what you want.* It was a glaring example of what most people *don't* do. They don't have capacity to be virtuous; a virtuousness which is not peevish and needing recognition, not martyrish – they just can and want to.

Now ... say we both hadn't have had enough energy for that particular thing (he'd had a new diagnosis for fibromyalgia, or a viral thing that was leaving him wan and exhausted), then maybe spreadsheets and chats *would have been* practically needed.

Or perhaps, had I been able to rise to it, I would have done all those tasks, and he might have contributed in alternative ways. He was good on computers. He often contributed a light and humorous vibe. Many scenarios are more likely than what happened. Hopefully, we would have found a generous way to share the space, and fairness may well have guided how we worked that out. Fairness is fine; it's just that sometimes we use the argument of fairness to muddle ourselves on other things. Obsessed with fairness, we can sidestep *decent*.

I think I used to do this and mistake it for feminism. (And I don't regret that phase of asking, checking, raging.) What I want to explain now is very ... *delicate*.

Sometimes people are arseholes and give very little.

Sometimes, they contribute *differently* from you.

It is *so* hard to spot the difference. And it's hard to wait things out a little, to check if you know which is which. For a long time, I was a bit too *quick*. Too quick to decide that I was being ripped off. That others were taking advantage of my goodwill. I felt morally 'obliged' to insist on 'fairness'. I knew that patriarchy got women to do a lot of stuff. Still does ... but, as a friend might say, I was insisting on 'sameness', which misunderstands what modes of equality we might want, and thrive with.

Sometimes I could do a lot 'more' than my fellows, and sometimes I couldn't. Sometimes I was flattened by neoliberal bleakness and I could barely move from my bargain-basement futon. Unwashed hair, no fresh cake coming out of the oven. Veins transporting concrete not blood. Some days feel like that.

But ... at some point, I decided to start from the assumption that people are contributing all the time. If it doesn't at base feel like that, then try to arrange a new arrangement. Select your situation differently, so you won't feel resentful and begrudging all the time. We tend (call me crazy ...) to prefer to bring something to the spaces we share. Sometimes your housemates *are* freeloading, and sometimes they're just weak, or depressed, or stoned, or defeated, under-confident, badly trained by indulgent mothers. Sometimes they had childhoods from *hell* and they have not begun in the slightest to unpack what that is doing to them. (It is making them sad, Spinoza might say.)

These days, I have the energy I have, and I don't pour too much *other* energy (of thinking, of worrying) into a paradigm where I fret that I'm being diddled. I probably also live nowadays with more loving people than I once did. I'm older, too, and have more skill when asking plainly for what I'd like. I don't frame it as My Right. Hindsight is a murky beast.

The fact that this sharehouse experience ('I'll do *all* the cleaning') happened, and that I got a glimpse of why *those with capacity have scope to be generous*, was a good moment for my understanding of what I'm like when I'm within my power of acting, my *puissance*. When I am within a stretchier capacity, I can wait; I can be kind; I can reflect; I can be honest and bear the consequences; I can abstain from petty destructions and cruelties; I can listen. I can *not* get too busy with the fact that today I can do more than you, and tomorrow you might do (differently) more than me.

While you read this, and your warning signals flash, just remember that capacity doesn't always mean 'of a physical kind', and contributions aren't always 'pragmatic'. The direction of this argument is going to concern you and your own slides (joyous, sad) more than comparisons with others ... stay in your seat for now.

Sometimes, I don't have this kind of energy. This is just the melody of living, but – think back to Springer – I might also have complied with some socioeconomic practices ('widespread ways of being') that have siphoned off what energy I *had* into a bigger, loveless economy that cares little for me (for my baking art, poetry playfulness, admin flair, sleepful skills).

Pouvoir and the Sadness of Others

Let's recall the distinction between *puissance* and *pouvoir* that I mentioned in the last chapter. Here's the lecture quote from 20 January 1981 where we hear Deleuze explain how they differ and why this matters for understanding Spinoza:

[There's] this denunciation which is going to run throughout the *Ethics* [Spinoza's main work], namely: there are people who are so devoid of powers of action (*tellement impuissant*s) that they are the ones who are dangerous; they are the ones who seize power (*pouvoir*). And they can seize power (*pouvoir*) given how distant are the notions of power of action (*puissance*) and of power (*pouvoir*). The people of power (*pouvoir*) are the impotent (*impuissant*) who can only construct their power (*pouvoir*) on the sadness of others. They need sadness.

Spinoza did not pull punches. Should I summarise again?

Puissance = power of acting; it is in you, of you. It goes up and down.

Pouvoir = something one tries to seize or 'have', usually (if we believe Spinoza) sought out by those with little '*puissance*'.

Spinoza creates a new distribution of how we think about this (Deleuze might call this a conceptual distribution). We see that we might have conflated capacity and this other thing, for which we need the French spelling, so as to disambiguate between power-of-acting (*puissance*) and some other structural thing '*pouvoir*' which is a sadness-generator. The latter needs sadness. Those impotent power-seekers are always cultivating the sadness of others.

Any examples, Antonia? This is pretty abstract.

How about we say that if I try to create instances of people envying me ... I'm in this second group (I want power-over/*pouvoir* because I don't have capacity-to/*puissance*). I need to make others have the downward slide of sadness, and I do this by showing them something they can envy which I seem to have. Sounds fairly 'off', right? But we often do this – we act in these ways, to squeeze some power/*pouvoir* out of things, but this is not the *puissance* that Spinoza is praising as capacity, as power-of-acting. Sometimes when I absentmindedly open a social media post, at the wrong time of day, and then see a post that someone has shared which makes me slide downwards, I just note that I decided to open it. I'm a big girl; I could have instead decided to keep on with my project, reading, thinking, making. But no, I got busy in the Lalaland of scrolling and there we are! Sadder. Which means, maybe, less capacity, and my being more of an arsehole (out of reactive obliviousness) in the next little while.

You think this is going too far. Okay, then. But please do some personal experiments before you decide.

My old housemate who does all the housecleaning. He was, in that moment, an example of jubilant *puissance*. He could do it; it was quicker for him to do it than to have fights about who would do it. We would both have squandered our life force if we'd had petty squabbles about which task, when and who. In this case, we didn't need to. (In other cases, I've had the fights. Or I've found creative ways to get around the fights. Sometimes, I do it, I do far more, because I have the capacity. If I force myself to do it, and it's beyond my capacity, this isn't what Spinoza has in mind. If we live beyond our organic limit, we fall towards Ugliness. It's quite subtle.)

Spinoza was also wildly unpopular because of this, or at least among certain groups of people. And fair enough. Even Deleuze's take above is a hard read, hard to take in – since one must thereby face in oneself the fact that plenty of stuff we might 'do', is really motivated by this weak seeking to create sadness in others, and when we might also try to construct power [*pouvoir*] over them. Gulp.

So, we see that 'weakness' (impuissance, being devoid of acting powers) comes in many shapes, even though its branding is confusing. Presentations of what is 'tough' in the public sphere don't align tidily with this conception of what puissance is. Weakness, Deleuze explains, is often to be found in those that want to hoard 'power' (*pouvoir*) too much, to get power 'from' or 'over' others. If they 'had' power (read: were full of powers-of-acting), they'd have better things to do than get busy with this weird behaviour, right?

Deleuze has already said, earlier in this same lecture series, that this approach is rubbish anyway. It's when he is talking about how people misunderstand Nietzsche's Will to Power. We learn:

> And obviously, one can understand nothing about will to power in Nietzsche if one thinks that it's the operation through which each of us would be inclined toward power of action or would want power of action. *Power of action is not what I want, by definition; it's what I have.* I have this or that power of action; I have the power of action of this or of that, and that's what situates me within the quantitative scale of beings.[5]

Getting power (*puissance*)? Not possible! Power ('*puissance*' – power-of-action) is not like money. You can't amass it. You have it as vital force, and sometimes you don't. Depends on the mixtures or encounters you are having.

Power is not what I want, by definition, it's what I have.

This! This is why we trawl through pages of brambly philosophy – for these unrivalled gems of clarity and beauty. Step outside a moment to recover. Take a quick and luminous stroll. The world looks different after you've just read this …

Nietzsche has this notion that the vital are going to be virtuous. Now, we might quibble with that. Or perhaps his thinking is an invitation to recast a number of assumptions we have about what virtue and strength are like, as we've seen above.

We do tend to think of oppressors as strong. Maybe they aren't. To want to oppress implies, following Nietzsche, a profound weakness. (And the weak ones 'in power', misrecognising themselves as 'strong', are attracted by the prospect of seeing others, the ones they resent, as needing curtailing … it goes around …) To be able to oppress isn't strength. Wouldn't the strong rather be lying in the sun, resting? Or serving at a soup kitchen? Playing a violin?

Walking in the forest? Rearranging the furniture to dust behind the couch? Making an ice-cream bomb from scratch, with an interlude of kitten soccer? Wouldn't the strong be translating poetry from their third language into their first? Wouldn't they be doing What Life Is, rather than the misguided project of smothering the Life in Others?

If you have capacity, using it either to contribute, play, learn or invent, or just to dwell, makes more sense. Moving when one has energy to move is gorgeous. (I'm wary about all this presumptuous talk of laziness ...) Why would destruction – ushering in a bleak and awful atmosphere – be what someone strong would want to do? Why would the strong even want to waste a second of vitality doing the unpleasant work of oppressing, even a couple of steps removed?

Notice I use the word 'want' above? Why would one want to do stuff that brings on sadness or oppresses others? Well, arguably one perhaps doesn't want to do it; it's more that one can't do otherwise. This is a kind of weakness, right? Thus, maybe the point is that one does the stuff, but it is disconnected from wanting, proper wanting.

You might argue back that one can't curate (organise, cultivate) various kinds of wants. That one's wanting is trained by society, class, convention, LinkedIn ... Maybe I can learn to want to oppress others, and then I'm stuck with that repertoire. You may be on to something; it's true.

So, what if I suspect that I am one of Nietzsche's Weak? Egad ... I think this is crucial to think about, but also exactly what people who are weak and who read Nietzsche rarely do. We often prefer to associate ourselves with the flashier side of how marketing has appropriated him ... we fantasise we are stronger precisely in those moments of weakness. This is the contortion that Nietzsche tries to grasp with the concept of resentment. *Ressentiment*. Two Sad Nos Posturing as a Begrudging Yes.

∝

TO EXTEND THIS QUERYING OF WEAK AND STRONG, we can go another layer into nuance.

If we go along with the famous reader of Nietzsche, Pierre Klossowski, then it's *also* unlikely that weak and strong could be anyway about fixed identities. It can't be that one person is born to be strong always, others weaker: nah. If I read Nietzsche generously, it's rather that we have modes of both weakness and strength in the communities that constitute us. We are communities of sub-processes, *gell*! And our actions, decisions, company-kept, routines and even reading material, can send us more towards one or the other, and this lurching happens at different layers within us.

We are weaker or stronger versions of ourselves. A moment of strength might be when I can face that I have had a stretch of slightly grimy, 'weakish' behaviour, and I want to work differently, and I want to cultivate what makes me a little stronger.

More dreamy walks in the park? A little more/less sleep? Touching the glassy oblong device less? I don't know. I can't program this for you, for anyone. The thought experiment invites just that: experimenting. For oneself. No guarantees, and no lists you can tick off.

If it's about 'weaker' and 'stronger' versions of myself (with weak and strong being fairly unconventional takes on these terms anyway), my curiosity might be, then, how not to gut my capacity, how to squander a bit less?

To what could I consider saying 'No', in order to be more capable of saying a more general 'Yes', such that I could step away from voluntarily trashing myself?

Apparently, I can look after my capacity via considered encounters, through experiments, but not endless ones. If I have more capacity, then I'm less unlikely to be able to be virtuous. My strength, riffing off this model, is likely to mean a capacity for more joy – joy as this slide towards more capacity – thus I might be less likely to peddle so much suffering (since not cultivating my own impotence), thus less likely to dole out carelessly cooked-up anguish to others. If I'm stronger (in this unusual interpretation of 'strength'), I may not invest so much time in making other people have a worse time.

We are now within this glorious vicinity of Affirmation (the Yes, in spite of all the cracks, and holes, and bitsiness, and *Dukkha*, and unavoidable harms), and of the No of critique which supports its possibility, its feasibility. To what do we say No (an experiment we'll enact many times, until we make it a site of reason)? And how do we take care of ourselves in order to have the mettle for this same No? This circles back to the cardinal virtue of temperance, of spine.

What comes next is quite yogic, but I'll put it in general language, to keep you on side.

Harming ... Less

According to the *Yoga Sutras* (and a bunch of Eastern stuff) harming is what we do on default mode. Being alive is bumping into ourselves and other beings. We bump too hard, and others are harmed by our very Being Alive. The only way to *mitigate* this default mode – and I include here carelessness, obliviousness – is to have a bit more capacity. The texts speak of attenuation ... *thinning out*. How can we thin out our propensity for being shabby, for being oblivious arseholes? Here 'strong' would mean having the capacity to contain one's harmful default mode and put something else out into the world.

This is another way of joining up capacity (carefully defined) and virtue (also carefully defined).

We do, sadly, *always* dole out a little suffering, or so say the yogis. Because living itself involves a bit of harming. For example: I don't know who made the metal tea pot strainer I just used. But it looks to me like it is old, factory-made, and the persons who were part of its construction probably were not paid enough, had dangerous work, and may have been injured at a time before any employer took any responsibility ... *that's* just my morning cup of tea.

It's about *amounts*. Life and *some* harm go together (the yogis insist on this). *And* it is not something to celebrate. We can bear to witness it, yes (without turning it into spectacle, without blaming the 'victims', without a certain heart-deadened flip into cynicism).

Then, just because *some* suffering *is* inevitable, this isn't reason to throw up one's hands and abandon all efforts to mitigate the bits of it that aren't necessary, given, essential or structurally predetermined. Put more personally, it depends how much more, how much *extra* suffering you're keen on creating as you live. I think when we create suffering for others, we feel sad. Or *I* do. A legacy of lots of suffering is not *my* idea of a good legacy. Of course, of course, this is a matter of taste. Some might quip here that it's a fantasy that our sufferings (made for others, made by others for us) could *ever* be less. We just dance around the chaos we make, excusing it with various modes of ideology, with various kinds of veils that mask its reality.

I think we can lessen some of the harm we make.

Wow, how unclickable is that? It's modest, measured, seems Not-Hopeful-Enough. No grand gestures. No confident declaration. Nothing 100% to see here. Just a step by step, daily effort. A direction that we don't let up on.

(The all-or-nothing stance is very widespread. Isn't it a kind of defeated tantrum that can masquerade as 'cool' but is really scared, grim and listless on the inside? I think yes.)

To reach a place where one can tolerate soberly the little bit of brokenness that comes along with a life, is arguably to do with a hard-earned maturity. This position abstains from dodging the fact of pain by doing a manoeuvre where one appears to be *on the side of pain*.

The Not-100% (just a bit less) is *not* on the side of pain. It's on the slope of hope. Right?

There's commonly a part of us that, when faced with the fact that there's no way to totally avoid harming, has the dysfunctional response of claiming ('identifying' with) an inbuilt taste for making others suffer. (This would be because of our difficulty with anything less-than-'totally'; our inability to tolerate the partial nature of being alive.)

This posturing of being on the side of Dark, Harmful, Brutal, Cruel, Cold (blah!) has been in vogue in many moments, many places. It's tedious. It's a sign of great mediocrity. (As a dear friend of mine says about art shows that use the words 'brutal' or 'chilling', &c. in their marketing, 'Only people who have never faced real brutality, find its notion tantalising or sexy.') This prancing about, all pro-Awful ... it's the outlet of the weak, right? Sorry to say it sans sugar coating, but 'tis so.

It is another form of resentment, if we channel a little of Nietzsche's acuity. Its double fake 'yes' of resignation makes it look like a position; but really, it's the abandoning of position. It gives up on taking a position. On deciding.

There is, furthermore, a kind of obsessional tantrum hiding in a logic that won't tolerate 'a bit less', 'quite good', 'on the whole faintly wonderful'. Under the guise of insisting on precision, on thoroughness, our sulky ultimatums want to make nothing (since it's *not* everything) worth any effort. This constitutes, I reckon, a bind in which we purport both to *know* everything and can *do* nothing. A stance that goes nowhere, and which also doesn't dwell or rest.

Are you exhausted just reading about it?

To not know everything, to proceed with a bumbling, unglamorous courage, to dignify our human foibles while not identifying stickily with them, to resist the flip that wallows in cynical cool ... to stay alert to the everyday practices that would trash your capacity ... how on earth (since for now: no other planet) could we manage this?

*Consider cultivating some inattention
for that which doesn't deserve your time.*

Rigorous Kindness

I've just been doing some after-work *asana* (yoga poses).

After a day of switching between the smart device, work-computer and the digital team platforms, I can feel *very* scattered. Or wrung out, wan and weak. There's a solid kindness, an attempt at plain, non-flashy kindness, going on when I decide to (and then do in fact) practise a little.

The wan, weak and wrung out version of me will try to approach slowly and manageably the preliminary actions. Feeling utterly incompetent, I'll roll out the mat, then probably drift around my space a little more. I might touch the phone screen thinking it has a command for me. (It doesn't.) Trying to begin, I'll still struggle to settle. Drink of water? Eventually, I'll drift back to the mat, risking a modest set of poses.

It can feel vague, listless, sometimes right-dreadful. After years of practising, I know to do whatever version of it I can. Imperfectly, fragmented, laced with reluctance ... that day. And the next. Some days are smoother, others inelegant. Some hold together. Some rare days stall completely – if exhaustion is too much. (Then it's dinner and early bed.) Some days, initially, seem more-than-hopeless and yet they *still* manage to open out into an ease I never suspect is possible. The (self) assessment, anyway, which one learns to do less and less, is irrelevant.

(I'm describing my *outer* actions here, the 'what's happening'. Of course, you know that there's an inner set of words, ideas, sentences which accompany lots of our doings. In a chapter on kindness, I want to tell you that alongside these prevarications, these bumblings towards an activity that tends to be kind, I've also learned to be kind to me, *in the bumbling itself*. The nasty words, the tough self-talk, have – after these decades of practice – fallen away. It's pretty quiet in there, I confide if people ask. There's very little chit chat going on at all.)

At the end of the practice, there's another kind of person standing there. Neither a portal to productivity, nor someone who's wasted their day. Actually, just a Person-Person. The practising slips you free of that dreary dyad of evaluation.

It's nice. Yep. (I know you have your own version of my *asana* session, your own version of a steadying activity.)

What's *less* nice, what's quite confronting, is how relaxing within the known sequences invites something else *in*. It accounts for why people might want to *avoid asana* – the breathing along with studied transferring of weight, sensing of body bits, 'inside' and 'out', sequences done thousands of times. During all that my organism is able to dredge up ... stuff, recollections, moments, happenings.

The thing I've found about *asana* (which might be the way it involves, like many practices, the body and noticing the body in a kind of bracketed and less instrumentalist way) is that it tends to recall to me the most recent times in which I've been *awful*, or a bit grimy, a little dishonest, a bit covet-y, a bit shrill and insistent.

I find this far from *un*interesting. I find it *gripping*. But it's scary too ...

Asana reliably brings me face-to-face with instances of my own unkindness or shabbiness that I hadn't clocked at the time. With the weaker, squirmy bits. Perhaps, even the bits of me that want to squeeze out *pouvoir* rather than cultivate their own *puissance* (with these two modes bearing a non-relation to one another)? These instances that aren't so splendid, I may have either not noticed or repressed. *Same same*. Likewise, *asana* can recall to me ways in which I was *on the end of* unkindness (and hadn't seen it). Asana is a clarifying force, an honesty machine. It's part rehab, part alignment work, part body conditioning and part Face the Less Likeable Bits of Yourself and the World. *Neat, right?*

Every day, *stuff happens*; this is why the texts say to practise daily, if you can. Just to have the metabolising space. Chew through the *things*, before other *things* go in on top.

When I was done, I went to mandolin some cabbage for dinner. As I was doing it, this childlike wondering came to me: *Why don't we want to make our shared lives nicer for each other?*

Embarrassing, right? I mean who would ask this daft and ridiculous question? So ... gauche, Antonia.

A less exposed version might read: W*hy does kindness matter if you're trying to think about a Plain Life*?

Yes. Why, indeed?

No matter what you've gleaned about plainness so far, whatever it's led you to think about on your own terms (which is arguably more important that 'getting' my angle on it), perhaps it's already obvious that a plain life simply wouldn't seek out meanness as much as we often do; it wouldn't mistake meanness for 'exciting'. It wouldn't, furthermore, underrate what can happen if meanness takes a back seat. (Cue the mindfulness playlist on the stereo, and pass it a rusk and a phenergan, if you must.)

Much of what cultivates the *conditions* for a plain life involves considering kindness in its different (and inventive) forms. To 'cultivate conditions' is a fancy philosophical way of saying that kindness is like the mattress upon which a plain life can have its rowdy, breathless pillow fight. *Or* – without the conditions for kindness, plainness has no good soil into which to grow its generous roots. Lush and muscular. The absence of kindness is arguably part of what sows the seeds for *both* neoliberalism's ease in capturing us (our time, our eyes, our heartminds, our energies), *and* also for plainness' becoming elusive and vague in our imagination and sensibility.

Kindness, if we're talking about a plain life, is a useful criterion to help sift through what might be making us sick, sad, sullen and subjugated.

There are ways we make our own lives *unnecessarily* hardened. We can be confused about what helps, and then make of our habitual unkindness a *resentful* 'virtue' – calling it tough love, calling it self-discipline, calling it 'being realistic'. We often tell ourselves (having been on the end of the same logic) that it's somehow *useful*, *best*, *sensible* to make other people's lives harsher, to accustom ourselves to excessive harshness (even when this is not all intelligent, and doesn't work in fact). Harshness as 'good for us all'. Harshness as The Realistic Remedy We Need.

The point of this chapter is to inject into this belief (which I reckon you *might* entertain, even if it's buried, hidden) the tiniest sliver of doubt. To introduce a little worm into your cabbage of confidence in Harshness as Necessary, into the certainty that more kindness risks making us all indulged, pathetic and feckless.

∝

ALONGSIDE THIS WARINESS ABOUT HOW IT MIGHT make us lose our edge, 'kindness' *as word* has lately been cropping up everywhere. It's very confusing.

As I drafted this chapter, the frequency of its two syllables – on the device, on billboards, on office coffee mugs, in the feeds, among your aunt's fridge magnets, in the window of the hair salon – confronted me with the likelihood: you've already heard about kindness; you're sick of being reminded about kindness.

I suspect you know all 150 ways to bring kindness into your days; you've got the tote bag, a Kindness app, and a collagen kindness supplement. Thus, I fear I'm massively on the backfoot if I want to approach it again.

What gives?

How can we be party to an enduring cultural suspicion of what passes for kindness, of its impulse, and at the same time be newly inundated with it as word?

We exist within an unsettling tension that orbits the notion and practice of kindness. This can keep us confused and leave us unsure as to which thread to pull if we have an interest in grappling seriously, rigorously, with the unkindness that goes hand in hand with the mean habits and poor-thinking that neoliberalisation likes to dole out.

Kindness is a noun, but it doesn't name a material thing in the world that we can grasp or seek a storage solution for. Kindness, as noun, names the quality of the things we do, the decisions we make, the stances we take, the situations we select.

There is kindness that is something *added*. This might include positive actions that meet the criteria for being kind, for having a kind quality. This seems to be the reading of kindness that's popular currently; this isn't necessarily a bad sign. Alongside this, however, is the blatant prevalence of rampant unkindness. It's not, you see, always the absence of explicit gestures of kindness that muddles the world, but also our long-term apprenticeship in participating in auto-pilot or intentional modes of unkindness (untracked, unmentioned).

Kindness added is one aspect of two that in tandem might intervene on what shuts us out of plainness. Along with adding explicit kind things into the mix, the intervention I'm suggesting also requires at the same time the concerted and unglamorous work of subtracting unkindness. Our own, and the unkindness we play along with.

I guess I gave you the *asana* example because: i) it *is* explicitly kind to do asana, yes; but also ii) while doing *asana*, I get to notice my recent difficult-to-admit moments of being unkind.

Working on this chapter took me a very long time. Rather than seeing this as a sign of failure (always tempting), I sensed that I was trying to say something difficult, and the material was curling up, twisting and not sitting easily on the page. I was trying to spot the mechanism that leaves kindness exposed to our derision, our disbelief and scepticism. Not only in our moment! It's arguably the reason why kindness has been viewed historically with varying degrees of suspicion, of contumely (what a word! – it's worth a web search).[1]

We have mistrusted kindness, we have come to view it through slit lids, and you might be justified in concluding (lately) for good reason.

Quite simply, it's become commonplace to talk kindness, to plaster its image as veneer onto things, behaviours, decisions that remain mean, neglectful, undermining and dangerous. We might agree that kindness can be active (and I'm going to give you a convincing example later), but also that adding pseudo-kindness on where the underlying fabric is a bit ... rotten ... opens us to the danger of becoming cynical about kindness.

An ethos that would pursue and cultivate both of these aspects – being actively kind, but also sincerely practising abstaining from meanness – might be a kindness we could take seriously. Maybe we could even call it rigorous.

Unlearning Meanness

To make convincing steps therefore towards a serious kindness involves a necessary *abstaining from what isn't kindness*. This is less gratifying than the flourish of a kind gesture. It means abstaining from the mean, the miserly, the murky, &c. Less flashy, it can easily drop out of our contemporary kindness make-over.

Capturing something good and co-opting its shell, or its façade, to render the first thing seemingly shabby, or 'like everything else' is a special trick of both long-standing capitalism and more recent technocapitalism. It's a despair cultivation method, and one must see through it. This has arguably befallen kindness in our recent experience. The empty co-opting of kindness makes it difficult to conjure a rigorous concept of it, so we can lose hope in kindness having political muscle, world-altering clout.

Now, we're hardly immune to the idea that kindness is nice enough. It's a workable *look*, right?

Kindness, in our marketing-filled worlds, risks being used primarily as *style*. It can just be one gloss of many that could be painted across any sort of action at all – irrespective of whether the substance of that action had benign, beneficial, heartening, comforting, generous, safe-making, enabling, protective outcomes, or not.

In our worlds, where we might be encouraged to invest in and cultivate our Personal Brand (this is normal now, but also *a bit* unpleasant; revise Chapter 1 if you aren't sure why it's unpleasant), a palette we might call 'kind' has lately been on offer. Gendered, sure?

Now, it's not that I don't want a 'kind' interaction when I go to the shops. I'm happy if the person behind the counter has some stock-standard phrases of politeness happening. *Fine.* (Google reviews are vicious. One must not offend the customer ever … we are co-ensnaring each other with this review culture, just sayin'.)

What makes us further prick up our ears is that the label or gloss of 'kind' seldom lives up to its own, self-proclaimed branding aspirations. The business, for example, mightn't be at all *kind*, in its structural make-up. (Ask the workers, always talk to the workers …) Its industrial practices and environmental sincerity might not be kind (to anyone, at all). If there are shareholders and greed in play, the likelihood of kindness drops off again.

Kindness-washing. *Yeah.* You can spot it.

It's another form of blithe hypocrisy, and that's nothing new.

As a little kid in Catholic church in my country town, I would listen, during the coffee and tea, to the adults who sat in the front row of church (which meant something about their 'status', one imagines). I was confused that they had listened to the same sermon as I had, which – given by Father Stanley, who was actually very sweet – had included only gentle words about being kind and patient, with no trace of brimstone, damnation or nasty vibes. But these same adults, in Sunday Best, stepped off the worn carpeting of the aisle, only to step into the hall and get straight on with the vicious and snide running down of someone less fortunate or different. My kid-brain didn't get the contradiction. I decided heretically that they must not be praying to the right god, since the God that Father Stanley seemed to be on okay terms with, to whom I decided I was praying when I said my nightly prayers, *clearly* wasn't so on board with such levels of nastiness. In a way, my reasoning was true ... there *are* always 'gods', and these churchgoers were likely to have been worshipping some other persuasive ones.

Kindness – as sham word, as insincere aspiration – can thus be a sort of 'colouring', an add-on. We can slyly wash our brand in the tone of 'kind', the way a décor mag can show us how to lime wash an expensive wall. Not profoundly kind, this is only *apparently* kind. It's siding with kindness as something trending, in vogue as notion, but not very thoroughly.

Alert, as we are, to mere kindness-posturing, our longing for a kindness that might not be a sham can get further trampled. Worse than the word being used emptily, is when it's used *perversely*. Colleagues grind their teeth when 'kindness' suggestions are bandied about, coupled with unsettling workplace subtexts. The brain can 'grind' its synapses when faced with these torrents of dissonance, and to splint that condition may require medications, entertainments, blankness, various addictions, screen time.

We know that technocapitalism's Kind is just a kindness wash over the top of business-as-usual Unkindness. This is what we hate. Kindness as *veneer*, as a way to muddle us in our spotting of structural unkindness. It can make us crazy, angry and miserable.

Greedy people selling us apparently kind-sounding shit that we, and the environment, *don't* need. We're done with this, I think. We are fully over this method, *but* ... we can tread carefully in the face of the danger of throwing out Kindness (baby) with our refusal to participate in a Sham of it (bathwater).

Harder than acting kind of Kind, harder than branding ourselves as selling pseudo-kindness, is getting really very interested in how we are programmed to be averagely mean, to be casually careless, to be *Schadenfreudic* (not a word), vengeful, spiteful and spikey. This, however, is harder to make clickable.

If you know how 'kindness' can be twisted, re-marketed, re-purposed and thoroughly fucked, to the point where you no longer think it exists, are entirely sick of its flouncey hum, and slowly join the silent ranks of those too tired, too jaded, too heart-sore to deal with it, I'm sorry and this itself is worth some grieving time.

It's rough. Yes, seriously. It *is*. Don't harden, for my benefit, and guffaw it all away – this fact of Not Much Kindness – just let the little droplets run down your face and into your ears, making the world arrive muffled and strange.

Pseudo-kindness *is* at risk of becoming our flakiest of affectations, apt for accompanying – as cosmetic overlay – structures that are hyper-nasty, moderately cruel, run-of-the-mill murky. We feel the dissonance: kindness mantras whirring on beside persistent fear about housing, employment, health and civil society. Often, then, we are flung out of this wicked smoothie of experience with a built-in suspicion of something we are in dire need of...

Critical Kindness. Non-resentful kindness. What I'd call *rigorous* kindness is more of a practice and an evolving intelligence than a branding. The first stage of this less spongy, less smug kindness would be a grittier grappling with abstaining from meanness. We'd need to return and return to its difficulties and solace for decades, *lifetimes*. Not-Easy, it's also soberingly fulfilling. It has a plain, dignified taste that can really grow on a person. When you next feel sick to your stomach with the aftertaste of Averagely Awful, just recall that there *are* other flavours. You're allowed to want them, to prefer them, and to try to experiment with how to coax them into your worlds, into your own behaviours.

Kindness as Critical Lens

Consider this summation –

We are disturbed by unkindness (it does things to us), and – at the same time – we struggle not to collude with unkindness as mode, as norm, as structuring principle.

Does this reflect what you know or what you see going on? Do you pause when this sleight of hand shows up – the inconsistency between the degree to which unkindness unhinges us (fuelling a whole culture of anguish, of complaint, valid and less valid), and the extent to which we nevertheless remain a little too tolerantly within its paradigms.

We 'entertain' ourselves off the back of its variations.

We 'motivate' ourselves with it.

We squeeze pseudo-humour from its fibres.

Unkindness, I mean.

While reeling under the systemic impacts of absent kindness, we can nevertheless press on with our complicity with it as normalised, as something not to quibble about. Our complicity might take the form of: receiving unkindness (from others and pretending its fine); being unkind to others as habit, as learned/absorbed tendency; and/or just existing without questioning within a logic that sets the kindness bar very, very low.

I find myself somewhere between bemused and outright shocked at our collective dismay at the extent and intensity of so-called 'mental health problems'. It's no longer news that we might be wary of this common sleight of hand, whereby an attempt at broader societal critique slides responsibility for everyday fallout onto the small person. Onto me, onto you, onto your childhood friend who jumped from a building and apparently no one saw it coming.

'Mental health', as a notion and way of talking about a certain kind of now-acknowledged suffering, is not without its ideological context. As neither historically neutral nor objective, it comes from somewhere and it arrives with a certain historical punctuality. A term for our times, it both does some work for us, and it trips us up. If we lump all our non-meaty ills together without discernment, we can get a floury, curdled scramble – a meal that's neither delicious nor nourishing.

(Imagine here that I write a paragraph that lists all the valid modes of mental health disturbance which we can respect and differentiate carefully, that we can sometimes medicate, that sometimes correspond to precise and rigorous categories, which we sometimes can hold at bay with old–new techniques, that sometimes we genuinely inherited in neural matters. Imagine that paragraph, then read on ...)

Some of our disturbances, though – call me cray-cray – are the mush that emerges from the jaws of the unkind/kindness inconsistency: we would like to live more kindly (because kindness makes our capacity soar). While preferring to be on the end of more kindness, we still however extend tacit approval, or approval by default, towards so many things that train us to swim willingly in the Waters of Unkindness. Blech. These waters are murky, taste bad and give us runny poo. Yet we frolic on. We can accidentally on-purpose forget to name this inconsistency (what we'd prefer, what we are complicit with). We fail to query it regularly. We could be sterner about what parts of it we contribute to, and this could amount to risking the 'No' of critique in the face of certain modes of unkindness. I'm regularly persuaded that such unkindnesses directly contribute to what gets called 'mental health problems'. These ingrained modes, practices, trends and vocabularies of unkindness could be met with less cheery inclusion, less laissez-faire languor, at the very least, less admiration.

Rigorous kindness here, I'm suggesting, is a method for and an experiment in withdrawing our participation in certain broader tendencies and 'givens' that skip over the problems that unkindness sows in our shared worlds.

Rigorous kindness, then, will only *seem* oxymoronic, since deep down it isn't at all. To spot the inconsistencies we are taught to live with (and with which we are barely managing to live) is a first mode for something I'm calling kind.

Maybe it's just me, but I think people often fob off kindness as something that doesn't apply right now. Maybe later (like 'Miss Ohio'). Good in principle but it's for someone else: for the rich, for women, for the placating, for the retired, for when I've built my nest egg, for those recovering from cancer, for after I'm promoted, for the community workers.

Kindness – let me be clear however – has nothing to do with what the weak do, or the slack, nor is it a mere habit of those aligned with a particular gender or who are richer, safer, post-ambition, even manipulative or oppressed. Kindness here becomes a clear-eyed decision, linked to a practical hunch that certain styles of being, certain assumptions about how we can be, are due for reappraisal. The reappraisal has to go step-by-step. What is kind to oneself under neoliberal paradigms is to spot that there is a paradigm full stop. To check that the behaviour one might have classed as 'natural' is actually produced and encouraged by a larger order that is very invested in your Enduring Faith in Unkind, in your belief that you are at base ... well, base.

Kindness, too, is hardly rare. It's less rare than the world would have us believe (in those hard moments when we're alone, frightened, sleepless and destabilised ... probably by an unspotted unkindness that day). People, in fact, are kind, have immense capacity to be kind, all the time.

Barbara Taylor and Adam Phillips, in their book, *On Kindness* (2009), argue that one very ordinary situation where kindness can be regularly witnessed is between parents and children. These authors claim that the kindness parents extend daily to children – solid proof that we are inherently also very kind – can be easily overlooked. (You might be reading this with decades of experience enduring family dynamics that were very unkind, or a confusing mixture of kind-then-mean. You might be in therapy exploring some ways in which, in your family of origin, kindness wasn't.)

This is what can make the brain hurt: contemplating, front-on and together, both the ingrained examples of assumed unkindness-as-given (see: big, wide world any day and our own hypocritical modes), and the fact that vast numbers of people are kind (patient, forgiving, unselfish, restrained) quite often.

When I see a car being cut off, for a good long moment, in heavy traffic, by another driver who is struggling, and the first car waits, and they just let the less competent driver find their way to a good lane, and they miss a light cycle, but they remain unfazed, launching no scene of mockery or bad-mouthing … then I note that many people are kind. They have this capacity for it. A capacity, since it takes something to pull that off.

I'm presenting an argument for a dual approach to rigorous kindness. There's a first subtracting moment (grappling with our own unkindness, the unkindness to which we're exposed, and our approval for, collusion with, modes of unkindness that are neither given nor natural). It's less fun but bracing. Then there's a second moment – shaking off our cynicism – when we freshly consider the possible dignity of gestures of active kindness.

Taylor and Phillips imply that humans are plainly nourished by exercising this active capacity. It's a reliable source of something good for us. We like to be kind, they say, and it's curious how much stick we give ourselves for wanting to be kind. Our kindness can occur in odd places and moments, with strangers in encounters that were neither foreseen nor socially likely. Kindness, therefore, might be our most honourable mode of promiscuity.

Speaking of promiscuity, I'm going to digress now via a little anecdote about how I ended up reading an unlikely book that contains an example of astonishing, world-tilting kindness. It was the other time when I was pretty young, overseas and solo.

∝

AT AGE FIFTEEN, MY PARENTS SENT ME ON AN EXchange to France (I turned sixteen there). Sound glamorous? Twasn't mostly, but it *was* 'elsewhere'.

'Do you want to go to France on exchange, leaving in two weeks?' my dad asked me. (I was transparently unhappy in an Australian country high school, so why not be transparently *malheureuse* in a French regional *Lycée*?)

I hesitated barely (and hadn't even heard of Deleuze's *Nietzsche* book then ...). 'Yes,' I said. *Yes*.

(If an alien spaceship had come down and asked me if I wanted to climb in, I would also have said, *Yes*. No doubt about it.)

My dad *sold* something, I think, to pay the exchange organisation's admin fees and the flight (our money situation wasn't very easy at the time) and I promptly left my classmates at school, and my little sister, for a good part of the coming year. In my odd socks, with no pocket money, I ate the French meals kindly provided by my family, getting a bit fatter eating excessive dollops of hand-whipped mayonnaise, and chocolate bars on baguette at the kitchen table for afternoon tea.

Unhappy and *nerdy*, I was hopeful I could learn French and had a hunch about how language acquisition needed to go. *No lapses*, was my logic. You had to enter the language, and not leave it, until you were done. This was way before the internet, even before rudimentary mobile phones (of the Nokia kind), and so it was easy to 'stay Française'. Long-distance phone calls were very pricey, so you almost never made them. Usually I would only speak to my parents weekly on a Sunday night. Sometimes I would only prank them and hang up at a stipulated time, so that they knew I was alive.

The other side of my commitment to full immersion was my sly method to delay it a little. *Kind?* Perhaps.

I decided I would take the translation of the massive tome of Victor Hugo's *Les Misérables* with me and, once done, there'd be no looking back to any English reading material until I was home. That was ten months off.

The book, at the time, was having a revival, and was therefore accessible. Bookstores were stocking it since the musical version was touring the world with its cast of talented waifs and urchins and busty barmaids. Every white female child with dramatic aspirations was singing 'Castle on a Cloud', posing implausibly as ashen and thin in local Eisteddfods.

Another advantage for my Strategy of Delay, was that *Les Misérables* is a very *fat* book. As literary work, it had size, narrative arc, and culturally relevant content – all pluses. It was *très* thick, and thus it let me put off full immersion for a solid while and prepare myself for a withdrawal from eloquent. To learn a language, you have to give up at first being witty, funny, charming and concise ... otherwise you never become witty, funny, charming and concise in the *new* language; this is a hard weening to face and endure. Thus, I came to find myself very invested in reading *to the end*, a (loooooong) novel in English.

I was confident the work would be a rollicking read – rousing, just like the anthem 'Do You Hear the People Sing?' from the barricade moment in the musical. (I mean, deep as we are in neoliberal times, that song seems practically militant compared to what passes for 'alternative' now. You could queue it on your chosen music platform immediately and cancel twenty of your faux-spiritual, self-care app subscriptions. *Je vous remercie.*)

What I didn't anticipate was how *vast* the novel would be. Artistically, philosophically vast. Big old works of literature. They are flawed, sure. They have some tacit icky politics (so, eyes-peeled, please), but still. These people *can write*. Inside this corpulent tome, I came across the example I've been hinting at – a gesture of kindness that I would call rigorous. A sobering, mind-blowing kindness that floors me every time. It exposes to what extent our usual logics (for 'drama' anyway) are soaked through to the core with unkindness-as-assumed.

Hugo's example, which I *am* withholding intentionally in a way I hope won't prove unkind, isn't just 'nice'. It involves both a daring act and almost imperceptible acting *else*wise, a snapping of time in two. It looks to the 'law' beyond established law, that is also the condition for any justice, if you like. The kindness that Hugo stages subtracts itself from our ingrained sense of *how things go*. These are our entrenched schemes of normality, of things rolling on regrettably, but as they 'must'. This is why I consider it a good example of *Kindness as Critique*. This act simply ignores the unkindness we are supposed to enact, thoughtlessly, zombie-like. *We're very sorry, but*...

It behaves like a raw but non-shiny courage. It arrives as a simple sentence, as a series of regular words, available all the time, but in *that* moment, in *that* order, these words change everything. A kind of *decision*, too. It *doesn't let happen* what we'd anticipate of that relation in that moment and in those circumstances.

Disambiguating Kindness

My argument, then, is that for kindness to impress us in its active guises, kindness also needs to function as critique, as a way of enacting a 'No'. Non-resentful, this No marks a boundary and signals a non-participation, a ceasing of going-along-with, so as to take a new direction less complicit with a corrupt (or tired, or confused, or miserly) order. (Remember that *before* Nietzsche's affirmation, one needs a boundary constituted by a kind of No, a retracting one's energy from the stuff one has critiqued. It's a specific kind of No, towards a specific kind of Yes.)

Part of this critique, I think, does involve reconsidering how one feels about unkindness more generally. There's a curly argument that might try to derail us here: that lots of people like unkindness *as kink*.

We've had authority figures, moments of trauma that we've honourably tried to recast; we've learned to turn unavoidable into desirable, and we do endless emotional gymnastics to placate our Super Egos. *Yes, yes*. Many have done and do. This is fine, but it is just a distraction from the less raunchy point. *Most people don't appreciate the grinding forms of daily, non-accessorised, non-negotiated, decidedly unkinky unkindness*, those that don't have much shimmy, much agential staging, to them at all.

Being harassed at the checkout (when you work behind it). Being made irrelevant in an employment setting. Being on the end of cruel gossip. The dropping of casual menace from someone who has power over your situation. Real structural unkindness – that can come packaged with all sorts of 'corp-kind' packaging, but which fucks your life. Put-downs, that you can't even recruit as a form of artless innuendo, but which are just average and demeaning. Wan and mediocre forms of saturating unkindness. Being mocked (for clumsiness, for slowness, for not understanding straight away ... for nothing! The mocker might just like mocking.) Even for the card-carrying masochist, even for the scared, smug person who is 100% Signed Up to Neoliberalism's Reality TV Show and wants to 'be realistic', I don't think that even they find these more humdrum modes of unkindness very racy, very enriching.

My illustrations, which are gauche, are also unavoidably broad. I don't think I can do this work of sorting and filtering in your place. You have your lived examples; you know the unkindness to which I'm referring. You might also know that you can find yourself *at once* complying with unkindess, while *also* despairing how it colours the world that you wouldn't mind inhabiting with less of *that* stinging hue.

Working out your position on this is a long process, if it interests you to begin it at all. It pertains to a personal ethic (which means: project of experimentation). How does kindness look? When is it possible to be kind? When can't I? When don't I want to? What prevents me (internally, externally) from activating kindness I'm otherwise on board with?

How can I refocus on my own meanness if I'm getting too much enjoyment out of pointing out and inventorying everyone else's? *Hahahahahaha.*

In therapy, there can be *both* the slow accompanied sorting through of the unkindness that one took for 'normal' (this is an aspect of certain therapies), *and* the thornier project of sorting through one's own habitual modes of unacknowledged unkindness learned from these early contexts and now activated as … *ours.*

Understandably, people might want to avoid therapy because it may ask them the harder question, *how did you contribute*? If this is too hard, too much, then off-the-shelf pharmaceutical cuddles might be how it goes for now.

Imagine a bully ends up in a serious-enough therapy. Usually, they existed in a home that was organised by bullying in some way. They don't necessarily know they are bullies, at work, or socially. They might be appalled to know. How much grief would this 'insight' unleash? *Gawd.*

Their learned mode of bullying is simply how they operate (often 'efficiently', often 'effectively' … intimidation can really 'get people moving' …). They'd be undone by facing how their impatience with others, their unwillingness to come up against even mild querying, their social methods, or strategies in 'conversation', all land poorly. To face the fact that aspects of one's way-of-being spread unkindness around, like a toddler at the fingerpainting station, is highly unpleasant. Who wouldn't prefer a tablet?

Facing *how we roll*. This involves facing one's modes of habit, or of incapacity, that culminate in unkind ways. No one really enjoys this. This is no party. But, for certain kinds of profound unhappiness, it might be the only way through. And it requires precision.

Our world arguably is facing a crisis that we label 'mental health', but – *seriously*, people – we know there are angles we could take to query why our collective hearts are sore, why we are wracked with fear and loneliness, and why our interior worlds are cloudy, erratic, unpredictable and (often) cruel.

(Sometimes 'no one likes me' because my learned behaviours are not very likeable. Who or what process could help me to work out *kindly* how I internalised all the unkindness to which I was subjected, and to invent something else? Serious project, *n'est-ce pas?*)

If you're sloppy with your analysis of 'how did I contribute?', then you can just replicate a certain foundation of patriarchy ('women blaming themselves for men's bad feelings'), or you can stall the exploration in a cul-de-sac of finger-pointing and not proceed beyond that. This project – where we pick through how our own collusion with unkindness, now or then, has contributed to our mental instability, our joy–sadness ecosystem, to our fulfilment palette – is finnicky and difficult.

It is a form of strange and non-flashy critique. You can't do it constantly (it's so painful), but you can *do it a bit*. That's my provocation.

And, as you know, being oppressed more generally (by patriarchy, by *unspeakable* colonial crap, by all the haters, or anything else) doesn't get anybody off the hook. It *explains* many things. It can encourage you to forgive yourself, to permit yourself to move in fits, starts and collapses, or to conjure patient expectations, to grasp non-reactively in moments why you can't-so-well. I don't think we want our pain to operate mostly as *excuse*. This precludes us from the dignity of which we're in dire need.

I can be oppressed, yes. And I can be a real *unit*. At the Same Time! Chances are they're linked. Because being exposed to unkindness is very, very, very likely to draw you into the same logics of unkindness. We tend to end up mirroring the company we keep. This is so hard. (I hate this fact; I might need to curl up in a ball under a blanket for a bit, then walk slowly near some trees, then let a few tears out, and press on ...)

Logics (or 'vibes that organise what seems normal') are very contagious. Once you're swimming in an unkindness logic, whether you're on the end of it *or* dishing it out can get murky. You've been sucked into the logic; and methods for getting out of, or pausing, that scene are often elusive. But we keep looking. *Fail again, fail better* (as Badiou quotes Beckett).

There's a line in the incredible documentary *In my Blood it Runs* (2019), where Dujuan, a ten-year-old who's at risk in an education system that's failing him and other Indigenous kids, names a method for pausing his own likelihood of being sucked into an existing unkind paradigm. He says something like: 'When you go out bush every week, you learn how to control your anger, and you learn how to *control your life*.'

This floored me. It left me speechless and in awe. (At this stage in the film, it's not yet explicitly mentioned why he would have anger, but the film unfolds very clearly the enormity of why he has it, and why it puts him in danger.) What's your method for giving yourself a chance to not be drawn in, not to be sculpted to the very shape you're wanting to avoid, that makes you sad, that trashes your capacity, that even puts your life at risk?

We're all a little bit a part of the problem (or we *react* to the problem in an entangled way). There's no way around that. So don't get purist about it. You can be part of it, *and* you can be slipping, wriggling, bike-riding free where you can.

∝

OKAY, YOU SAY, BUT WHAT ABOUT THIS FRENCHY example you're so keen on?

Yes, let's go to Digne, of the France of Hugo's tale – to the character Bishop Myriel, who was based on a real person: Bishop Bienvenu de Miollis (1753–1843), also known for his kindness, his wariness of complicity, and his grappling with non-greed to the letter.

In the *fictional* tale, Jean Valjean has been granted parole after serving nineteen years for stealing bread for his sister's children. Having served his sentence, he now has to present what is called the yellow passport (*passeport jaune*) that identifies him as a former criminal.

He cannot find anywhere to sleep, and no one will offer him any hospitality. Desperate, he knocks at the bishop's door.

These stories don't talk about trauma. It wasn't their lingo. Of course, we could read it like that, knowing that Valjean has been horribly treated in, and absorbed by, a system founded on cruelty. He's just been hit with a new wave of crushing despair, since the parole that should invite some relief from suffering instead means that he faces a new form of punishment and ostracism *in* the community. He is a marked man. The world will always be able to *know what he is*. The law of the time ensures there's no way out of that.

The bishop, however, welcomes him in for the night. Valjean is offered food, a place to sleep, a chance to wash and gather himself after the exhaustion of two cruel decades. They eat together off the best crockery, and silver candlesticks adorn the table. When Valjean questions why the bishop has allowed him inside – 'you don't know me' – he's reasserting his own internalised identification as outcast, as dangerous criminal. The bishop replies: 'I know who you are. You are my brother.'

Holy moly.

When I find this scene in the 1978 film excerpt on YouTube, I fall to hard, painful sobbing. It's, like, 10am in the morning, and I'm at my desk, and luckily no one is around because I'm weeping in my office chair. Shaking and snotty, and it just takes me over. It's what Alain Badiou would call egalitarianism. The *generic* set – see *Being and Event*. The bishop is not doing identity politics of the kind Badiou thinks is not necessarily taking us where we long to go, namely towards *justice* irrespective of categories. Valjean is doing a usual manoeuvre of asserting that he belongs to a 'set' of humans known as 'criminals' and that the bishop belongs to a 'set' of humans known as 'clergy'. Valjean is all of us, more than ever, who are primed to declare a lack of common ground, that never the two shall meet – a former 'criminal', clergy – let alone eat a meal together, simply, plainly. A plain meal. On some nice plates.

The bishop, in a moment of Badiouian truth, a moment that is arguably *political*, says: *we are brothers*.

Now ... I'm a *rampant* (frothing at the mouth) feminist, and *I* don't care that he says 'brothers'. I know what this means, and it is world-changing. If he were around today, he might use a fancy, theory expression like 'kin' to try to loop the various categories together. Don't quibble!

So, they eat a meal together, and Valjean – perhaps for the first night in several decades – has the chance to sleep soundly and safely. (A precious thing, that many folk then, and many *now*, do not have.) He wakes in the night, however, and the strategic part of him, the part that knows how horrible the world is, how harshly it will treat him, recalls the bishop's silver collection.

We're not surprised that Valjean would be captured by the scheming part of his psyche – his trashed and tortured psyche, that has been thoroughly formed, trained and brainwashed by nineteen years of merciless incarceration. Give the guy a break. Valjean is a part of all of us – the part that *already knows* the danger of hope, and which opts for the cleverness of anticipating unkindness.

He makes a move, in the face of kindness-so-far, since he does not imagine this kindness as likely to last. Inside the finitude mindset that we all live with, it mostly *won't* last. After this brief brush with a decent person, he'll then be on his own. One meal. One sleep. *Sure*, but only more ostracism and indifference ahead. In the fictional story, he makes a move.

I say this to emphasise that this is a predictable moment –

prepared, manipulated, inculcated by systemic logics – but *still*: Valjean makes the move solo, and no one *makes* him. He is the doer of this verb, this action. He *does* something.

We make plenty of moves in relation to our position on kindness, on how much we anticipate kindness to be possible.

∝

WHEN I WAS DRAFTING THE EARLY VERSIONS OF THIS chapter, I found myself sprawling into rabbit holes, sliding into long-winded accounts and anecdotes, detailed particulars.

That's the *unkind* way to describe it. It may be that there's simply a lot to say regarding the details of kindness, in various situations, such that I could pen a long, exhaustive *manual*, a fat reference work, full of situational, fine-grained illustrations.

At the same time ... asking about the fine-grained particulars of kindness in each moment, in that situation yesterday, for a gnarly conflict that's coming to a head, as a way to parse what has happened and what options I have for my imminent moves ... well, this is a further grappling with kindness, and less easy to capture in a lip balm, or even a team wellness day. It's applying kindness as a crisp but confronting lens to hold up in front of situations, to cast differently what might have been in play.

It's all very well to have meta-theories about inconsistencies, social malaise and dissonance eating our heartminds, but it's going to contribute zilch to changed behaviours – in myself, as a humble starting point – if I don't follow through with something more *nuanced* and practically *tested*.

This pertains to how we choose to cultivate ourselves, if we bother with such things at all. Programmed to be a little bit mean (by neoliberalism, by poor parenting, by some institutions, by the assumptions grounding capitalism as logic) and if – as organisms – we are anyway prone to be reactive and aggressive, we would need to *really* apply ourselves to operating otherwise.

Letting things flow (although it sounds nice 'n' natural) isn't really going to cut it. *Desolée*.

One morning, as I grappled with this idea, the internet threw at me a quote from Fredric Jameson that says it another way: 'Ideological critique has to end up being a critique of the self. You can't recognise an ideology unless, in some ways, you see it in yourself.'[2]

Thank you, FJ. Without a further step (the one I'm aligning with putting kindness to work as a practice), I won't be able to follow through on spotting ideologies that are ruling my life, and my own role in perpetuating them. Notions about ourselves are fine. Noble. Nice sounding. Gratifying. We do not perceive ourselves clearly. Zen says it. Psychoanalysis says it. They *say* it, and then – instead of swerving into swoons of *Oh well*s – they proceed into the sticky porridge of incident and reaction, of close reading, of delaying decisional haste (about *what went on*). Politics is less remote from all this than we'd reckon. Wrestling with the ideologies that *have* us, that constitute us, maybe ... this demands a difficult work. It's daily, quiet enough, fortifying.

I'm making it sound tedious. It both *is* and *isn't at all*.

Kindness can well be a lens for observing the matter of everyday life. It's detailed and often *thrilling*.

When I uncover a veiled move that I make, that gets squished together but is in fact an action that I was doing behind my own back, it's astonishing. These are the lush details that surface with practising, with kindness as not just a nice *tone*, but a trusted methodology for interrupting the meaner reactivities, the awful autopilots, which determine much of how we operate, often without realising (or caring to recall) it.

Personally, it makes me uneasy to know I'm doing (and responsible for) a whole lot of things about which I don't know *anything*. You could say (though I wouldn't) that it ramps up my ... 'anxiety'.

Living behind my own back, so to speak. We *must* live like this (since we have an unconscious), but appreciating that one lives like this, and that we can't/don't know everything about ourselves ... holding this incongruency without resolving it somehow makes for a gentler Unease.

Here I could do a plug for meditation. Not with an app. (Or with one, if you must.) The approach I've mostly practised involves just sitting – still, straightish spine, timer on, candle, *whatevs*. And train yourself (AKA 'play around non-preciously') to have more space between the molecules of reacting. Change how 'time' itself happens.

For most of us, time is a concentrated *hoik* of stuff all at once. This is just what happens if you let things run spontaneously in a regular human life. The organism streamlines what it perceives, what goes in and registers. It *has* to; this enables us to practically get through the day. In this same streamlining, however, details go missing, and sometimes those details include layers we might care to have a closer relation to.

Meditation horrible? you ask. Well, obviously. Sooooo horrible. It is a big slap in the face, worse than that blockbuster scene, where you can't look away. Our internal cinemas – behind the peaceful facial features – can be confronting and dismaying. Noisy and a letdown. Lots of fornicating, murder, shopping lists, minor fretting and rivalry. Sometimes in meditation we just replay old, old griefs. Sometimes, however, small fledgling ideas, that we've never glimpsed before, flicker into view. We face both the less salubrious aspects of ourselves, beyond our curated self-image, *and* sidle nearer to something dignified, something we can plainly live with.

This rigorous kindness? It could involve how we might speak to ourselves at the very least. (I know, I know – the Super-Ego isn't evaded that easily ... but *still*, it is possible to giggle it into retreat, lovingly jostle it with a sly chuckle just out of your spotlight, into a contained corner with a lunchbox full of cheese sticks and fruit chews ...) The kindness tone, its voice, would not be indulgent, and it would not pass the blame elsewhere.

There's something about kindness that is very subtle – hence my rabbit holes in wanting to illustrate it for you. It steps softly clear of the flakiness we might be concerned about, while also casting clarity across our penchant for resentment. Kindness: neither resentful, nor pandering. Kindness: artful and unique in each instance. To be decided. Resentment, on the other hand, is reliably a bit *mean* (like those front-row church adults). Resentment hides meanness inside its folds of tut-tutting. Resentment and generosity rarely meet.

To read kindness in relation to something we could activate *in practice*, as a kind of practising, gives us umpteen instances in which we can ask, for real, about kindness, and track the degree to which it *can drop out* of how we make decisions.

When people treat us badly, there must be the tiniest part of us that joins in. If we can see this, peel away its sticky tendril, and notice the awful thunk: *that happened* ... (they were mean, and then I mean-retorted in retaliation – at myself even, at my partner, in some other sneaky way ...) then we may be able to subtract ourselves from that feeling-reacting. It might fade out, become gradually harder to recall and less likely to activate.

However, that's not Jean Valjean's situation ... yet. He makes a decision that night – wakeful in the bishop's house – a decision not so much grounded in kindness. Fair enough, I say. Fair enough.

∝

WHEN I DARE TO, I CAN RISK NOTICING IN WHAT WAYS I comply with a broader, deeper, saturated regime of unkindness, in boring, small ways. (This bears little relation to sweeping impassioned arguments, which are good, but it's less grand than that; it's about more subtending detail ...)

There are so many ways I don't know my unkindness. If I have some capacity, I may withstand the awkward scene of your telling me about how I am unkind, how my ancestors were unkind, about how I don't see how a certain 'benign' practice is effectively unkind. This is crunchy, difficult, harrowing work. I will try not to bite when you tell, if you can try not to luxuriate resentfully in my unease and shame.

My little internal responding patterns, which I have been taught (no doubt about it) by the surrounding culture, the waters we swim in, are how aspects of the complicity persevere. These aren't glamorous. For many politically engaged folk, they might seem too small to bother with. But there's a bigger system to challenge, tear down, reinvent. Yes ...

... but things aren't unrelated.

Kindness requires an odd mixture of softness (which isn't flaky), capacity (to face how Awful we often are), along with something else, which we can call strength.

∝

IN A DISCUSSION SOME YEARS AGO ABOUT WHAT'S called *Tapas* in the *Yoga Sutras*, my teacher had something very interesting to say about kindness.

Tapas does not refer here to delicious small plates of Spanish salty treats, but rather the thing in Sanskrit which is often translated as 'austerity', or the 'heating practices'. These would be trainings in minor or more exacting difficulties, which however are not destructive (the twentieth-century commentator Aranya emphasises this last point[3]). In the yoga curriculum, meditation itself counts as serious *Tapas* (it's a rigour to sit mostly still for long periods); or the *asanas* (poses) that challenge the strength, balance and alignment to a constructive extent. These are all forms of *Tapas*.

Aranya also says that if the rigour disturbs the practitioner too much, then it stops working. Cool, hey? One works just up to the limit of capacity, recalling what Spinoza also knows.

Yoga, too, if it is to matter, needs to strike the right balance between kindness and strength. Strength doesn't mean a cliché of 'strength'. Here, strength would mean an ability to remain steady and non-reactive in the whirlwind of everything. Strong enough not to join in (the unkindness, the grimy joke). Nietzsche, as I mentioned, might call it not going along with the herd. It does require a kind of material substrate – mostly – and this might be seen in a vigorous body, but really it tends to proceed, as one skills-up more and more, towards a less-meaty version of this. In the experienced person, it becomes strength and stability at the energetic level. More elderly practitioners are an example of this – their considerable strength is located at a different register than, say, someone in their twenties, whose meaty vibrancy might be strongish, while their other layers are still developing themselves. Meaty but flighty, often.

Anyway, my teacher gave the following provocation (possibly in relation to why one might need to do enough *Tapas* in yoga): one needs to be strong enough that one's kindness doesn't land as weakness.

Wow and ow. This is immensely pragmatic advice. It was probably directed at us as fledgling yoga teachers. If you're not sufficiently leading the space, then your kindness will just seem flaky. At one level, too, there is a sobering aspect to this pithy aphorism. It is a pragmatic reminder that our cultural stance on kindness remains ambivalent, since we need it packaged up with strength to make it land as *kindness*.

I don't know if I'm explaining well. I find this question in yoga fascinating. I think about it a lot: *himsa*. 'Wounding'. Deciding, experimenting with how *not* to wound – *ahimsa*. Non-wounding. How it looks in every unique instance? Can I pull it off? Why don't I? Why can't I?

Kindness can be structurally difficult for us to enact. I don't think we look at this enough. It's so awful to look at. I doubt whether most mortal, small human brains can bear to look at how structurally kindness is not possible for them, not on offer.

This is why kindness genuinely disturbs the status quo.

It's a reason to work on oneself a little, just enough. Some movement, some sport. Some difficult tasks for the mind. Some abstaining, just to check that one can. Keep the whole organism somewhat capable, in relation to its overall potential capacity. You see, this is not comparative. (It's not a 'who's stronger' between people, but rather a 'how am I strong as myself?') It is internal to us, really. It becomes tricky when extrapolated as a principle of comparison. For yourself, what's a way to be strong enough that you can let yourself be kinder?

∝

JEAN VALJEAN IS KNOWN FOR HAVING THE STRENGTH of four men. It's as if Hugo paints for us a picture of immense *capacity*, but a capacity also twisted in on itself. Just now, I referred to some internet notes, to check I wasn't misremembering details, and ... I found myself crying. *Again* ...

Crying! From some *notes*, made for students who can't be bothered reading the actual book (or probably who don't have *time* to read the book, since they're juggling multiple neoliberal side hustles alongside their literary studies ...). *Lordy.*

Predictably, what I'm going to say is: read it. The whole fat thing. People aren't afraid of thickness, these days. People love the mega-brick fantasy series. Come on. Get yourself to a bleak moment in Parisian history. Indulge in long passages of philosophical reflection from Hugo. I'm sure I disagree plenty, with some aspects. *Still.* The tension at the centre of the plot can still make me cry on an internet site with an ugly font, and some ads for jorts and anti-ageing crèmes in the sidebar.

Jean Valjean has capacity, but he has also lived through the extreme consequence for his 'misdemeanour', if we can call it that. It is unthinkably horrible. We know Australia had a good long moment when it was used (*illegally* we'd say) as a place for putting people in precisely Jean Valjean's position. People stealing out of sheer need. And, thus, likely hardened, angry, violent, broken and dangerous. Doomed to horrific quarters, treatment, loneliness and unhinged company, in a land that belonged to another people.

I digress. Jean Valjean is also a predictable product of the system that Hugo is out to critique. The story would be accurate-enough but far less readable – or *there wouldn't even be a story* – had not a very rigorous, a very stern act of kindness occurred close to the start of the narrative.

Recap: the bishop is atypically hospitable; Valjean sleeps under his roof. Possibly made uneasy by a level of kindness he can't really bring himself to believe is safe, and swayed by his own history and its exigencies, he pilfers all of the bishop's silver (my memory is of his stashing it all in pillowcases … but I'm not sure). He runs off in the night. Discovering this upon waking, the bishop waits and prays.

Predictably, Valjean is apprehended by the *gendarmes*. They drag him back to the bishop's home to confirm that Valjean has indeed stolen the silver. The breaking of the public law sits alongside a breaking of a personal fledgling trust. With Valjean having betrayed the bishop's kindness as well as the law's letter, he has doomed himself to an immediate return to incarceration, now with an even more punishable crime hanging over him.

We shudder. Verily, we shudder at what awaits him.

Hugo *stages* this philosophical scenario. He puts all the elements into the mix, offering us an ethical theme park in which we, for ourselves, might grapple with the problem. At this point in the tale, a reader could respond in various ways to the tension raised by the dramatic tangle, by the sad, devastating incident that's just unfolded.

Like a program. It happens like a program that 'could not have happened another way'.

We understand why. We understand why Valjean would steal the silver. This remains *within the logics of the program*. This is how the program, how the systemic concatenations work. All is as normal, as it should be. Valjean isn't doing anything interesting here. His 'criminality' (at this moment) sits harmoniously within the order of things. Like most 'transgressions', the system has no problem with it. The system *loves* our transgressions, mostly.

There is a difficult passage in Deleuze's early work, *The Logic of Sense* (1969). It's slightly impenetrable, so let's start with the gist. Deleuze is talking about Good Sense. The average person assumes good sense is, well ... *good*. Deleuze has specific reservations, as he might. He says good sense isn't always appropriate to philosophical thought; it's not always useful when inventing concepts, let's say. Good sense is bound up with the risk of being too colonised by dogma, with stuck ways of thinking. When we go along with (what passes for) 'good' sense unquestioningly within our status quo, we can also just travel well-worn ruts (in thinking, feeling and deciding). *So* ... we don't throw it out wholesale, but we do appreciate what it offers specifically and where it isn't always suited. But it gets more interesting.

Good sense is grounded on something else: the *paradox*. Cool. However, Deleuze points out that good sense – despite its name – is *less* about determining *which* sense you go in (I'm simplifying horrendously here ...), but it's more the principle that tells you *that you will* choose from *between two directions*. WOW! At its basis, the message of good sense is: there are two ways, and you will (bossy voice: *you will*) end up choosing between what's on offer. (Remember, *sens* in French means both meaning and direction.) It's like when the maps app gives you two trip options but (oddly) both of them include tolls. *Hmmmm*. Let's read the excerpt.

> Good sense is not content with determining the particular direction of the unique sense. It first determines the principle of a unique sense or direction in general, ready to show that this principle, once given, forces us to choose one direction over the other. [...] The opposite of good sense is not the other direction (*sens*), for this direction is only a recreation for the mind, its amusing initiative. (p. 88)

Thinking we have a genuine choice, when actually what's on offer is the constraint, is a 'recreation for the mind', a way to while away our time. The 'opposite' of good sense is *not the other direction*. It's not flipping into an opposite. So much for transgression. It's spotting that you've been cornered into choosing-between. We can't be content with swapping between ostensible *opposites*. This changes nothing. Working hard for the Man or slacking off in a heroin share house. Same same! It's all within the same double direction which is practically one direction. It ends up the same. Jean Valjean steals the silver. Transgression? *Yeah-nah*. He just does it, and it changes nothing for the system. It isn't even an Up Yours to the system (it might be a pragmatic win, if he got away with it; in Hugo's tale he doesn't).

He seems to be stuck in the bind that good sense has provided for him in his socio-historical moment. He apparently has two choices – steal or suffer – but these are both somehow within the same reality. He's in the bind of the vulnerable. None of us could expect to 'do' better, frankly.

We are trucking along *within* the dominant order very nicely. In the story, the character who we can align with earthly 'justice', with the order of things, is the police officer, Javert, who is committed to maintaining law to its letter. He will not waver, cannot bear to. His system is so brittle, it cannot stand a variation of any kind. He's adamantly in the good sense camp. His passion for hunting Jean Valjean will form a backbone for the narrative's unfolding.

We've jumped quite far. We were having little daydreams about making life nicer, not getting caught up in harshness as a remedy. The idea of kindness. I was saying there could be something like a rigorous, reality-warping kindness, and you were waiting for me to deliver on that. Well ...

At this point in the story, we're at the door of the bishop's home, the police have a helpless Valjean, for whom the rest of life seems now fully determined. He may well be hung for this, or at least indefinitely incarcerated. His tiny moment of freedom, which was crap 'freedom' anyway – freedom with a yellow card that doomed him to ostracism, to being shunned and seemingly blocking any kind of new start – has been cut off forever. The system offered a lousy 'release'; it did not take care of Valjean ... (We could leap forward several centuries to First Nations young men sentenced to Australian prisons, but that is another discussion, and excellent scholars, activists, community folk and elders work tirelessly there.)

The series of events is, at this point, *as if determined*. It seems an already-given future just needs to spool itself out from a predictable present. Nothing to see here. Nothing out of the ordinary. Misery begetting misery, even by its own hand, assisted by the hand (and the hand's training in harshness).

Then the police say to Bishop Myriel: 'This man claims that you gave him this silver.'

Myriel's social programming should have him inform them of the theft. If we adhere to a version of private property, social division and normal temporality, this would be an accurate statement. However, Myriel operates on another register. He had said everything that's mine is yours, and so he simply replies in conformity with that reality. He confirms that Valjean was *given the silver*. (I'm such a sook; I'm even crying as I write this out.)

What kind of kindness is this, people? It's hardly weak, soppy kindness. And yes, Myriel can do this from a privileged position.

He can afford to lose the Conspicuous Consumption items called Household Silver. Cutlery. Dishes. Vessels. Trays. He has nothing to lose, but still! He could have done what the world prepared him to do.

Tell a *minor* truth and condemn a man to death or to a life worse than death.

Was it a lie? Well, perhaps not even. If Myriel in his heart, upon discovering the missing silver, after having met the man who took it, let go of the object, of his ownership of this particular fiction of private property, per se, source of umpteen evils of this world, then he told the truth. In his heart, if he had already given it away, wished Valjean well with it, then *he wasn't even lying*.

That he is a man of the cloth is not irrelevant. Jesus, after all, advocated poverty. Now, this has slipped the Christian (Catholic) church's mind for much of its history, but Jesus was no capitalist. Someone who practises their faith *better* – Myriel? – might indeed have the nimbleness to move fast, to see through a scenario with a kind of lightning perspicacity, one that allows a swift and magnanimous response ... to effectively SAVE A PERSON'S LIFE. Shouty font. Sorry. I'm just so damn moved by this example. I'm moved *still*, decades later, in an entirely different moment in my own life. Still moved by this plot twist. Sure, it's been copied, structurally replicated, bastardised, and now we probably collapse it with the schmaltzy stuff of the worst of Hollywood. *Still. Nevertheless.*

An imperceptible hairline fracture appears in the fabric of the reality as those characters live it, and Myriel, a devout man – someone perhaps trying to follow less the letter than the *spirit* of a kind life – he wedges an action, not an identity, not some cheap chit-chat, but a statement *that has consequences*, into that fracture and he changes the world. The world of the novel. Definitely the world of Jean Valjean, who himself will change other people's lives (Fantine's, Cosette's).

Do I misremember? I think the Bishop also says that it's great that Valjean came back since he forgot to take the candlesticks!! And Valjean is given the candlesticks, worth several hundred francs.

Valjean, after that, tries to live in tune with this note struck by Myriel. Towards the novel's end, when faced with a defenceless and captured Javert, he decides *not* to execute him – the man who has made his life a living hell of flight and fear. Valjean lets him go, and the latter, so disturbed by this kindness, this example of an unflinching personal ethic, of remaining true to the promise he made Myriel – rigorous kindness of the most hardcore kind – in response to this, Javert drowns himself in the Seine. He does not indeed have the capacity to rearrange his world to accommodate this most unthinkable of mercies, from a man he had decided was *only* and *essentially* criminal.

He cannot understand what tilted the logics of his worldview in such a vastly unexpected direction. He is unable to alter himself to welcome the invitation of this new reality, and thus instead he opts to erase himself from that very reality. Spinoza would have plenty to say about this, but we press on.

Rigorous kindness, you see, might not leave the world, as we know it, intact. It replaces our assumed misery with a vista that's unrecognisable. It may not leave our brokenness broken in the ways we were certain were inevitable.

How do you cultivate the strength to carry through on these fracturing kindnesses when their possibility appears? If I borrow from Badiou, I'd call their appearance-disappearance 'events'. He says after an event, what lies ahead is our 'fidelity' … a commitment to something that you create as a stepping stone just before you place your foot on it. Sound like love? Yes, it's that, and other forms of the unimaginable that lend life a texture which the loudest version of our current order simply doesn't have frames to accommodate.

(I fell in love with a person I made love to in a stairwell at the end of that trip. It was just after I told someone else, the previous evening, that they should follow their 'good sense' and resist the madness of infatuation, since it seemed hardly practical. The kindness of destiny turned around and whacked me on the head with my first blazing, impossible love, that couldn't be lived out, but which was ... in fact, as experience, a kind of *kindness*. The kindness of being welcomed into the ranks of human creatures, who are rarely practical, often unreasonable and very regularly kind with enormous, unruly hearts, which can forget obedience to any known direction, to any 'good' sense.)

On the basis of what principles would a training operate that would allow us not to squander our encounter with events (like love, like politics), if and when this appears-disappears in our usual worlds? Yoga, for me, has had something to offer. And you'll have your own version of 'yoga' that accompanies you, when the unkind normality gets too rugged. It's the thing that helps stop the slide towards compliance that is good for no one. I take this up in the following chapter.

The Middle: framing vastness
ordinary magic and being an organism

In the philosopher Gillian Rose's famous book *Love's Work* (1995), we read in the first chapter about her 'Intelligent Angel'. This is Edna, 93 years old, who believes in an overlooked magic. According to Rose, this magic is not one of tricks, elves or fairies, not spells of life-hacking, not strategic combinations of futuristic cunning, not first-world 'manifesting' ... Edna's intelligent magic was rather 'the quiet and undramatic transmutation that can come out of plainness, ordinary hurt, mundane maladies and disappointments'. (p. 9)

Rose's comment emphasises how plainness, as idea, has something to do with the dignity of the ordinary. I want to give these words upper-case importance: Dignity of the Ordinary.

Rose points her reader towards a hunch about life; it could be deemed a kind of wisdom. It distinguishes itself from another widespread and deceptively benign-seeming tendency, which often threatens to engulf steady seeing and ruin a life with *unplain* thinking. This tendency consists in only wishing for, only tolerating (or else a tantrum) the full, the positive, the present, the cheerful, the realised, the exceptional, the flawless &c. This list could continue, and you'd know how to extend it.

This tendency stems from a worldview that's 'in' the drinking water, but which also emerges from something inherent in thinking itself. In its grasp, solutions to things lie in whole, purified, totalised, complete and unmarred modes. We imagine that everything could be 'just so'. When we respond like this, too, we place a lot of faith in the *finality of solutions,* as being full of promise, as able to wrap things up, as the point after which there will be a particular kind of (existential, psychological, bodily, emotional, sexual, spiritual ...) relief.

This tendency – widespread, usual, understandable, ever-promising – is *not* the magic of Rose's intelligent angel, the nonagenarian Edna.

Rose's hunch – about what kind of magic is worthy of our trust – arrives from a different place, one drenched in perspicuity, mishap and spattered with the usual stains that come with living. Something kinder and more inclusive, it has a nagging suspicion about this other shiny tack, which trucks in fantasies of wholeness, completeness, presence, &c., which are common-enough notions to reach for, especially when we are trying to evade suffering or when we're in its grinding mechanisms. Rose guesses, as I'd also guess, that this other kind of thinking, sadly, leads to a slow poisoning, despite its encouraging label.

Sometimes it delivers a quick rush, but then there's a wan slide and stall. For all its slickness, all its neat and accomplished promise, any shiny magic almost inevitably swerves towards or collects much misery on its way; it validates and cultivates *extremes*. Extremes 'read' well – maybe – but they can 'live' badly. This stance on how life should be often doesn't deliver. It doesn't live up to what is written on the packaging.

I've just acquired one of those easy-to-use blenders. You flip it one way, fill it with stuff, and then, once blended, flip the other way, turning it into a drink bottle. I tend to use the kitchen appliances I buy, so I'm not concerned that this will be an impulse moment leaving me with an obsolete item. I noticed on the box that there were marketing words like 'fast', 'easy', 'efficient', 'compact'. Those kinds of words. Describing a machine like this is fine, of course. It's a good machine and will probably last a while. I wonder somehow about how much we, as humans, nurture expectations of being machine-like. Or I wonder what the lure of the *tidiness* of these words does when it meets our messier (thank goodness) and more-nuanced (hooray) manners of navigating a unique life.

At the start of this same book by Rose, there's an arresting epigraph. From Staretz Silouan, it reads: 'Keep your mind in hell, and despair not.' Naturally, this aphorism plays on a counter-intuitive logic that we don't at first see coming. Keep your mind in hell *and* don't therefore despair ... Very interesting. While there is slightly more flourish to this aphorism than I'd personally go for, I am definitely on side. It reminds me of a phrase that turns up (in my own mouth) when I'm teaching yoga. Trying to imply lightly an attitudinal caution in the practising methodology, relevant to the advanced aspects of yoga, I find myself jesting to my students: *Stay negative!* I count on them appreciating my humour, having worked with my teaching for so long. *Stay negative*! The combination of explicit content and twinkly delivery signals the open secret, which (like Silouan's sensibility) knows that there is something necessarily oxymoronic – something that requires a holding of opposites – involved in a life that, at the end of the day, you can mostly stand by.

A life in which others can mostly stand *you*.

The wise know to stay negative, to stay in hell, in the unsure spaces, and not to 'know' too much. Despair, you see, is a presumptuous 'knowing' or certainty about the future. It suffers from confidence that its grim picture is flawless and complete. From this, it settles into to something dire, but seemingly *justified*. Despair lacks the cracks of doubt, of not-being-sure. Despair prefers solid (horrid) certainty over the accidents of grace, and things not turning out as badly *as you'd hoped* ... If you aren't so arrogant as to assume you know, then despair ceases to be so accessible, so plausible. Pessimism, as I said once in an interview, is very imprecise.[1]

∝

RILKE ONCE WROTE TO HIS YOUNG POET CORRESpondent something like: the question isn't whether you should be a poet ... it's more along the lines of *Only be a poet if you absolutely cannot avoid becoming a poet.* He said the world definitely didn't need more of them (poets!), and I read this to mean only select this path if you can't become an accountant, a swim instructor, an elite bartender. It's almost the same with my trajectory towards yoga teaching. (Seeing it written *still* gives me the heebie-jeebies ...) I absolutely did not want to become one. But the world kept placing yoga teaching in my path, repetitively. Out of concern for legality, insurance and general competency, I began a series of trainings, to give shape to a vocation that seemed to be pressing itself upon me.

(If I tell you a little bit now about how I ended up doing something unavoidable, you can ponder your own version of this. The thing (*things*) you almost didn't want to do/become but which hounded you, and turned out to be exactly the thing(s). We are also rarely *one* thing. Usually we live with several 'hats'. Yes, usually.)

Experimental Frames

There are a lot of ways to talk about what yoga is. If you're not a self-identifying yogi, when you encounter this kind of talk, you may find it landing badly, getting on your nerves. For me, at least, and for years, it landed quite badly and got on my nerves. While the person talked, sometimes with a calmness of voice or demeanour that I simply *did not buy*, I had visions of bad scarf-wear, sickly incense and good dollops of cultural appropriation.

This was a while back. And now, when someone who isn't a yogi encounters the contemporary, commercialised yoga thing, they may well meet contouring active wear (releasing microplastics every wash), quick-dry caps with secret society branding, slick ponytails, running jackets, elaborate nails, and ergonomic cross-body bags. I wouldn't know. I stay in my house a lot, doing stuff that may not look anything like this.

What seemed to be yoga – way back then – when it was presented by an Anglo-person from Moonee Ponds, or Byron Bay, or Paddington, or Culcairn, struck me as unbearably irritating. I was on high alert for Lashings of Pseudo. For Over-Earnestness. For Virtue-Signalling. I was impatient with what seemed to be extraneous accessories, saccharine affectation, and a Performance of Goodness that boded badly.

As it turns out, I've just finished practising and, indeed, I did spend some time wrapped in – well, not quite a scarf per se – but yes, a big bit of light fabric (pale pink, stretchy) that I bought in Munich years ago. I'd traipsed on foot through the hot July streets to find a fabric store and had given myself foot blisters as a result. Big, white, round blisters on the soles of my feet, not even on my heels! I was headed further south the next day, for yoga training, and I'd forgotten to pack a practice blanket. I did find the store, and I did buy the big length of soft fabric. In the quieter bits of yoga, it's nice to have your skin wrapped up, to have something around you. Like a little, soft room, that you wear. It's like being given a departure hug as you embark on something whose destination is suitably indeterminate and always a little risky.

Like love. Like parenthood. Like art. Like death. Like waiting. Like apologising.

The people whom I encountered, who were performing this version of yoga-ness, were probably just beginners and probably not as annoying as I perceived. (I would also have been annoying, playing my part of eye-rolling cynic.) They were trying on the trappings, I suspect, which could work as talismans for an important experience or a genuine encounter they'd *had* and were still digesting. Perhaps they'd crossed paths with long-term practitioners in India, China, England, Spain or elsewhere, and they couldn't yet distil (into a more personal expression) what they'd felt there, so they reached for the material things that surrounded that less tangible event. My guess is, that what they may have encountered, without words to name it, was a kind of plainness. A plainness like water – which tastes of *less* and tastes *better* for that. Thus, they could only bring back – as interim talismans – accessories seeming to pulse with those unfathomable moments. Scarves. Incense. Performed and self-conscious calmness. After all, sometimes we can only fake it for a while before we make it.

(In front of me, beyond the window where I'm typing right now: a pool of fallen, mauve Jacaranda petals, across a lawn. Not quite a circle, but a rounded carpet. Pale purple against a timid green. Kangaroos jump through here on dawn, and then dusk. Two parents and two joeys.)

I think most people find yoga *and stick with* yoga if their suffering (or their fear of something yoga seems to counter) is very great. Yoga is an expert on the mechanisms of suffering. It is with suffering very precisely that yoga concerns itself. You may not see this in the fancy signage in the main street of your regional town. In the self-satisfied bounce of the proselytising newbie. Still, I promise you it's true. Serious yoga has eyeballed suffering and is learning not to flinch, while also deciding, working, experimenting with how not to succumb to life being wholly determined by its mechanisms. Or ... people do yoga because they are mystics, or becoming a mystic is their vocation.

Many years on, I no longer shirk the moniker 'yoga practitioner', since that would be disingenuous and inaccurate. The fact is, I spend many hours doing yoga (and others spend many hours doing dressage, doing breakdancing, doing gardening). I find myself wanting to attempt something difficult, something ill-advised, something gauche. I want to attempt to tell you, from my own window of experience (limited, finite), about what this thing *is*. For me, now (and I barely understand it ...).

I feel like a small child, holding out two eager handfuls of debris: pasta shells, a smooth stick, cicada wings, tiny stones, a cracked leaf, a bright, bruised flower ... wanting to give you – the reader – *everything I have* which concerns this topic. I want to hand it all over to you, to condense decades of engagement into just the right words, so that you can be alongside this experience. Such an ungainly want; I note its impossibility, unviability, and prepare myself for something far more ordinary than that. Ordinary but perhaps worthwhile.

I could pretend, too, that yoga – or more precisely, *practising* (of many possible practices, so insert your own) – has nothing to do with a plain life. I could refrain from making that link. Given, however, that I can only tell you what *I* know about the plainness, I cannot – in good faith – cordon this knowing off from years of practising – for me, yoga (including sitting) and, of course *writing*. Somehow in among the practising, the importance of plainness has shone out. A plain life doesn't equal yoga (or sitting, or other similar kinds of engagements) in any straightforward way; but if I talk about yoga, I might be able to circle around what plainness is, and why the ordinary is more interesting, and even urgent, than it seems.

∝

YOGA IS A HARD THING TO TALK ABOUT *WELL* – perhaps a good reason to remain silent on the topic. Often the advice given from the inner circles of practising is that it's best *not* to speak about practice. Talking about the showing up, the repetitions, the mistakes and the bafflement, the humble insights, the reversal of insights ... it can be a tricky content to work into verbal exchange. Tedious for others? Charmless, perhaps? At worst, a little bit self-congratulatory. Mystical posturing, a posturing of diligence, or it sounds *flaky*.

We can speak about yoga as both a tradition and as a kind of live, ongoing *experimenting*. People – regular, non-yogic people, *you*, for example – are making experiments everywhere, all the time. *Aren't you?* Artists are. They are the quintessential experiment-makers. But also, lovers. Also, parents. Also, children (– they never stop experimenting until circumstance thwacks it out of them). Also, our comrades in the sciences. Also, athletes. Also, permaculture experts. Also, the guy who controls the big crane at the construction site.

All of us are experimenting, right? Almost every day. Almost all the time, whether we dignify what we are up to as an experiment, or whether we don't. This tiny difference makes an enormous difference. Do we dignify these ventures and efforts, these attempts and noticings, as intentional undertakings with an unknown outcome to which we apply every intelligence we have available? Our body experiments with more sleep, less sleep, more caffeine, less caffeine, more talk, less talk, heaps of sex, less sex, being alone, being with others. These regular experiments go on and on.

This would be why the 'elderly', to use that term, are likely to be so interesting. In them, a dense collection, an archive, of happened and happening, experiments!

Sometimes when I'm with a group of people, I think about this experiment angle and I'm overwhelmed by contemplating the depth, the cumulative layers of time, the hundreds of thousands of hours of informed and meandering, courageous and ill-conceived, personal and collective experimentation – standing around with me in the shape of very regular folk at the shops, on the bus, at the demo. I try to take in the idea of all the discoveries generated from that, the atmosphere of it all – thick, intricate – swarming closely. We're there together in a fine cloud of invisible, tacit intelligence. Sparkle-arkle.

In those moments, I can also get a bit sad. I get sad about how the ways we can be with each other (culturally, habitually, defensively) would seem to specifically preclude, to make less likely, that I'll hear about this knowledge from anyone. While I'm at a pub, or an event, or on a plane, I regret that it will only be by rare fluke that this person and I will find a way to communicate any glimpses of what we've each discovered through all the experiments of our lifetime thus far. The third meal pack will arrive, and the hostess will ask us if we'd like coffee with that. Or we'll probably say our jobs (if we have one), whether we have siblings, or we'll repeat something we've read on the internet lately. The experiment-gems tend to get put through the sausage-mincer of opinion.

We'll set going our default talk-program about some news event or global scenario. This is also fine. This, too – this bit of disappointing – is life as we live it. And all the while, the library of understanding is there – in the queue at the bakery, or patiently waiting near the swings, simmering below the surface of the postie, of the person who sells me tahini; it's there as someone pores over the sponge choices in the cleaning aisle. It bowls me over.

Take parents. They have devised trillions of clever work-arounds, ways to see and notice, nuances of affection, care, methods of working with time and physical capacity, relations to fatigue, to joy and to money. (My words are going to fail here ...) Yes, parents. They have been doing intensive, often-urgent research. They have been making experiments in real-time and finding things out.

My point is that, in a life viewed from a certain vantage point, a lot of experimentation goes on. Yoga would be a mode of experimenting, which comes with a guidebook (called the *Yoga Sutras*, as well as thousands of other associated texts and commentaries) and then all the unwritten stuff, the embodied knowledge, you might call it.

Yoga comes along in the shape of a practical teaching (accessible or less accessible, reliable or less) – what might nowadays get called a Learning-by-Doing approach.

How? How does it come along? Well: you take your body. You take it and get it onto a bit of floor space, and helped by some minimal equipment, you begin mucking around. Or you head to a class and – assisted by (hopefully a sincere and well-trained and practising yogic teacher) – you follow some verbal, visual and tactile instructions, so that you have a thread to follow with your own experiments at home, at other times.

This is one way to talk about yoga – as a big set of experiments that you do with whatever makes up your human organism – bone, skin, fat, organs, nerve-networks, brain matter, breathing apparatus, muscle, fascia, blood, lymph &c. (And I'm not insinuating that other creatures don't also do this; I simply can't talk about it for them.)

There is, however, a further way to say what yoga is, which I learned from my yoga teacher, Orit Sen-Gupta. It's one of my favourite ways to say it. This is how I remember it:

> Yoga is a practice of staying in the middle. In yoga, one tries never to compromise the middle for any thing, for anyone, or for any pose.

I can't recall when I first heard her say this. I had done a lot of yoga classes, even yoga retreats, and I'd heard many things about what yoga was. I had never heard it put this way.

Yoga. The middle. Trying not to compromise it.

Now, this might sound like a rule, and many people are allergic to rules. So, we can say it another way. I can turn it around and make it a recipe for an experiment.

Let's find out what the middle is, and then we can apply these three instances in the above maxim, to see what emerges.

What is the Middle?

The mistake would be to think that the middle was some *thing*.

Perhaps this is why I resist the term 'centre'. Being *centred*. I might resist it also because it's become a cool thing to say, and when things become cool things to say, it's easy to feel disdainful about saying them. For this notion we're considering – the middle – we could say that we want a term that specifies a region, without specifying a substance. I'm not sure which word is best – centre, middle – it doesn't matter really.

The middle, the centre – these need to be regions and not *somethings*. To stay in the middle might mean to 'locate yourself in a certain way' but it simultaneously intimates that one relates to a discrete perspective in a different, unnatural way. The middle might be both at the very heart of you, and also where your 'you-ness' pauses for a bit. The middle as a space where individualised perspective is both strong, and also evaporates.

Delicate? *Yes*. If we said before that *in general* being-an-Organism means that you have a unique perspective, then the middle challenges this in a paradoxical way. In the middle, hypothetically, one might no longer be shackled to a single perspective. One takes a tiny holiday from a fixed perspective which is usually a given for an organism. One departs from one's state as organism, strangely by coinciding as closely as possible *with it*. As middle. Weirdly, one is very stable in this centre of no-perspective. Because the small-you, which reacts, fears for its petty (or less petty) interests, isn't behind the wheel.

'To stay in the middle', here, works as a kind of poetry. It is an incantation for a happening that might be difficult to say without sounding trippy, but which is very precise in its experiential nature. A body that orients itself in relation to its own middle, will be a body that can move in particular ways (see above). The wager is that this body will have access, like a key in a lock, to its own capacity. It will be able to have the capacity that is its own. At the same time, due to what I'm also hinting about the middle, this body's capacity will somehow not be calculable, not in any usual quantitative terms. It will not relate to its limits as it usually would.

The body will 'have its own capacity', but under these counter-intuitive conditions of middle*ness*, the meaning of 'own', the implication of it, can be recast radically. When you are in the middle, due to the latter's nature, you are ... well ... simultaneously *everywhere*. In other words, it becomes *im*possible to say anymore with any accuracy, what exactly *wouldn't be* possible.

(Put simply: you simply don't quite know what you *won't be able to do* when you embark on yoga. The whole organism, as you've lived it, won't remain the same. It's not that it will become some cliché of a tanned, slight thing in orderly monochrome, with a beige drink bottle. *Nope*. It's that you won't recognise the feeling of being inside yourself, and the old images you have of yourself become quickly obsolete. They *un*mean ... peel away from their typical meaning, these images. Or the self is *uncertained*. Who you are? Well, nobody knows.)

The open secret of the middle, which I find breathtaking, is that the middle is the site in us where our original nothingness is located. The middle is a space. It is a void, an emptiness. Call it a vastness, if that phrasing works for you. At your very core, you aren't you. You aren't anything, and you *aren't not-everything*. You are founded on nothingness and (if I don my bossy yoga teacher personality) this is a place you *need* to inhabit fairly regularly. I'm not one to use the 'need' word carelessly (I'm strict with this word), so I say it again:

You *need* to inhabit the nothing that is part of you fairly regularly.

And thus, you'd seek the middle by going looking, against every typical logic, for *nothing*. As the name suggests, this nothingness can be located – yes, *physically* located – somewhere along the body's midline. A region of probability. Every bodily structure is unique with its own idiosyncrasies and, thus, this middle can't be located using a formula. My middle won't correspond necessarily to your middle. (Just as my method – yoga – for experimenting with this middle, might differ from your practice of, say, climbing, sewing or bonsai ...)

Often one is instructed to look for this middle, as a supple line, a length which lies along the dark front face of the spinal column. It might be the darkest place in the body. You can't find it in a mirror. The mirror doesn't even hint at it. It's protected, held close against the spine, behind a wall of skin, fat, muscle, organs and more, and it's protected from the back by the relative hardness of the vertebrae.

Looking for nothingness, for Nothing, sounds obscure. Yes. But yoga is those sets of practices which can point you in a general direction, give you a fond shove in the back, and say: *Off you go. Good luck out (in) there.*

I remember being in an online yoga seminar with someone who was a Traditional Chinese Medicine person. They'd recalled a theory in TCM that the heart function, what gets called 'the heart' in that system, is seen by some theorists to corresponded to sheer emptiness. The heart wasn't a *thing*. It wasn't the muscular structure that contracts and expands. TCM has another function – the pericardium, the heart-protector – which might, I wondered, be analogous to the western heart muscle. I speculated to myself that the pericardium, then, might be the vessel *with* substance in this cosmology, whereas the heart itself was what was *without* substance – that which this fleshy vessel protected, the former constituting a space, a clearing. Sheer potential, and how we must leave that blank, otherwise nothing can move, get in, arrive, or surprise us. The heart was what this very system existed to protect. The heart was space not substance. Middle ... nothingness, not-You, and also the You-est bit of you.

We protect the heart. We preserve the middle. We don't compromise it; we don't abandon the nothingness that must be included.

That there would be an organ function in this system of medicine whose sole job is to protect space – to check that one isn't filling up the emptiness – feels astonishing and completely logical all at once. Don't fill up all the spaces! Don't think fullness is always excellent. Stay negative! That is: protect what *isn't* there. That which isn't any kind of *there-ness*.

Protect your Not-Having. Your Not-Doing. Your Not-Knowing. Everything in the worldly-world is baffled by this. And faced with it, the world (your internalised outer-worlds) can threaten you with everything from accusations of laziness to being-unproductive, from becoming irrelevant to being a kook. The world can imply that if you leave space for the empty centre, you might be becoming unhinged. Hmmm. There's no need to give airtime to this kind of standover tactic.

A system that only values that which shows up, that which is present(able), ends up in its own cul-de-sac. A person, trained to devote themselves only to substance within such a system, ends up … unwell, or unhappy, unlikeable, or … unable to survive, along with the culture that champions this filling at all costs.

The middle, then, starts to have a few different poetries at its disposal. *Stay centred. Follow your heart.* Eek. Being a words-person, I struggle with these phrasings. I strain against their apparent populism, their sloppiness, and yet, I suspect that they – like all truisms – are shorthand efforts to indicate something hidden in plain sight.

Hidden out in the open doesn't mean easy to access. It doesn't mean readily available, although it does imply not needing to venture very far. With the middle, as you'd suspect, it is indeed right there. But people travel to distant locations; they attend remote retreats; they curate their time to allow some window for practising. Sometimes you've got to go far to get close.

Staying in the middle. Inhabiting the middle *a bit*. Looking for the invisible vastness. Or listening in for the big silence. All of this has something to do with yoga (or your version thereof), and what it's about.

Working Intentionally with Middle:
The three instances

Recall the maxim I heard from my teacher: *Yoga is interested in the middle. In yoga, one tries never to compromise the middle for any thing, for anyone, or for any pose.*

Yoga is interested in the middle – what is it? where is it? And then, in addition to this curiosity, it further proposes that as you go searching for this middle, you play around with staying there (trying to) and also departing from this middle. You find out the flavour of these modes. You see what happens to your body, brain, ideas, mood, and so on, when you stay closer to 'middle' or move further from it. You have experiences and notice how they affect your middle, or your middleness. You start to learn about kinds of circumstances that are middle-wobblers, and other situations that cultivate this middle, and make it easier to orbit in its vicinity. You might even notice that around some people, it can be easier to stay in your middle, and that other people pose a big challenge to any middleness, *gell*? You could theorise why this is, or simply notice it, and make a decision about it – or not.

That's the first part of the middle-experiment recipe. (My German friend, C. from Chapter 2, might wire me a few thumbs up emojis. Experimenting with the middle, incidentally, is not unrelated to tracking one's slides in capacity …)

The second part is also interesting. The second part names the ways in which the middle might get compromised. Three aspects of possible wandering-off. We can leave our middles because of …

Things.
People.
Poses.

Things – this is pretty general and not so mysterious. You experiment with (not) compromising your middle for stuff. Your middle is precious. It's something you might want to care for, cherish, make Pretty Important (if you're a yogi, but also if you'd like to stay averagely sane). Things, any kind of things, can throw you off it. And being thrown off it can also be interesting, might be what currently floats your boat.

Here's an example of the middle as lens. When I went on overseas yoga retreat, I tended to take one really massive suitcase. I had a monstrous white number, which held a whole 30 kilos. It contained enough clothing for me to sweat three times per day and not have to do much hand-washing. (I don't prefer the hand-squeezed out clothes ...) Now, mostly I could manage this object alone. And sometimes I could not. Sometimes the station escalators were out-of-order. Sometimes the train only had overhead luggage racks. And then I was stumped, unless a pleasant, more largely-built human turned up and offered to ship it up to the platform, or throw it onto the racks, on my behalf.

My teacher would always tease me for having this large suitcase. That was fine. The teasing felt affectionate, and I had no intention of adjusting my packing philosophy due to teasing. However, at some point she said: 'Antonia, you're a yogi. You need to protect your shoulders, and this bag puts your shoulders at risk.'

Is this a good example? I'm not sure. You probably have some better ones from your own life. I'm just trying to say that this was a thing, and I was kind of compromising my middle unwisely (or unwisely in the long term, if not exactly then) for this thing. If I muddled my shoulders, then it would probably just cost me money at the Shoulder-Fixers. Or I could experiment with being in pain. Could be interesting? Or tedious. Yeah, but nah. This wasn't middleness.

(I now have two bags, which add up to 30 kilos. My shoulders thank me, and I thank my teacher for the advice. If I move the bags separately, it is wise-enough. Wise-enough isn't the worst thing to aim for, right?)

Other examples? Your 'middle' might be your primary relationship (better said: the Love of your Life) and you're compromising it for a notion you can't relinquish about status, or your career, or gaining your (dead) parent's approval.

Your middle might be your creative practice. And you're compromising it because you think you can scroll the alluring/sapping social medias everyday endlessly without something going pear-shaped. You are compromising something that has definite quality for something whose quality and crucialness are debatable or not reliable. Or you might draw your creative energy from the socials ... It just depends, and it depends for you.

Your middle (last one!) might be the food that you've worked out is good for you. Your own special combo for now. For this year, for this passage of your life. And you're compromising it slightly too much because you don't want to 'put people out' or rock the boat of convention. So, you keep eating it, and you keep making yourself privately sick. No one cares, since they're not there for that. And actually no one would muchly care, if you didn't have a parma at the pub.

This is a question of how you want to relate to that which appears, after some experimenting, to reduce your capacity. In this example, this food isn't for you and repeatedly makes you have less oompf.

Okay, so there are some sketchy, clumsy examples you might consider when querying how you leave your own middle, abandoning it, for things, and how that reverberates into your life. We might say that abandoning the middle for things is fairly widespread. It is even culturally encouraged, in the dominant culture I see around me. It's how not to be a Party Pooper, how to be upwardly-mobile, how to Enjoy Capitalism™, how to not rain on the current paradigm's parade. Compromising your middle for things is good for (other people's) business. And that experiment might (or might not) be an interesting one for many of us, and for a good long while. (I want to emphasise that this maxim isn't necessarily anti-things. It's anti-compromising your middle for things. That's different. Maybe the trick is learning to discern the things that un-middle you and those that don't.)

What about the second aspect of my teacher's example – people? Not compromising the middle for anyone.

I'm not sure I'm daring or skilful enough to go here. I'm not entirely sure whether our relations are anything other than movements away and towards our middles. Seen from one angle, our relations are this overall movement, somehow. If we never left our middles for anyone, we would not have so many relations. I guess, I could reframe it slightly – using the experiment mode – by saying that yoga notices the way other people affect our connection to our middles. It takes this seriously, and it provides a way to think about and even to track intelligently how this kind of compromising goes.

Sometimes it tastes nice, and sometimes it gives you reflux.

Falling in love might seem to be a total abandoning of one's middle. Sure. Maybe. If I follow French philosopher Alain Badiou, on this point (which I do), one's life is liable to transform, to become unrecognisable, when one falls genuinely in love. The amorous event opens the old life to a new trajectory. One world meets another world (a person is a whole world, right?). The procedure that true love is involves embarking on something unknown (for both parties), taking off in a direction that only appears-disappears in that moment, and is painstakingly invented and invented repeatedly at each fresh encounter. It is invented by the Two, who stumble forwards into uncharted territories. The couple create something that is genuinely new. That's why it's good and difficult (see Chapter 3), involving, for Badiou, a flavour of 'terror' (meaning: genuine trepidation, profound unsettledness at times). Your life is going to become unrecognisable, but that doesn't mean less 'itself' ...

The way love upends our humdrum apple carts could look like leaving-middle, if we are trying to follow the advice above. Yes, but it might depend on whether one was in one's middle before the love showed up. The lurch, which the love precipitated, might be a lurch back towards a middle, a new middle, that needs fidelity and courage, which needs some big, strange feelings, since these will grow important roots for this new middle to grab hold of.

Maybe, however, it's more helpful to think about this question – about the middle and how people affect our middle – in the sense of stretching *too far* in our relations with others. Or, put otherwise: to hold open questions such as: *do our relationships consider us?* Not always, not every second – that's unrealistic – but often and enough to not throw us off our middle frequently? This would ask whether we are included, in a dignified way, in the relations we give our time to.

Sometimes the answers is … 'not-so-much', or 'too-seldomly'. And this is where the concept of the Yogic Middle provides a litmus test.

The thing is, when you turn the 'rule'-based version of the idea of the Middle, into the experiment-version, everything becomes less a question of 'should' and more a question of 'what do I feel like?' 'What do I want?'

As I say to my yoga students (something I learned from my own teacher), in the practice pranayama (constraining the breath) we meet an amazing stripped back version of wanting/not wanting. With all flouncy anecdote removed. We tend to feel muddled about what we want – if we've complicated it inside ourselves to the point of the strands now being an almighty, matted knot. Think of the Lindor Ball example from earlier. Pranayama is a yogic technology that plays with the question (over and over) of whether one wants, or doesn't want, in that moment, and the next and the next, *to breathe.*

In breathing practice, one repeatedly asks one's organism – quietly, without words – *what do I want now?* Hold this breath longer, exhale it, let it out in little sips, bring it in on long, smooth ribbons, press it out heftily, in a steady beat? The options are pretty fabulous.

On the basis of this sketching with breath, we can then find our way towards wants that get slightly less murky, and which perhaps have more ornate content. (Do I want to continue to work at this organisation; do I commit to attending this event; do I raise a difficult matter with a friend? &c.) And this can involve middleness experiments concerning our interactions, the people with whom we spend our time.

Personally, I try to dignify all the things I do. Even the things that turn out to be less brilliant. I don't call them 'lessons' (that feels too infantile for me, but to each their taste). I just decide that I wanted that experience, that I did that thing, and that I can then do something else when I want to.

To give an example of this (which isn't autobiographical, by the way), I might *want* to leave my middle for fifteen years co-habiting romantically with a person who reliably makes me uneasy, to see what that *does*. If this is what I end up doing, then maybe I can at least *dignify* it. I can notice it, perceive it crisply without running myself down, and then make another move. There's a freshness to living, noticing, moving on. We don't need to be embarrassed (even if we spontaneously *are*) for following leads that didn't – for as long as we thought, in the way we imagined, or because at the time of embarking we just didn't know – work out.

In yoga which *isn't* a religion, which does not set up the idea of the gaze of a big Other (who decrees, approves, hands out rewards, or punishes), no one is watching.[2] It's just me, my plain life and what I feel like doing with it. There's no one to blame (on this count, in this specific respect), if I experiment and find out that I don't like it.

Fourteen years and three months.

Fourteen years and eleven months and five days. Whatever.

I can make that experiment. It's not a lesson (coming from

someone in the sky, or the 'universe') it's me, testing stuff with my intelligence, finding out some more info, trying a next move.

My teacher's advice about the middle, then, is simply that it frames yoga in a way that doesn't interpret it as wellness gymnastics, personal improvement, or a means towards more seamless productivity (*ugh, ugh, ugh!*). The middle, here, becomes a *pretty* interesting and not inaccurate framework to apply. It affords us dignity, but also a direction that isn't uptight, and which includes us.

But what about the final aspect – poses? *Yoga is about not compromising the middle for any ... pose.*

Whoah. Wild, right? For any yogis reading this, for any folk who head down to the local sweaty room with fluorescent lighting carrying a fraying, crumbling yoga mat, or for those who pull up in the e-vehicle, in full designer lycra, to then wander past the single white orchid at the reception desk towards the large timber-floored room ... not compromising the middle for any *pose*? This does feel a little renegade or out-of-touch.

For most people, hanging out on the apps, or googling for classes, or using some kind of universal pass (bringing the gig economy right into the heart of things – *blech!*): yoga *is* poses. Right?

Well, *no*.

Often, I sit around in nerdy, philosophy reading groups, and sometimes I dare to raise yoga to make a theoretical point, and sometimes someone in the group tells me, with the confidence of the non-participant, What Yoga Is. Contortion is often mentioned. Often fitness, or flexibility. Often mastery, discipline, &c.

How can I square up this instruction – about not compromising middle for any pose, coming from a very serious yoga teacher – with what people think they're doing at the fancy studio, or on the app, or assessed from the scholarly sidelines? I think it's a nicely surprising bit of the middle maxim. *Yoga is not compromising one's middle for any pose.*

What does it even mean?

The first take: no matter what practice you choose to do, practising itself finally will train you in not compromising yourself for the surface content of that practice, if those contents are not good for your middle. Climbing when hung over, or when you didn't do a thorough check of equipment. Obeying the apparent demand to do 'steps' on the sports watch, even though you know you have a strained Achilles and should rest. The practice *should* make you robust enough (lead you slowly over decades towards this), leave you clued-in enough that you slowly don't even let the gross demands of the practice itself throw you off. *Wild*, right?

As a yogi, I know it means activating the framework of the first yama of the *Yoga Sutras*. A yama is a restraint, a thing we abstain from, experimentally before we embark on further yoga activities, and always informing any activity that counts as 'yoga'. (Artists know these as creative constraints.) There are also five such constraints listed in the second chapter of Patanjali's *Yoga Sutras*. The first yama, which is considered the base for all other yamas, is *ahimsa*, 'non-wounding'. It is generally rendered as non-harming.

As I like to tell students on retreats, or when I discuss with my international colleagues, I doubt whether this yama has anything to do with being 'nice'. This would be misreading the vibe of the serious, early yogis. I don't think they were 'nice', as such. It's not a floaty, wafty, new-agey kind of instruction. It is strategic, mechanistic, procedural. It is linked to yoga's working or not working. I reckon they are saying – without any moralistic slant going on in the background – that yoga *won't* work, if you are mostly violent, bullying, a bit of an arsehole, and if you disregard the suffering of other living beings, including yourself (since these two can't be separated).

Ahimsa is a deal-breaker for yoga's being effective. This is a big provocation, I know. Go test it. See how it goes for you. You probably are testing it all the time – but start noticing the results of your own tests. *Don't harm yourself*: falling off rock faces, overdoing the tendon injury, ignoring your children and partner for some irrelevant sports goal ... if extremity was all we needed, life would be *easy*. It's not all we need, and living, thus, is an ever-artful, difficult thing.

Thus, the thing that makes yoga not Active Wear Gymnastics is that you try out the sequences, the poses (*asanas*), you muck around with movement, *without* harming yourself, *or* others. I mean, anyone could theoretically get into a difficult posture, if they were willing to tear some ligaments, get a disc bulge, and traumatise themselves. Or, as someone joked recently at a party: 'You can do anything *once*.' This would have nothing to do with yoga.

You consider yourself a practitioner in your field (think of your own middle practices, the things you can't avoid, as per Rilke's advice) if and only if you can *sustain this practice over the long term*.

Yoga, as I understand it, also wants you to make this more nuanced, sustainable experiment: to find ways that your organism can be comfortable and relaxed in unusual, but also ordinary, awkward or just complex, situations which we call poses (but you could also call them 'scenarios'). This is what the maxim is getting at. Yoga is about staying in the middle while you are (for all intents and purposes and viewed from the outside) not at all in a conventional middle.

Let's try it out.

It means *stay in your middle* (try to, experiment) *when you are standing on two feet, plainly*. Okay.

Even standing on two feet *well*, which might be viewed as a common posture for an adult human of a certain ability, is not really very easy. There is something about an external gaze that draws us outwards. We orient ourselves, as Lacanian psychoanalysts know, via an other who is not where we are. It can be the mirror, as we recall it. It can be the imagined gaze of someone who sees us. It can be our 'own' gaze, when we position ourselves as if outside of our skin. Standing in the middle, simply or *plainly*, is a decades-long undertaking.

Our accreted posture, arguably, results from trillions of instances of a gaze landing somewhere on us and pushing us ever so slightly in those many directions. Our posture is also pushed from within – injuries, surgeries, emotional or other wounds, growths, cysts, tightnesses and protective micro-gestures, all of this adjusts us constantly, too. However, the gaze is very influential, and we could include in this idea all the instructions, criticisms, our responding efforts to please, and so on, that mark our demeanour and poise. On the other hand, if we orient towards a 'middle' (which we are also looking for, researching the nature of …) then the impact of those gazes – the way they've struck us over the course of being alive – might be slightly off-set. We might orient via the middle, rather than mostly via a 'being-seen', being an object of a gaze.

The maxim means *stay in your middle in meditation practice* (try to, experiment) when you've just learned that your work is restructuring and you might not have a job, or a home in a few months. It means stay on the cushion, at least until the bell goes, and don't send any text messages now, and – perhaps – not even later. Not quite yet. Stay in the middle. The 'middle' as a protection against the extra mess that your reactivity to this difficult news is likely to unleash.

We *have* problems. This is a fact. And we *make* for ourselves greater problems. This is a reactivity to the lived experience of the first fact, the domino effect that will happen unless we train to counter it – via the middle experiment.

So, these middle examples from the yoga curriculum are mere rehearsals for other more embedded, consequential, and off-putting scenarios where holding the middle is very hard, maybe impossible, but where we (or people we love) are more exposed to risk from our wobbling. We *will* wobble. Wobbling is how it goes, and yoga doesn't fantasise that away. But there is a small chance that we will wobble for less long, with less violence, with less blinkeredness. Just maybe. And probably not, and then we will deal with our scenario, with what it threw at us, but more relevantly: what 'extras' we made in our reactivity to it. There was the first suffering, and then there was everything after that which we added to it – all on our own. Yoga, like Buddhism, is interested in the bits of suffering that *we add ourselves* – to the usual, and quite normal miseries that come bundled with being alive.

As mentioned, suffering tends to topple. Its organic tendency is precisely to turn domino-like, to collect *more* in its wake. Reducing this tendency is highly *non*-natural. This is why I tell students that yoga isn't going-back-to-nature. It follows hunches one can read off 'nature', but its way of working is an artform, not a lucky given.

What's definitely quite 'natural' or commonplace is to add to one's own suffering manifoldly. However, the non-naturalness of yoga means that we intervene into this likelihood via minimal, very precise techniques, with a trained lightness of touch. For me, maybe, so many years in, I pause for two minutes longer than I might have, compared to my teenage, or early adult self. I halt my brain's topplings, or I still touch the phone screen, penning a too-long, outraged message, but I *don't press send*. I pause a fraction before I assume and project. Just a wee bit. I still suffer and add to my suffering, but a sliver less than I may have. Is this something? It might not even count as anything.

I want to circle back to the idea of not compromising the middle for any pose. What could this mean for anyone – perhaps for you, dear Reader – who may have no interest in poses at all?

Striving for States

Poses can look like things to 'get'. People can become proud of themselves about poses they can do. This is irritating to be around. It's not so different, however, from someone who needs to let you know what car they drive, what awards they've won, what school they went to, how many beers they sank, how virtuous they've been. *Yep.*

And we know why people posture, and sometimes we are the posturers (embarrassed about it, as we might afterwards feel). We're humans and we hunt recognition (though sometimes, too, we manage to cultivate conditions in which we'd need to hunt recognition less).

People 'posture' when they're a little wobbly, and yoga involves 'postures', which allow you to learn about ur-wobbling (the wobbling that is our very foundation). It's possible that we start in yoga postures hunting for approval, and we end up with them more like big, generous planes of experimenting (think of a sculpture garden, a sacred canyon, an atopian scifi city, a desert full of silence and strange florae) that we can wander about in, that can surprise and unmoor us, and provide little spots where we can take a rest, gaze into sparkly darkness, breathe in strange, arid perfumes. Petrichor from your own pores ...

Poses in yoga can appear to the onlooker, and even to the in-looker, to be a 'thing' ahead of you that you might one day 'get into'. And it's not that you won't. If you are practising intelligently, carefully, there might indeed be some positions that your body becomes able to do more comfortably than you could at the start. This is normal. It can feel nice to find a way to be in a new pose. It also becomes irrelevant, weirdly. One ceases to care much. Yet, the body-that-couldn't and the body-that-can are indeed, technically, different bodies. New pose, new body. But also new day, new life. (That kind of thing.)

Strangely, these blips of transformation tend to happen when one is not fleeing the body that one is. The fastest way to elsewhere, in other words, is here. Stepping *from* here, while curious and open to something else happening. Depending on the degree of struggle that was involved in understanding a pose, if you do find your way with your body's version of that geometrical invitation, then you might shimmer a bit and appreciate a gentle bit of congratulating. Poses, thus, are fine, nice, interesting, and could seem sometimes to be the bulk of what people are doing in yoga. At the same time, it's not unwise to acknowledge the short-term nature of any attachment to yoga-pose-getting. The latter, I view as madness. Yes, maaaaadness. Why?

It's hardly news that we live in bodies that change dramatically across time. If ornate and fancy poses constitute the main focus of a yoga practice then this yoga practice is not looking far enough ahead in the viewfinder of time. The poses are just invitations now, and sitting meditation (as a kind of yoga pose, too: the central one, in fact) might turn out to be the pose you do into your 80s and beyond. (Or, it might be the pose of lying down, if you experience bodily or skeletal events that mean sitting up lengthily isn't for you anymore.) To focus on pose-getting is to have a skewed relation to time, impermanence, vulnerability and reality. I don't think too many yogis are confused about this. However, the impression that 'yoga is about poses' still prevails in some circles or in the wider media; it influences mainstream marketing and yoga's 'image'.

When I see runners running with two knee braces, I do wonder whether they are trying to hold on to a practice that needs adjusting to include all of them more, to include their changing knees, for example. Achieving milestones in practices is a very short-term focus. It can be nice to accompany these with a focus that can endure beyond our obvious physical prowess. Change is happening, folks. Running can also be a very good training in middle. If it is also this, then it can transform with the requirements of our years and situations, to include the reality of who we are across time. (Insert the version of this for any of your chosen practices.)

I admire, for this reason, my teacher's clever way of making the middle more important than the pose and stating this as the heart of what yoga is. (Yoga: not about poses; about ... middle. Keep that order of priority in the forefront of your practising brains, Baby Yogis.)

The grace offered by poses is that, essentially, they are both potential Middle-Disruptors and Teachers of Middle – all at once. Poses are tricky things that can tempt you away from your commitment to middle. They work like blatant metaphors; they work, in my experience, via the very vibrant and colourful experience called ... injury.

When I leave my middle to try to get myself into a pose which I can't yet do, I'm not saying I will get injured. I do know however that if I leave middle, I'm basically seating myself at the roulette table known as More Likely to Get Injured. I play around with being willing to harm myself for a thing I might (or might not) 'get' (and which, at the end of the day, isn't really that important). This can reveal a lot about a person. In short: how much self-harm for an ideology which doesn't even acknowledge you? Ouch. Apply wherever is apt.

Some people are a little bit mean to themselves, and they'll put themselves through quite awful things for an external affirmation, a kind of objective milestone, known as a pose. Many people are like this. If you point it out to them, they may show a minor curiosity, but probably not for long. Not unless they've had an encounter with this kind of risk-taking which turned out badly. One remains interested in and faithful to self-harm until one loses interest. This is what I've noticed. Arguing about it doesn't get you far. People like to harm themselves a bit. I'm not into it on paper, but my organism can still display its deeply embedded cavalier self-harm habits – perhaps less than I once would have. We bumble our way towards 'not being into harming'. (Do I think this is teleological? Well, maybe I do.) I don't believe this process can be rushed, or persuaded to move faster than it can. Our collective infatuation with a Little Bit of Hurt is one reason, I reckon, that the world often feels mildly bleak.

It feels bleaker when we realise how embroiled we are. We hate the effects. Then we see that we create these effects for others.

When I've silenced my body's messaging, its meek complaints and cautions, when I've pushed a little (often only a little) to then subsequently find myself injured, this real fact of having hurt myself, for an idea, for a concept, for something that is not that important, reverberates for a good while. It's not a hypochondria. No, it's seeing that there was a cost to a decision one made, even if the 'decision' seemed to happen on autopilot. Pushing without even noticing one was pushing.

I still did it. As a product of a culture, as a witless participant in a broader ideology. One learns to say: 'I hurt myself.'

Personally, I take Orit's provocation seriously. I do yoga and, among that curriculum, I do poses – but I work at not compromising middle for any pose. (I try, I fail, I fail better the next time, in that Beckett way.) The yoga-ness of yoga is the non-compromising. The rest is sporty, contortion stuff. The yoga isn't in the pose, whether you can or can't. (I'm sure some yoga-doing readers might not agree with me entirely, and I understand.) I can say it differently: experimenting with how far from middle you are willing to go, why you do that, what goes on for you, becomes a central element of what yoga touches and reveals, over the long term. Leaving middle is part of the middle experiment. And ultimately, agreeing with Orit, yoga gets closer when you leave the middle less and less.

And my friends who are runners might also – if I were to push them – say something similar, when describing the path of serious running. Or friends who are gardeners. Or serious cooks. (My mother is a serious cook. When she moves a spatula, she really works precisely and gently. Far more gently than I do, since I'm still a baby cook. I use too much energy. I waste effort; I bludgeon and bother the poor ingredients more than is required.)

Yoga, one can imagine, also builds a middle. Finds it? Cultivates it? Orients you towards it? The language lurches, and it would be better if you went and experimented, since the language will only take us so far.

Someone who thinks they don't have a 'yoga body' (whatever that might be) is absolutely suited for a yoga practising (or just another practice) that emphasises middle and not pose-getting, outcome-getting. For yoga, poses will be part of what is called the tapas aspect (the bit that 'turns up the heat'). Poses are pretty good *Tapas*. But the yoga-ness of doing poses (which distinguishes it from competitive gymnastics, or from dance that's for fussy audiences, or from circus) is the middle experiment aspect, the middle experiment which includes staying interested in the framework of ahimsa, non-wounding.

Poses that you try, which you try to do without lurching into self-hurting. You begin to notice how the trying (even without arriving) does something. Super interesting.

From another angle, why do all these silly positions? This might be the gripe of my academic bystanders, who wonder about the point of this whole hoo-hah. They are insightful if they are noticing that 'getting' poses is a fairly impoverished, skewed thing to aim for explicitly. A lot of effort for a flourish? What about world poverty? What about activism? What about rising sea levels and microplastics? Getting poses could even be interpreted as another kind of 'greed' – yes! – among all the kinds that beleaguer our fragile worlds. And it would seem (if it were solely about that, about achieving positions with your body) a very non-inclusive, ageist, very able-ist, kind of undertaking. I would agree with them on this, if they'd let me get a word in during their yoga-lecture. Hahaha.

Although yoga isn't about getting postures, the framework of the postures – which is truly a brilliant and nuanced curriculum – is one aspect of a well-rounded yoga repertoire, and not its only mainstay. If I were incapacitated due to any number of life misfortunes, there would still be 'poses' and a wealth of associated practices that I might be able to use as my practising scaffolding, even if these appeared to outside eyes as very humble, insignificant, barely any kind of movement or 'doing' at all.

Steady Sweetness

One of the most memorable of the *Yoga Sutras* is the one that describes how the *asana* (the pose) should be:

> II.46. sthira-sukham-asanam
> [The pose is 'stably pleasant' or 'pleasantly stable'.][3]

This means, if we're being fussy, it qualifies as a yoga pose *only* if it meets this description. If I harm myself doing some kind of contortion, and it has neither pleasantness nor steadiness, then it's something ... but it's not yoga.

For the non-yogi, all this talk about the quality of poses mightn't seem very relevant. However, in the word *sukha*, there lurks another translation, alongside 'pleasant', which is *sweetness*. If yoga is about steadiness and transformation (which I'd say it can be), then this tells us something interesting.

It is that when we find stability, and can tolerate it, *and* if that stability has a quality of sweetness, then we might be in a state in which we can encounter our own lives, the people in them – a brief and intensive passage.

I'm thinking of Gillian Rose describing Edna's magic as a transmutation, one that emerges from the plain and the ordinary, from mistakes and disappointments. Ordinariness, we could say, implies a kind of stability that isn't flashy, perhaps one that you barely notice when it's in front of you.

To the outside eye, plainness, too, gives an impression that nothing much is happening. The untrained, outside eye slides past the plainness, and onto flashier snags. The trained eye, a little more fatigued by and wary of that which doesn't deliver, catches the rare dash of nothingness at the heart of what is plain. It drinks it in like water.

What Rose notes about her friend Edna is that she hadn't in fact lived any kind of exceptional life. She had lived *her own* life. This is what each of us 'get' – a swift sojourn in the realm of embodiment, in the realm of squishiness and vulnerability. We get a chance to abstain from the knee-jerk programming of harm, as an experiment, which is dignified, imperfect, never known in advance. We are presented – *in every moment* – with opportunities to be kind. Sometimes, if we are stable, if we pursue the things that usher in a poised sweetness – rather than an onslaught of maxxx flavour – we can take up those plainer spaces where the logic of kindness becomes the dominant logic, a breathtaking logic. Not without its small sufferings, not flawless, but a logic that's less likely to wipe us out, one that can travel us much further than we tend to think.

So many words needed just to get a little, minuscule, impression across.

Gilles Deleuze, December 1980[1]

Risking Plainness

There was a moment – a handful of years back – when I was lucky enough to be travelling around a public art event in a minibus. Driven along dirt roads, I felt open and curious; I felt the usual harried, impatient suspicion that wheedles its way into the heart of a contemporary person fade out. Along the side of dirt roads, across paddocks, there were art works, mists, performances, sound events. I drifted in the kindness of unstructured expectations inside gently structured time.

All of this very ordinary, non-shiny spaciousness converged in a quiet thought: *it might be fine, more than enough, indeed so much, to live a plain life*.

I didn't understand then the importance of the sentence which had presented itself. The word 'plain' stuck out, however, since it seemed one which normally wouldn't get airtime. *Plain things* ... well, they just don't really feature much. The term was neither racy, nor despairing; neither glam, nor drab. It sat, instead, to-the-side of that kind of mental manoeuvring.

We are some years along now, from this first moment of my considering this term. I know for sure that a word cannot fix anything. It can, however, palpate the edges of new spaces. It can find the tiniest chink in a glossy surface, and burrow in some canny, sensitive roots, wait patiently for rain, draw in the sunlight through its membranes and sometime later – hey! – you're on a hike and see green, lush creatures growing unfeasibly out of the vertical rock of a cliff face.

The improbable occurs quite regularly.

A plain life, you see, mightn't look like anything. (Things have other ways of being, aside from how they 'look'.) From the outside, no one would know if I were living plainly, or not.

(There might be hints, might be ...) It isn't a style you can research and then emulate, recreate. It's not a way of furnishing one's situation with a certain set of accessories; it isn't lived via imitation. A stance in relation to one's own life, plainness, if I can say that, has to do with the fact of deciding, for oneself, that one's life is intrinsically 'enough' (and there may be new things you want to live, to try), that you want it and that you make it to some extent. (Perceiving the bits you make and the bits that come with the broader package, or harsher inheritance, then noticing that interplay is an ongoing undertaking.)

The word 'plain' offsets the demand of all kinds of fake binaries that would snare us in their measly offerings, keeping us busy and tired with a 'choosing-between'. These terms leave us with little gumption, unable to pan out to see clearly the shoddy scenario from which we could decide to withdraw.

The loudest example of these seems to whisper (constantly, constantly) that one risks being either a winner or a loser. This little brain-trap is obviously idiotic when one sees it spelt out, but when operating in the background, it is harder to spot. We fall into it often, and often its pressure accounts partially for why we treat ourselves, or others, so poorly. With so little regard.

(Everyone's idea of what specifically constitutes the signs of this winning and losing is different. For some it's trucking in sufficient amounts counter-cultural cool; for others it's masses of cash in the bank; for others it's idyllic family life with all the trappings, and so on. These fantasies might serve partly to guide our direction, this lifetime around, but when added to a winner-loser framework, they can get a bit nasty, a bit unscrupulous.)

Plainness withdraws its interest from choices that present themselves on these either/or, bossy terms; it turns away from an invitation to live mainly through that kind of thinking. Strictly speaking, it is thus other than reactive. Technically, it might not even be resistant.

Plainness, maybe, means that we might reconsider the ways we speak about ourselves and our lives. It coaxes us to be discerning about the words we use, savvy to the ideologies they bring along and the behaviours and pathways they activate.

A plain life would say (or mumble), 'Enough!' to a kind of conceptual bullying among which we all live, day in and day out. It's there in advertising (of course!). It's carried along in words that slide into popular usage. It's part of our complex relation to advanced technologies with which we'll increasingly share the world and to which we devote a lot of our time. Frames we didn't ask for, but with which we are (for my liking) slightly too easy-going.

With the term 'plain' – this choice of word as word – I've been trying to step free of a minefield of associations. As word choice, it intimates a space beyond a certain common way of thinking, beyond a pattern of ideas we traffic in collectively. Plain ('plain?!') is a bit unsettling and in a good way. Plain implies neither exceptional nor irrelevant, when it comes to assessing your own life. Or, when people offer us the option of being motivated or lazy, it gives pause before we take up these terms uncritically. If someone offers me that kind of choice, this way of categorising myself or my life, my relationship or my attitude, I'm more ready now to hesitate. What are you asking me to choose between? Who says these are the terms? Who says these terms are even plausible or accurate? Do I want them?

Any tight choice itself – its very shape of tightness – awakens my caution. These choices are depressing from the get-go and actively shrink what's possible. As well as tight, they are imposing and a little bit mean. With oodles of these badly formed pairs of notions forming the fabric of our wordy worlds, it's very easy to fall prey to them. We are tired and off our guard; we're sick of having to be alert, and the terms, the ideas are so pushy, we often just give in. Thus, we borrow from the popular lexicon and presto! suddenly our life is ruled by sets of spurious either/ors. Not even in any obvious way, because the logic gets under the skin.

It's especially dire when such terms come to seem entirely natural. (Are you productive or procrastinating?) We can trouble, or turn away from, this and similar binaries. These terms are considered by people (by you, your cousin, your boss, your pilates teacher) adequate ways to organise how we relate to what's very precious: this brief life. I wish to suggest that they aren't adequate at all.

People think that procrastinating is a real verb. Hahahahaha! I spoke to my sister on the phone this morning. She said she was procrastinating, and I replied that she wasn't. She was just doing what she wanted to do. She laughed and said: yes, it's what I want to do, but not what I need to do. Maybe. But still, couldn't we all consider saying that we're doing what we want to do? This has dignity. This leaves us in the role of adult. Procrastination as word (so popular, golly!) is like a little slap we give to a naughty child. We are too old for these slaps; we can unbelieve them.

In fancier terms, we can say these are Imprecise Distributions. (The word 'distribution' here means that what's in focus is less the ideas than the way ideas are laid out.) Distributions of various kinds cut up the world into categories and these categories come to seem so natural that we take them for 'givens', rather than remembering that they are just a human invention, often invented by those invested in maintaining some advantage, some *pouvoir*. Thus, we can question not only the ideas – one by one – but the general arrangement (distribution) and the latter's consequences for us. These Fake Binaries aren't any kind of useful or careful thinking. They harm us not a little.

People are good at spotting ideas (the idea of a horse, a house, a hose, a hoax, a hound), but it's harder to spot the pattern our ideas tend to make, the ruts our thinking falls into. This is genuinely difficult. Philosophers are people who are often trained to watch the way ideas flow, settle, drift, fray or stagnate. They note what ideas can conceal behind pleasant façades. For most of us, glimpsing the shape of ideas is next-level in the application of our intelligence. The brain can hurt a little, since it is trying to work on itself, see itself working, while it works as itself. Oosh.

Other folk, who have some chops with watching idea patterns, are meditators. There's much misunderstanding about what 'counts' as meditation, and there are many forms of meditative practice (with varying instructions, and 'ways in'). One thing for sure is that the brain will keep being a thought-machine while you meditate, and this fact doesn't mean that meditation isn't worth your time, or that you aren't suited to it. There are many studies that now concur with what's always been known: meditating may increase your tolerance for happiness ... (I hope you're smiling.)

It takes something, some intervention, to learn to *like* (a new level of) happiness. Of sweetness.

Meditators are those who do the unusual activity of non-activity – doing nothing for a while, and just watching, without many opinions, the stuff that trails through a mind within a body at relative rest. This practice tends to give us access to more 'head' space than regular life allows – which in turn impacts the body that now hums along differently in this spaciousness. Meditation invites us to spot how an idea pattern has set itself up and how it is generating all sorts of dreary treadmills. These treadmills don't always cease when you spot them, but they tend to lose energy, drop down a notch, when they are under a non-interventionist gaze: the meditating gaze. Even if the ideas or their arrangements apparently 'stay the same', they are simply not the same, once you see them.

At the beginning of this book, I felt cautious about coining a word, a moniker: 'plainness'. These things rarely turn out well. The shelves of self-help sections are lined with invented words which are doomed to imprecision through overuse. In these cases, the word (and its notion) risk sliding from being something useful, a playful provocation into being a something – a state, a label – that a person can 'get' or not 'get', embody or not, display convincingly or not. Imagine dinner parties where people conspicuously drop the word 'plain' in among their self-congratulatory banter. Oh dear.

Words, then, are tricky because we get worn out with them. They overuse our mouths. They keep inserting themselves, such that thinking – awkward, genuine, less definitive – gets stage fright, and the bossy, 'new', mass-produced words (packaged in ideas-patterns) topple out. You only have to read how we all speak/write to each other at work, via email. It's a horror-show, truly. And the AI bots, bless their good nature, will just replicate these habits we have, unless we give them another apprenticeship.

While this is something to watch for, it is also the in-built nature of language. Language is (as we teach creative writing students) both a means of oppression, as well as the very means to slip free from this same oppression. Letting the word 'plainness' take form and point to some ideas cannot but be a risk. It might, however, open something in passing for us, for a small while. If it hardens too much, we can abandon it. We can then perhaps think again, without words, and in a rawer way. Going back to the beginning, which can mean 'back into the middle of things'.

Helped by nimble philosophers, I've come to learn that mostly things turn out badly *and* well. Sometimes (and mostly) both at once. There is, in other words, no way to avoid the loss each moment structurally involves. There is thus no 'safe' path, although there are some paths that seem more likely to be laden with shrill, guaranteed suffering than others.

This is a fairly widespread definition of wisdom, or what Spinoza might call 'reason'. I recall my teacher quoting: 'The intelligent know how to get out of situations that the wise don't even bother getting into.' Yes ... well, indeed.

∝

YOU BEGIN TO GET INTERESTED IN PLAINNESS SLOWLY over time. Becoming interested in plainness also doesn't mean you abandon interest in things like flair, flamboyance, style, enthusiasm or magnanimity. Plainness *does* have something to do with losing interest in things that present themselves to you – to the collective 'us' – as ultimatums. This *or* that! In instances when the world seems to demand that you (or we) *choose*, it is what I'm calling 'plainness' which notes that the choosing itself, this kind of 'either/or' predicament, might in fact be what we could divest from … a little.

Plainness isn't another way to hedge your bets. It involves something other than a greedy, terrified or desperate lurching. A poet friend of mine wrote to me recently saying that they were feeling very 'unmotivated' … and that at least that meant they weren't desperate. I nearly fell over laughing. This friend is a certified genius (I mean, they really are). 'Motivation' is some fancy active wear that we clothe our desperation in and that we are encouraged to feel as often as possible. It's a very tricksy invention of a concept. It reeks of self-manipulating, internalised economised enthusiasm. Unmotivate! See if nothing happens. Something will happen, but less desperately perhaps.

While thinning out a relationship with what Nietzsche taught us to call resentment or *ressentiment*, plainness has little to do with cynicism. To sidle up to plainness, I think one has to let in the reality that one is an organism – a being embedded in fleshiness, a vulnerable, perishable, unknown-to-itself phenomenon. Plainness seems to involve testing the possibility that perhaps, in being-an-organism (and not another kind of machine), we are not only body, not only an assemblage of live processes whose destiny is primarily determined by the needs and aggressions that compel any bodily creature.

Or perhaps plainness allows for us to be less sure that we can fathom the complexities of Being an Organism.

Plainness refrains from taking defensive refuge in the pragmatic aspects of this being-organism. (It's not a signing up for a dog-eat-dog world view, for example.) It refrains from that all-knowing hurrumphf that I know in myself, or in friends, when we have found less-expansive solutions to our woundedness. One is truly an organism, and rather than this justifying a tightened and sad way of approaching the world, or a triumphant, proselytising one, it constitutes a persistent layer of that which needs to be navigated while being alive.

There is a matter-of-factness to plainness which distances itself – not from imagination, but – from (what gets called, accurately enough) 'magical thinking'. Plainness involves a slowly cultivated capacity for non-shirking. This is not for the faint of heart, to quote my friend (on ageing, on sickness, on misfortune, on power and exploitation). The world is no easy place. It is rarely fair. Plainness tends to generate, as its unique spin-off, a quieter gentleness that feels very composed because it doesn't disavow its falling-apart-ness. It doesn't attribute to anybody really that they have their shit together. Most of us are (at multiple levels) ontologically, existentially, energetically ... in honorable disarray.

To put it psychoanalytically: because one has (over and over, deeply, shallowly, at every level and with umpteen setbacks) renounced imagining there is a version of oneself that would be 'whole' and/or 'satisfied', or 'present', or 'realised', one strangely approaches (without coinciding with) something like those atmospherics that were previously associated with those very things.

Not despite. Alongside. Less 'knowing', more composure. Sorry to spell it out.

This both-at-once style in thinking – I'm pondering as I write – might be the friendly terrain that welcomes plainness ... Both organism (as body) and not-only bodied organism. With regards to the second aspect, there is again this aspect of making friends with our Not-Knowing. This is a practising of – I want to say 'training' in

– not being sure. What we do surely know is that we are organisms, and we don't know everything about what that means.

What might we know, or suspect, about being organisms? Many wisdom traditions are busy with this question. Because they are ancient texts, our modern sensibilities can find them quaint and miss what they are up to. Being an organism means we occupy uneasily a unique perspective. In our normal modes, we can't be everywhere; we are thus a bit 'finite' at one register, and we might not only be finite for now, being an organism involves an inherent vulnerability due to a hardwired dual yearning: both to persevere as itself and to become other – in other words to change.

By considering such a hardwiring – which goes in (at least) two directions – plainness arrives to help us grapple more warmly, even jovially, with our real predicaments. With our real situation. The Real has been associated with that which language doesn't (and cannot) capture or account for. The Real, in a tradition like Lacanian psychoanalysis, can designate that which lies outside of what can be signified, lies beyond what can be put into 'languages' (of various kinds), or subsumed under a consistent system. The Real, too, might be that which is indifferent to the rules of meaningfulness, of making-sense, of how (via the words and conventions we have absorbed) we think things should be. There is no 'should' in the real. There's just how things are, which we cannot (anyway, mostly) say in any consistent way, and much less think very well. There are traditions that try to think it. The ones that do a good job of this, we might grant the title 'wisdom traditions'.

To see plainly.

I care about this especially when plainness helps me to pause in my brittle knowingness with which I often am just trying to shield myself. Seeing clearly – to borrow a bit from Zen – is an exercise in allowing for, not blotting out, the depthless depths of our delusions. When I'm a little plainer, I reckon, maybe, that I hurt people less (and I include myself in this group 'people'). It's not that

I hurt them 'not at all', just marginally less often, and less blithely. We are hurt machines, and we are not only that. The *Yoga Sutras*, the Buddhist texts, many long-standing texts, are explicit here.

I've learned something about plainness from working, for a long time (as they say) 'with the body', but not with the body as 'means', rather as a site of curiosity in itself. The body as ongoing, open question, about which I don't expect definitive answers, although some 'knowledge' does tend to come out of solution, to crystallise, thanks to this kind of sustained engagement. You, too, have ways that you work with the body, with being-an-organism. Or I hope you do. It doesn't have to be sweaty, loud or horrible.

At a basic level, working with the body means learning how to handle, and listen to, the vehicle you can't but drive around in … rather than using the body as a 'means to' something else – like scoring goals, dancing to entertain a crowd, or doing your job efficiently (all good things). This experience has been a useful foundation on which to research plainness.

When you work with the body, you can't avoid the fact that you are an organism. It is never far from awareness. You tire. You get slightly injured. You are careless. You make mistakes and continue not to understand 'how' to do things (whereas before working with the body, you assumed this was transparent and straightforward). Your emotional experience reveals itself as curiously tethered to the state of the body. You investigate the ins-and-outs of that. The body (whatever that is) becomes a field of investigation, and it has open sets of logics and laws unto itself. The body speaks, in various ways. It has modes of inertia, of habit and invention, sites of intensity and void. The body isn't what we tend to 'think' it is. It may not be any kind of 'it', not an entity in a simplistic way. Plainness can be a methodology that emerges from, but also suits and sustains, playful and curious engagements with whatever we think the body 'is', all the while as the likelihood unfolds that it really isn't to be taken at face value.

When the body is not just the tool for 'sport', and not something one just tolerates having to 'live with', working with it becomes a direct experimentation with some basic building blocks of life and change; that is: with differences and repetitions. Before you doze off here, what I can say is that doing stuff with the body generally calls on structures (behaviours, actions, movements, &c.) which then get repeated, but which are also different each time. Sameness and difference. Repetition and structure. As it turns out, these operations are the very stuff out of which time itself emerges, and language definitely, and wanting probably ... and, and, and! I find this wild.

People tend to think that the way to variation is via extremity. For example: Want a new life? Do something rash! Instead, what I trust more is the counter-balancing phenomenon that surprise tends to lurk within the tissue of regularity. Surprise, or newness, or possibilities that seemed once impossible tend to be accessed by seeming to repeat, and consistently. The way one goes about relating to the regularity requires some fine tuning – but really, seldom do rash manoeuvres open many fresh pathways. At least, that's been my closely observed experience. Another way to say it is that, when I'm rash, I'm also less relaxed, and when I'm less relaxed this strained state tends to lock me into more of my deeper habitual tracts (even if the surface looks novel). Thus, I can find myself – despite all appearances – effectively staying in the same place.

It's weird how we've ended up talking about methods of transformation, when I was intending on talking mostly about plainness. It's because they are not so 'opposed', after all.

Plainness emerges less as a thing, then, than as a kind of ethos or sensibility. To court what's plain can mean entertaining the possibility that the shiny promises on the package aren't necessarily going to deliver in the ways they imply. Plainness might be seeing this, without a sulk. Seeing this and finding it somehow ... moving.

Plainness, too, involves a second moment, when one wonders about 'delivering' itself. Would anything 'deliver'? Well, not strictly. And things do deliver. They deliver in surprising ways, not what we made up in our heads. Life delivers in a way that's full of merciful less-ness, bursting with the ordinary, sating us otherwise. In plainness, our satisfactions (if we can still call them that) might be more jumbly, ramshackle, humorous and kind. They might have more flavour, actually. Not like a 7-Eleven slurpee, more like a meal at the local, unflashy but gorgeously skilful-with-ingredients-and-processes family restaurant. You might have one. You could make a booking there again, like that last time – to celebrate nothing much, just because.

∝

THERE IS THE LONG-STANDING QUESTION OF WHETHER to make politics (raw, hard activism) or Care [for] the Self (to borrow loosely French philosopher, Michel Foucault's term[2]). I do not believe in this opposition. The bodies of activists can be broken on this dualistic wheel, and they deserve our love. We are would-be activists because we have (some) money, and we decide where we spend it. We have some urge to connect with others, and we decide on which platforms we wish to do that, or *not*. We have thoughts and we champion their directions and implications, or we watch them closely to see where they came from. We have reactivities, which we let run or which we examine, considering ways to intervene. We have time and, although much of it (a lot of it under neoliberalism!) is not always 'ours' to organise, we can watch the way we surrender all the rest of it to the economical, or to economised thinking. We are very often too *generous* towards that which cares not a jot for us. We misdirect our good natures. It might be good to withdraw and divert this care elsewhere.

A plain life is one where we don't add quite so much to the tally of suffering that is already our lot, or the lot of others. Plainness, as I said, is probably not likely to be popular. It's mostly quiet and often sobering. It has terrible branding, but a nice singing voice and it doesn't stoop to sarcasm.

Coda

We find ourselves right back in the first chapter of this book, where to the cruel binary of 'there are only winners and losers' ... we countered (after Badiou):

There are only winners and losers, *except* that there is my life.

In the days following the US Presidential Elections of 2024, *The New Yorker* published a 'dispatch' by author and Buddhist practitioner George Saunders called 'Five Thought Experiments Concerning the Underlying Disease'. In this experiment (how wonderful!), Saunders puts to the reader a number of scenarios, in which the division of his fellow countryfolk along the lines of red (Republican) and blue (Democrat) is either emphasised or *deemphasised*. In the second experiment, where it is deemphasised, he poses the idea of a group of people in a local council, in a 'charming' room, and with a beautiful tree outside the window, working together on a small relevant issue: potholes. A budget exists but doesn't stretch to do *all* the potholes, and thus the people will try to work together to spend the budget they have. It was this line that caught my attention:

What may result among this group of people is something like fondness.

To see this word, this plain and gentle word, describing a feeling that may develop among creatures (yes, *actually* – including humans, and budgies, and pythons, and rocks, and plankton, and reed warblers, and lice ...) made the little, fierce fire that I have in me leap up with a surge of relief, carried on a cosmic giggle.

Fondness. Despite ourselves, no matter how much we protest, we sometimes can't help but become *fond* of each other. When we do things together (not simply 'meet for coffee', but sometimes that too). When we hang out clothes, clean out a shed, pick up sticks so the grass mowing person can come in and zip around to clear for fire danger, when we muddle through a poorly worded recipe, or wrangle a dinner for people, or wander along during a too-sunshiney demo ... we tend to not be able to help ourselves also develop *fondness*.

In this life, plain, not-yet-lived and decided, there may be terror, courage, anxiety and justice. For Badiou, rightly, these four affects mark the becoming-subject of a human who, encounters the possibility for something *true*. In the face of this opening in normality's weave, they decide *Yes*, and begin to act in fidelity to its direction. Fidelity sounds flashy, sounds prim, but it's just our daily stumbles, baulks and failures strung together with on eye on dignity.

Something *true*. We indeed are bodies (with all their reactivity and fear, and windows into pleasure and sensibility), *and* we are for the most caught in modes of language. At another level, Badiou claims, we are also, alongside this, *eternal*. We touch this potential for eternity when we devote ourselves to a picture that includes something bigger than the small 'us'.

This might sound quite grand, compared to what I've been exploring as a plain life, but I think the two are kin.

To be able to follow through on some events and the portals into newness they offer, whether amorous, political, and so on, we might need to take our leave from certain grinding modes of Awful, train ourselves to be less reactive (sometimes), dignify our modest attempts to make experiments in rigorous kindness. We might then get to encounter our fellows otherwise, do some actions together – nothing that flash, but something we may feel quietly proud of – and reawaken our basic capacity for fondness, for non-squandering.

As I've come to learn over my first half-century, there are certain things, certain practices, activities, actions, devotions, which *clear the heart*. Singing is one. Outdoor, simple work, that isn't for the gig economy, but probably just for your elderly neighbour, is another. According to Saunders, perhaps sitting in a pleasant conference room, with some other folk, biscuits to the ready, and working on a plain, but not unimportant pothole puzzle is another.

Some things, some company, some decisions, clear the heart. And then it opens to fondness. It might then want kindness, since kindness often follows on from fondness and clarity. If we spend our precious, earthly, fleshy time doing things that muddle and warp the heart, we end up in a difficult and painful, dangerous and … silly place. Silly and/or brutal. We almost guarantee the likelihood of provoking and exacerbating scenarios that are Awful. Without clarity in the heart, we are less likely to spot unkindness for what it is, and instead give it shifty names like: necessity, efficiency, expediency, rationalisation, 'getting ahead'.

Inside the heart, we are *every* creature, every time, all the contractions and relaxations of history. In the heart, you have to let go – for a second – of your little, frightened, short-sighted and perishable self. Decisions made on the basis of this self, if divorced from something wider, simply make no sense there. This isn't straightforward, but it is vast and it displaces empty 'hopefulness' towards a kind of *faith*. Faith, which might be a non-knowing knowing. It can't be a knowing of anything, but it is a stance of this same heart. Understandably, humans have often called this stance 'God', and then slid imprecisely to thinking their god was local, exclusionary, requiring specific rituals, &c. on 'their' side, something to be forced upon others. (You can write this paragraph for me, *gell*? It's such an old, old and painful story …)

God might be thinkable as a stance in the heart, a certain turning, which is an *un*orientation, a widening out of perspective, away from only-me, and including me. We visit the vast heart (like a punctuation, a spacing in all the 'thingness'), and tend to return to our more finite perspective to muddle on, perhaps then with less reactivity, a corner of our eye tuned to a felty, enmeshed eternity *here*, rather than to the know-it-all timelines of despair.

A plain life would be one where we take care to recall the portals to the heart, the collective and solo practices that build fondness, and the decisions that abstain from gutting our own capacity. We don't need for neoliberalism or our devices to love us. We have what we need, and the discipline required is that of rigorous kindness, letting in the pockets of nothingness, and building gently but surely, a bit of muscle to enact the affirmative 'no'. This 'no' is also a steady patience for that which aligns with joy, which affirms our fumbled failures, and involves *some* small harms that we cannot avoid and which we will grieve with every sincerity. It opens onto a perhaps unanticipated, yet probably quite astonishing and ordinary life.

Works Mentioned

(in order of first mention)

David Foster Wallace, *Infinite Jest*, 1996, Abacus.
Gilles Deleuze, *Difference and Repetition*, 2004, Continuum.
Wendy Brown, 'American Nightmare: Neoliberalism, Neo-conservatism and De-democritization', *Political Theory*, vol. 34 no. 6, 2006, pp. 690–714.
Alain Badiou, *Logics of Worlds*, trans. Alberto Toscano, 2009, Continuum.
Lauren Berlant, *Cruel Optimism*, 2011, Duke University Press.
Simon Springer, 'REPLY: Space, time, and the politics of immanence', *Global Discourse*, March 2014, pp. 1–4.
Jacques Derrida, *Acts of Religion*, trans. Gil Anidjar, 2002, Routledge.
Jacques Derrida, *The Gift of Death*, trans. David Wills, 1996, University of Chicago Press.
Rachel Cusk, *Kudos*, 2019, Faber.
Benedictus de (Baruch) Spinoza, *Ethics*, trans. Edwin Curley, 1985, Princeton University Press.
Alain Badiou, *Immanence of Truths*, trans. Kenneth Reinhard and Susan Spitzer, 2022, Bloomsbury.
Byung-Chul Han, *Müdigkeitsgesellschaft, Burnoutgesellschaft, Hochzeit*, 2016, Matthes & Seitz Berlin.
Alain Badiou, *In Praise of Love*, trans. Peter Bush, 2021, New Press.
F. Scott Fitzgerald, *The Great Gatsby*, 1970, Penguin Modern Classics.
G. C. Field, *The Philosohy of Plato*, 2nd edn, 1969, Oxford University Press.
Orit Sen-Gupta, *Patañjali's Yoga Sutras*, 2013, Vijnana Books.
Byung-Chul Han, *The Agony of Eros*, trans. Erik Butler, 2017, MIT Press.
Alain Badiou and Barbara Cassin, *There's No Such Thing as a Sexual Relationship*, trans. Kenneth Reinhard and Susan Spitzer, 2017, Columbia Univeristy Press.
Sianne Ngai, *Ugly Feelings*, 2005, Harvard University Press.
Byung-Chul Han, *Burnout Society*, trans. Erik Butler, 2015, Stanford Briefs.
Jacques Derrida, *Specters of Marx*, trans. Peggy Kamuf, 2006, Routledge.
Cecelia Watson, *Semicolon*, 2019, Harper Collins.
Gilles Deleuze, *Nietzsche and Philosophy*, trans. Hugh Tomlinson, 2006, Columbia University Press.
Mikhail Bulgakov, *The Master and Margarita*, 2010, Random House UK.
Friedrich Nietzsche, *The Will to Power*, 2017, Penguin UK.

Adam Phillips and Barbara Taylor, *On Kindness*, 2009, Farrar, Straus and Giroux.
Maya Newell (dir.), *In My Blood it Runs*, 2019, Closer Productions.
Swami Hariharananda Aranya, *Yoga Philosophy of Patañjali*, 1983, State University of New York Press.
Gilles Deleuze, *The Logic of Sense*, 2004, Continuum.
Gillian Rose, *Love's Work*, 2011, NYRB Classics.
Rainer Maria Rilke, *Letters to a Young Poet*, 1986, Stephen Mitchell (trans), Random House.
Michel Foucault, *The Hermeneutics of the Subject*, trans. Graham Burchell, 2005, Palgrave Macmillan.

Acknowledgments

This book has been made possible by many beings – human and non-human – who in having lent support, labour, love, expertise, space and time, I'd like to sincerely thank. Ann Vickery, who encouraged me to consider turning my essays into a longer book, and Zoe Dzunko, then-editor at *The Lifted Brow*, for accepting my odd nonfiction pitch about 'a plain life', and her astute editorial feedback. Other editors at the *Brow*, who read, improved and championed subsequent essays, especially Justin Wolfers. Colleagues in visual arts at Deakin University, David Cross and Cameron Bishop (and all the commissioned artists involved), for staging the *Treatment* art event at Werribee. Deakin's Faculty of Arts and Education, School of Communication and Creative Arts, and the Alfred Deakin Institute for research support. My fellow writer–scholars from *NovelLab* at RMIT, who included me in their residency at Bundanon, and the Bundanon Trust for hospitality, time and wombats. The team at NewSouth – Harriet McInerney, Elena Gomez, Joumana Awad, Katherine Rajwar – for enabling a steady, clear and often inspired process. Emma Cowan – for the incredible image and artistic friendship over many years. The Wenzelburger/Werder household. Orit Sen-Gupta and my yoga colleagues and dedicated students – for the slow research in good company. Fellow scholars, close readers and arguers – you know who you are. Of course, Paloma – who instinctively and instructively knows how to rest and how to bolt, thus setting an example in evading capture. MP and KP – for your faith, probing conversations, excellent cooking and love. Esteban (who epitomised the compossibility of 'plain' and 'flamboyant'). And LV – for reading everything and showing me, day after day, how plainly wonderful a human can be.

I extend heartfelt gratitude and ongoing respect, as well as my awe, to the custodians of the various lands on which this work was developed and written – Wurundjeri lands of Woiwurrung and Boonwurrung, and lands of the Dharawal and Dhurga language groups. May our ways and lives together cherish, protect and sustain these sacred lands, waters and skies, and may we hear, honour and heed the guidance of First Peoples' Elders, ancestors and future leaders.

Notes

In Praise of a Plain Life
1. Simon Springer, 'REPLY: Space, time, and the politics of immanence' (*Global Discourse*, March, 2014, 1–4), 3.

Deciding Capacities
1. If you would tend to use the names for these scenarios (decision, choice, &c.) around another way, this works too. It's less about what we call these things, and more about the mechanisms in each distinct case. Decision can also be a deciding-between, using Derrida's example which references legal decisions. A judge or jury must decide guilty/not-guilty. See 'Force of Law' in *Acts of Religion*, trans. Gil Anidjar, 2002, Routledge.
2. You can find the series, plus an earlier lecture from 1978, here in Purdue University's open archive: deleuze.cla.purdue.edu/lecture/lecture-00/
3. There is currently much research circling about concerning how our metabolic function (and dysfunction) interacts with what we call mental health, or Spinoza's sadness. It's very interesting.
4. This raises a very technical issue regarding transformation. There *can* be a jump to being something else, but rarely do we 'do' this action, since we do things *as the current version of ourselves*, and this version has to pause a second, for a newness to appear. This is complicated. I've written about this in more detail in *A Philosophy of Practising*, 2021, Edinburgh University Press.

On Love and Making Ones
1. See Alain Badiou, *Immanence of Truths*, 2022, Bloomsbury, Chapter C25.
2. See Han's *The Agony of Eros*, 2017, MIT Press.
3. And we also know that people are in situations where they do practically need support of these kinds, cleaners, food delivery, transport options, but we don't need a market solution for this; we can also consider social, governmental or collective ways to care for each other in various moments of differing capacity.
4. See Barbara Cassin and Alain Badiou, *There's No Such Thing as a Sexual Relationship*, trans. Susan Spitzer and Kenneth Reinhard, 2017, Columbia University Press, p. 57.

Being Bothered

1. Disapproval often signposts a triggered state for many of us. Trauma? Pain? Cascading sadness in a sad world? Yes. What's been triggered often goes missing under the dank tones of disapproval. When I'm wallowing in disapproving, I might need your kindness.
2. Could this be a conscience *before* having been manipulated, harnessed and tangled up by external third parties in relation to power (*pouvoir*)? My philosophical readers may protest: 'Antonia – you're positing something prior to these organisations, and we all know that priorness has been rigorously debunked and examined as a spurious, retroactive creation.' Yes, I know. Sceptical gears grind ...
3. Superego. (2019, May 21). *No Subject – Encyclopedia of Psychoanalysis*. Retrieved 12 February 2025, from nosubject.com/index.php?title=Superego&oldid=44474.

Virtue: falling out of love with Awful

1. Curiously, Guy Cromwell Field was the grandson of Jesse Collings. His first book was titled *Guild Socialism* (1920). The science fiction writer Olaf Stapleton was highly influenced by this socio-political model. Stapleton, for contemporary readers and film viewers, is the author of the story *Last and First Men*, which has been made into a recent cinematic work, with the same title (2020), voiced by Tilda Swinton.
2. Later in the book, Field notes that Plato was mostly busy with societal virtues, and is known for saying less on interpersonal virtue.
3. In her lecture on French Existentialism, given at Yale in 2023, Marci Shore gives the example of the children's book *Not the Hippopotamus*, by Sandra Boynton, to reference this ability to *not* join in.
4. 'The Velocities of Thought' lecture series, Gilles Deleuze, 16 December 1980.
5. *Pratipaksha bhavana*, sutra II.33.
6. Personal correspondence, teachings, 2024.
7. 'The Velocities of Thought' lecture series, 24 January 1978.

Envy: a case study

1. In the weeks when I was revising this book, I had another version of this with shame. Also a rough landing, but once I'd worked out it was shame, my stroppy, horrible mode (which activates when I'm defending against shame) dropped away. It was replaced by that odd, plain clarity of admission. It also feels *impersonal* then: shame has been around. *That – didn't you know, Antonia? – was a visit from shame.*

Four Nuances of 'Can'

1. See Sianne Ngai, *Ugly Feelings*, 2005, Harvard University Press, Chapter 3.
2. 'The Velocities of Thought' lecture series, 9 December 1980.

Wanting, Affirmation and the Plain 'No' of Critique
1   I use this term 'enjoyable' in a psychoanalytically inflected way. We can really 'enjoy' forms of our own ostensible suffering. We can 'enjoy' talking about how hard everything is; we can 'enjoy' our complaining. We especially 'enjoy' complaining about others and their faults, &c. Psychoanalysis is rare in calling out this tendency, which has a tone one learns to listen for. Mostly, I try to listen for it in myself. *Golly*, am I good at resentful enjoying! Hahahaha.
2   On this note, however, one reads about mitochondria and how we school them in particular tastes. This can become a taste for 'edible', undigestible substances, which they then crave. So, this is interesting. One might have to slowly retrain a community within ourselves, if we have accustomed these to things that are unkind to us more broadly.
3   It is discussed in Book II of *The Will to Power*, section 2. 'The Will to Power as Life', part (b) 'Man'. [para 685].
4   We can read without going along with something wholesale. This is crucial to keep in mind.
5   Lecture 3, 'The Velocities of Thought', 9 December 1980, emphasis added.

Rigorous Kindness
1   See Phillips and Taylor, *On Kindness* (2009) for an overview of attitudes to kindness across history.
2   *The Paris Review*. 'The Art of Criticism No. 5'. Winter Issue, 2025.
3   See Aranya's *Yoga Philosophy of Patañjali*, 1983, State University of New York Press.

The Middle: framing vastness
1   *Poetry Says* interview with Alice Allan.
2   The philosophy upon which yoga is based is called *Samkhya*. It actually does have a gazing Other, which is called the See'r, *Purusha*. It bears little relation, however, as I understand it for now, to a transcendent God figure in the sense that many of us understand that function. *Purusha* could account for the sheer operation of perceiving (and even that might not be the word ...) It could be thought about in relation to Derrida's notion of *différance* ... but that's another book entirely.
3   Orit Sen-Gupta, *Patañjali's Yoga Sutras*, 2013, Vijnana Books, p. 66.

Risking Plainness
1   'The Velocities of Thought' lecture series, 2 December 1980.
2   Michel Foucault, *The Hermeneutics of the Subject*, trans. Graham Burchell, 2005, Palgrave Macmillan.

www.ingramcontent.com/pod-product-compliance
Lightning Source LLC
Chambersburg PA
CBHW030612230426
43661CB00053B/1952